SUCCEEDING
AGAINST THE ODDS

Succeeding Against The Odds

How the Learning-Disabled Can Realize Their Promise

Sally L. Smith

Jeremy P. Tarcher/Perigee

Jeremy P. Tarcher/Perigee Books
are published by
The Putnam Publishing Group
200 Madison Avenue
New York, NY 10016

Jeremy P. Tarcher, Inc.
5858 Wilshire Blvd., Suite 200
Los Angeles, CA 90036

Library of Congress catalogued the Jeremy P. Tarcher edition as follows:

Smith, Sally Liberman.
   Succeeding against the odds: how the learning-disabled can realize their
promise/Sally L. Smith.
      p.   cm.
   ISBN 0-87477-731-3 (pbk.)
   1. Learning disabled children—Education—United States.
2. Learning disabled children—United States—Attitudes.
3. Learning disabilities—United States.   I. Title.

LC4705.S66   1992   91-34819
371.9—dc20   CIP

Design by Mauna Eichner

Cover design by Andrew M. Newman

Manufactured in the United States of America
10   9   8   7   6   5   4   3

This book is printed on acid-free paper.

To my three sons, Randy, Nick, and Gary, each an only child.
You have been my backbone and my pride!
Thank you.

Contents

Acknowledgments   ix

Introduction   xii

1   The Hidden Handicap   1

2   Feeling Stupid, Acting Smart   19

3   Masking Secret Shame   35

4   Talent   56

5   Drive   71

6   The Need for Order   86

7   Learning by Doing   106

8   Responsibility: Preparing for Adulthood   132

9   The Emotional Toll   145

10   Family Tensions   156

11   Socialization   166

12   What Parents Can Do   182

13   What Teachers Can Do   202

14   What the Learning Disabled
      Can Do for Themselves   226

15   Strategies for Success   252

Appendix 1   Resources for the Learning Disabled   270

Appendix 2   The Lab School of Washington   288

      Index   293

Acknowledgments

Elisabeth Benson Booz, one of my dearest friends in the world, I thank you profoundly for your enthusiasm, for all your sage advice, and for your professional talent as editor. You provided a beautiful and uncluttered existence for me in Yvoire, France, to write this book, and I am forever grateful.

To Mark Wurzbacher, thank you for your painstaking page-by-page critique and for your astute suggestions for reorganizing the chapters. I became far more organized thanks to you.

To Lois Meyer, my gratitude for the long hours spent studying the manuscript, finding its weak spots, and helping with Appendix 1. To Uncle Paul Elkin, my appreciation for your careful reading of the manuscript and for your careful attention to my grammar and punctuation.

To my dear friend and board member Garry Clifford, my gratitude for all the support and caring you have given over the years, as well as for your extremely helpful criticism on the manuscript.

My thank yous for excellent advice to:

Neurologist-psychiatrist Dr. Grace Gabe

Psychiatrist Dr. Brian B. Doyle

Learning disabilities and reading specialist Sara Hines

Learning disabilities and computer and writing specialist Paul Kaiser

Social worker Penny Durenberger

To my present and past staff at The Lab School of Washington, my profound appreciation for all your talent, ingenuity, dedication, and love. I feel privileged to be among you, and I delight in the work you do. You are unique, and together we create a unique learning environment. To all of you, our division heads and staff, and to Neil Sturomski, our Night School director, my thanks for turning my dream into such a shining reality.

Without an extraordinary Board of Trustees—volunteers who have given unbelievable amounts of time, energy, thought, and often money—the truly nonprofit Lab School would have closed. A most grateful thank you to all of you who have served on our Board of Trustees. Particular thanks go to Pauline Schneider, Sergius Gambal, James Rosenheim, Ambassador Timothy Towell, Dane Towell, Fred Brennan, Dean Howells, Samia Farouki, Susan Hager, Max N. Berry, Ann Bradford Mathias, and my very good friend Judith Terra, who have helped the Lab School thrive and reach even higher to meet its goals.

The Parents of the Lab School have been unbelievably supportive of the school and of me. Thank you. You have made the Lab School's work more effective. Those of you who have been board members of P.A.L.S. have given much time, energy, and thought to The Lab School of Washington and made us a better place.

Our students have taught me so much! Thank you, Day School and Night School students. I admire your hard work, your problem-solving abilities, your courage, your resourcefulness, and your honesty with me. You have been my finest teachers!

My appreciation to The American University for prodding me to publish and to continue to develop new ideas. You gave me the chance to train teachers in my style of teaching and learning and then to employ many of them. Thank you.

Thank you, Lab School of Washington Outstanding Learning-Disabled Achievers, for giving of your valuable time and energy to offer great hope and inspiration to the learning disabled everywhere. Also, my gratitude to you for letting me quote you! And to Joy Galane, who has given me the tapes of all our galas, my appreciation for all you have done for me and for The Lab School of Washington.

Special thanks to Mrs. James Totten for letting me print quotes from your father, General George S. Patton. Dr. Florence Haseltine, Elizabeth D. Squires, and Nonnie Star, I thank you for letting me quote you. You are models for others with learning disabilities who are inspired by what you have done with your lives. Leah Gambal and Gary Smith have also given me valuable help on this book. Thank you.

Thank you, Ruth Switzer Pearl and Ann Charnley, for seeing the big picture of the Lab School. God bless Anna Hilt, who turned my purple pen scrawls into typed words. My friends the Behrens, the Rosenfelds, the Stephanskys, the Klaidmans, the Poppers, Mildred Wurf, and Gloria Gaston, you have been my Washington family. I thank you all for your support.

Introduction

It all began with one child, my child. My introduction to learning disabilities was as a parent, a desperate one. Why couldn't my child, who looked normal, learn normally? Why was he not like his two older brothers? Why did he behave differently? How could I help heal his deep hurts and teach him to learn? The search for answers to these questions became an obsession and then a vocation. As my son later said to me, "I gave you a career, Mom. Something good came out of this thing called learning disabilities." Something good, indeed. Out of it came my finest teacher!

What worked for my son is now working for countless others like him. As an educator, I have devoted my professional career to creating, for people like my son, schools, curricula, and teaching methods based on

> individualizing
> building on strengths
> learning from doing
> using all the senses
> setting precise, reasonable goals
> organizing, step-by-step
> problem solving
> challenging the intellect
> tapping the imagination
> reframing remarks and questions
> careful pacing
> valuing effort and availability for learning

giving visible proof of progress

encouraging independence and self-advocacy

building self-esteem

In 1967 I founded The Lab School of Washington, an elementary school for children of average to superior intelligence with moderate to severe learning disabilities. To this school I soon added a junior high and then a senior high. Today the school serves 250 children in grades K through 12. In addition to its academic programs, the school offers clinical services to the surrounding community, including tutoring, psychological and diagnostic services, occupational therapy, speech and language therapy, and career and college counseling.

When I began to work with the learning disabled, I soon discovered that they are for the most part quite talented, but their talents do not show up in traditional schooling. It's as if they have different intelligences than ordinary people— intelligences that set them apart and that make their childhoods miserable but that often make possible astonishing creativity and career success later in life. Unfortunately, too many adults with learning disabilities never get the opportunity to identify and to nurture their special talents.

In 1984, to meet the needs of adults with learning disabilities, The Lab School of Washington opened its Night School. In my Tuesday-night seminars with the adults at the Night School, I have learned what it's like to have grown up with an all pervasive feeling of not being OK. Again and again I have been overcome with how rotten these adults feel about themselves. Again and again they have shared with me their pain, their attempts to mask their disabilities, the devastation that they experienced from feeling stupid.

The material for this book came from those adults and from conversations with former students of the Day School. College students with learning disabilities from The American University also contributed insights and strategies. Since 1976, I have been head of the Master's Degree Program in Special Education: Learning Disabilities at The American University. I am a professor of special education, with thirty to forty graduate students each year in my program.

Some of the material in this book comes from letters sent to me by adults with learning disabilities—people whom I have never met but who write because they have heard of my school. Much of the material comes from adults around the country and in all walks of life whom I have been fortunate to meet in the course of lectures, seminars, panel discussions, and conferences. I have dealt with thousands upon thousands of adults with learning disabilities. This book presents many of their stories and, I hope, begins to answer some of their questions.

Further inspiration for this book has come from celebrities who have risen above their learning disabilities to achieve eminence in their fields. In 1982 The Lab School of Washington initiated luncheons at which celebrities spoke about their learning disabilities. The luncheons grew into daylong celebrations at which the Lab School presents its Outstanding Learning-Disabled Achiever Awards. The awardees spend part of the day meeting and talking with students at the school. Then, in the evening, there is a formal awards ceremony attended by eight hundred people from the diverse community of Washington, D.C. At the ceremony, and in conversations with our students, many celebrated people with learning disabilities have shared their secret pain and their strategies for success. These, too, have found their way into my book.

Three of my five previous books were about children with learning disabilities. The young people whom I wrote about in those books are adults today. It is fitting that I write a book for them—one that tells their stories in a way that reaches out to others with learning disabilities and to their parents and teachers.

This book has several purposes:

to give voice to the despair, the fears, the anger, the guilt, and the anxieties of the learning disabled

to show how these people grapple with adversity—the diverse strategies that they use to avoid failure and defeat

to suggest ways to reduce the pain and heal the wounds caused by growing up learning disabled

to demonstrate the crucial roles played by parents, teachers, friends, and mates in the lives of the learning disabled

to trumpet to the world that the learning disabled can soar to any height and can do anything if they receive the support that they need

To build a decent future, America needs the best minds. It needs energy, creativity, and resourcefulness. America needs to call on the learning disabled. Let the world profit from their gifts!

I

The Hidden Handicap

"I barely squeaked through high school and college, but nobody ever questioned if something was wrong."

"I went to the psychology clinic and I said, 'Somebody's got to help me. I'm going nuts because I'm spending ten hours a day and all day weekends studying—and I'm still flunking.'"

"You know, I thought I was retarded all these years."

"What a relief it was to discover that I wasn't really an idiot! I simply had a learning disability."

Imagine the frustration felt by those otherwise capable people who persistently fail in school. Despite normal intelligence, the will to succeed, and many highly developed skills, they find themselves unable to learn by traditional means. Their parents and teachers are baffled. Their frustrations and failures mount. Many give up entirely. A few are lucky enough to meet a psychologist or teacher who can help, one who can say, "You are not stupid. You were not born to fail. You suffer from a *learning disability,* a condition that can be diagnosed, accommodated, and overcome."

AN EDUCATIONAL ENIGMA: TALENTED STUDENTS WHO FAIL

Educators have long been puzzled by students who fail in school and yet go on to achieve greatness. Gustave Flaubert,

William Butler Yeats, and F. Scott Fitzgerald were all extremely poor students. So was Auguste Rodin. Hans Christian Andersen, that spinner of magnificent fairy tales, could not read and so had to dictate his stories to a scribe. Thomas Edison, the most prolific inventor of all time, could neither understand a lecture nor write a readable sentence. Woodrow Wilson, perhaps the most intellectually gifted of all American presidents, was called "backward" because he didn't learn to read until he was eleven. Nelson Rockefeller, who became governor of New York and then vice president of the United States, struggled all his life to read and to spell. He became an extraordinary extemporaneous speaker in part because he could not read fluently. General George S. Patton, the brilliant tactician who led the Third Army to victory in Europe in World War II, didn't learn to read until he was over twelve years old, and he never learned to spell properly.

Many ordinary people suffer from similar problems and demonstrate similar talents. Their parents think that they aren't trying hard enough, that they *could* learn if they only *would*. Their teachers call them "lazy," "willful," or "inattentive" and decry their lack of effort. Being for the most part good kids, as most kids are, they usually believe their parents and teachers. Worse yet, they sometimes believe the people who think that they are retarded or slow. At times, especially if they are hyperactive or impulsive, these students are called "troubled" or are said to suffer from emotional disturbances or behavior disorders. Most of them are labeled "stupid," though they are, in fact, normally intelligent individuals, endowed with special gifts and abilities, who happen to be learning disabled.

Only in recent years have some scientists and educators begun to understand the problems that cause intelligent people to experience learning failures. And only since the 1960s have these problems come to be known as *learning disabilities* and to be recognized as hidden handicaps to be dealt with as other handicaps are—through legislation, special schools and training programs, and other accommodations. For hundreds of thousands of Americans who suffer from learning disabilities, the recognition of their problem has brought hope and relief, even liberation.

What scientists and educators began to recognize in the 1960s and 1970s was that learning disabilities often have a neurophysiological base. Some problem or group of problems in the physiological mechanisms of the brain causes learning not to occur or to occur intermittently or inefficiently. To understand how this might happen, it's useful to think of the brain, the nervous system, and the senses as a computer and its peripherals—a central processing unit and a storage or memory unit that is hooked up to input and output devices. For the computer to operate well, each piece of hardware must do its job. But suppose that something goes wrong with the hardware: the keyboard is improperly wired and scrambles the incoming letters, information is sent to or retrieved from the wrong address in memory, or the printer fails to recognize instructions from the central processor and starts substituting random symbols for particular numbers or letters. In short, one or two specific problems in the hardware can cause the whole system to malfunction. This is what happens to a person with a learning disability.

DEFINING LEARNING DISABILITIES

Public Law 94–142, the Education for All Handicapped Children Act, defines *learning disability* as "a disorder in one or more of the basic psychological processes involved in understanding and using language, spoken or written, which may manifest itself in an imperfect ability to listen, think, speak, read, write, spell, and do mathematical calculations."

A second part of the federal definition appears in the regulations used to interpret Public Law 94–142. It states that a specific learning disability exists if the student does not achieve at the proper age and ability levels in one or more of several specific areas when provided with appropriate learning experience, and the student has a severe discrepancy between achievement and intellectual ability in one or more of these six areas:

1. oral comprehension
2. listening comprehension
3. written expression
4. basic reading skill
5. mathematics calculation
6. mathematics reasoning

The National Joint Committee on Learning Disabilities, an organization composed of leaders of associations in the field, came up with a more general definition. The committee's definition stresses that learning disabilities "are intrinsic to the individual and presumed to be due to central nervous system dysfunctions" and "are *not* the direct result of any external conditions or influences." Even though this definition is more general, including as it does non-language-related problems, many specialists and parents would still consider it inadequate because it is not general enough. It excludes many learning-related problems that could legitimately be considered learning disabilities, such as social immaturity.

There is no common agreement among all specialists in the field about who is learning disabled. Specialists do not agree on

- the best way to diagnose learning disabilities
- ways to measure potential, particularly in the non-verbal child

- how great a gap between potential and achievement should be considered important
- how to educate students with learning disabilities
- who is properly trained to work in the field of learning disabilities

Because specialists cannot agree on who is learning disabled, there are no reliable data on the size of the learning-disabled population and thus no way of knowing the true dimensions of the problem.

Whatever their disagreements about the scope of the term *learning disabilities,* specialists do agree on one thing: *learning disabilities are not a single condition but a group of related and often overlapping conditions that lead to low achievement by people who have the potential to do much better.* A given person can suffer from one learning disability or from many and may have problems in several distinct areas.

The illustration below shows some of the areas in which a person with learning disabilities might experience problems.

Areas in which learning disabilities occur

No one person has difficulties in all of these areas, but problems in more than one area are common.

The following is a preliminary, nonrigorous categorization (or taxonomy) of the problems that can occur within each area.

Attention Problems

short or very variable attention span

trouble-shooting

problem focusing on thoughts

distractibility

difficulty sticking to and completing tasks

poor modulation of response or activity (over-reactive or under-reactive)

Left-Right Confusion

reversals

trouble following spacial directions

Visual-Spacial Problems

poor discrimination of one object, symbol, word from another

trouble discriminating central figure from background

difficulty isolating letters in words, words in sentences and sentences in paragraphs

inability to perceive and/or remember letters in a word in proper sequence, or numbers or telephone numbers

inability to visually organize mathematical problems on paper difficulty with puzzles, mazes, etc

inability to read a map. Getting lost easily (even in familiar surroundings)

Motor Problems

trouble with general coordination (for example, in sports)

clumsiness, tendency to bump into things or to drop things

poor eye-hand coordination (i.e. catching or hitting balls)

difficulty with tasks involving fine motor control (i.e. buttoning)

difficulty with handwriting

difficulty doing several things at once

difficulty with motor planning (i.e. trouble figuring out how to do an unfamiliar motor task)

Memory Problems

difficulty following instructions

difficulty remembering what has just been said or seen

difficulty getting into memory what has just been read

tendency to lose train of thought

difficulty remembering things learned after some time has passed

difficulty remembering names, dates, or places

difficulty remembering abstract material

frequent feeling that a piece of information is "there" but cannot be retrieved (the tip-of-the-tongue phenomenon)

Symbol-Learning Problems

  unusual difficulty with basic mathematics, algebra, geometry, or calculus (numerical concepts)

  unusual difficulty with chemistry

  unusual difficulty with foreign languages

  unusual difficulty with phonics

  unusual difficulty with reading and spelling (usually a slow reading rate)

  difficulty using or making graphs, tables, and so forth

Language Problems

  poor listening skills

  difficulty comprehending what has been heard

  frequent "mishearing" or gaps in what is heard

  trouble understanding subtleties in language

  trouble expressing thoughts and ideas

  disorganized language

  immature speech, trouble with tenses, or with other specific aspects of grammar

  trouble retrieving words

  poor vocabulary

  difficulty decoding written symbols

  difficulty understanding what has been read

  poor spelling

  poor written language

Cognition Problems

  difficulty separating main ideas from details

  difficulty separating the whole from its parts

difficulty understanding abstract thought or expression, as in a metaphor

difficulty making abstract comparisons

poor synthesis of ideas to make a point

difficulty drawing inferences

Organization Problems

difficulty organizing information coming in through the senses

slow processing of information coming in through the senses

difficulty breaking things down into sequences (first, next, last) or performing sequential tasks

difficulty seeing the parts that make up the whole

difficulty categorizing and classifying

difficulty establishing priorities

difficulty organizing belongings, materials, notebooks, and so forth

difficulty keeping track of belongings, materials, notebooks, and so forth

difficulty organizing space (for example, a place to work)

difficulty organizing time (for example, meeting deadlines)

difficulty organizing research (planning, notetaking, outlining)

difficulty synthesizing different points of view or complex ideas

Social Behavior Problems

difficulty perceiving or interpreting the facial expressions, gestures, or body language of others difficulty understanding cause-effect relationships

difficulty evaluating how personal behavior affects others

inflexibility, rigidity, resistance to change

poor timing of remarks

impulsive behavior, impulsive verbalizations

inappropriate responses

tendency to become easily overstimulated

tendency to become easily frustrated

overreaction or underreaction to events

egocentrism, trouble empathizing with others

trouble establishing and/or maintaining relationships

excessive perseverance in doing or saying one thing

emotional lability—mild mood swings, somewhat erratic and unpredictable behavior

guilelessness (naïveté)

failure to apply rules of social behavior in an appropriate manner

A person with learning disabilities is likely to have some specific combination of the difficulties listed above. Some adults are very verbal but don't listen well and can't write. Some are not verbal at all but understand well what they hear. Some have no socialization difficulties. Others are plagued with social problems. Clusters of difficulties often indicate the presence of learning disabilities. The simple fact that a student is having trouble in a math class would not, for example, suggest that he has a learning disability. However, one might infer that the student does have a learning disability if he also displays problems in several areas such as attention, motor skills, and cognition. Particular clusters of difficulties connote particular learning disabilities, of which there are more than twenty different kinds. As the illustration below shows, *learning disabilities* is an umbrella term for many overlapping conditions that adversely affect a person's ability to learn, causing him to achieve below potential. Research has not yet produced a rigorous taxonomy of these disabilities.

CONFUSIONS OF TERMINOLOGY

Lewis Thomas called his book on medicine *The Youngest Science* because modern scientific medicine is only about a hundred years old. However, the field of learning disabilities is much younger, having emerged during the 1960s and 1970s.

As in any relatively new field of study, there is in the discipline of learning disabilities very little agreement among specialists about the names and definitions of key terms. Strange as it may seem, there are problems even with the term *learning disabilities* itself, which is not listed in the standard psychiatric

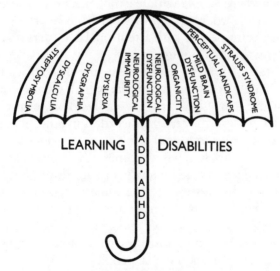

Some common learning disabilities

reference work, the *Diagnostic and Statistical Manual of Mental Disorders,* III-R, 3rd edition, revised (commonly referred to as *DSM III* or as the *Psychiatric Handbook*). The term *learning disabilities* doesn't appear in this handbook, even though terms for a few specific, isolated disabilities, such as *developmental reading disabilities,* do appear.

Today, the terms *Attention Deficit Disorder* (ADD) and *Attention Deficit Hyperactivity Disorder* (ADHD) are confusing the public even further. Both ADD and ADHD are listed in the *Psychiatric Handbook,* a fact that is significant because the handbook is used for communication between practitioners and insurance companies. Doctors use the terms *ADD* and *ADHD* frequently because the official status of these terms makes it possible both to prescribe medication and to get insurance companies to pay for services.

ADD and ADHD have been classified by some professionals and parent groups as conditions entirely separate from learning disabilities. I see these three conditions as closely allied, since many people with learning disabilities suffer from attentional disorders that also stem from neurological dysfunctions. Some people with attentional disorders do not have learning disabilities, but many do.

One term from the field of learning disabilities that has become widely accepted is *dyslexia,* which comes from Latin roots meaning "to speak or read badly." This term was originally used to describe reading disorders in otherwise normal, intelligent people but is now often used in a wider sense to describe trouble with language in general. The great currency of the term *dyslexia* has led many people to think that dyslexia and learning disabilities are the same thing. However, dyslexia is usually simply a symptom of more general learning disabilities. Very rarely do we find a pure dyslexic whose only difficulties are breaking down the code of reading and spelling, though there are some such people.

Why has the general public so taken to the word *dyslexia?*

The answer is that the word has few negative connotations. Parents find that people know what they mean when they say that their child is dyslexic. *Dyslexia* denotes a reading problem but connotes no lack of intelligence or other gifts. In contrast, if parents say that their child has a *learning disability*, people tend to think that they mean a *developmental disability*, a type of retardation. The term *learning disability* has not yet sunk into the public consciousness and is not yet completely socially acceptable.

WHAT CAUSES LEARNING DISABILITIES?

Learning disabilities seem to derive either from hereditary factors or from specific problems that occur before, during, or after birth.

Hereditary Factors

In many families, reading and learning disabilities can be traced through several generations. Specific difficulties with spelling, math, coordination, and/or handwriting may also appear at various times in a family's history.

Problems Before Birth

maternal malnutrition

bleeding in pregnancy

poor placental attachment to the uterus

toxemia in pregnancy

infectious disease of a pregnant mother (German measles, a viral disease, influenza, or a chronic disease)

alcoholism during pregnancy

the use of certain drugs during pregnancy

RH incompatibility

Problems During Birth

long or difficult delivery, producing anoxia (insufficient oxygen in the brain)

prematurity

breech delivery

cord around neck

poor position in the uterus (such as left posterior position)

dry birth (caused by water breaking prematurely)

intracranial pressure at the time of birth due to forceps delivery or to a narrow pelvic arch in the mother

rapid delivery, exposing the infant too quickly to a new air pressure

Problems After Birth

a significant delay in the onset of breathing after birth (which often occurs in cases of prematurity, difficult delivery, or twins)

high fever at an early age

sharp blow to the head from a fall or an accident

meningitis or encephalitis

oxygen deprivation due to suffocation, respiratory distress, or breath holding

Unfortunately, the sciences of neurology and psychology are not yet sufficiently advanced to identify unequivocally the specific central-nervous-system dysfunctions that cause particular learning disabilities. Since the actual physical basis of a given disability is generally unknown and subject, at best, to speculation, it follows that the exact cause of the disability would also be unknown. That's basically where we are today.

The day may come when medical breakthroughs will offer specific treatments for learning disabilities, but that day is, for most such disabilities, a long way off. Fortunately, people with learning disabilities do not have to wait for the neuroscientists. They can begin, now, to take control of their own lives and to work through their own problems. In the next chapter we shall meet some people who have done just that—amazing people with learning disabilities who have found a light at the end of a very long tunnel. First, however, you or someone you care about may want to answer the following questionnaire, which is designed to reveal whether a person should be tested for learning disabilities.

SHOULD I BE TESTED TO SEE IF I AM LEARNING DISABLED?

Check the box each time the answer is yes. No one item here means you are learning disabled. Even a *yes* many times does not necessarily mean you are learning disabled. If most of the answers are yes, it might be useful for you to be tested by a diagnostician who is experienced with people with learning disabilities. (This questionnaire could also be read aloud to another; copyright 1991 by Sally L. Smith.)

☐ Do I hate to read?

☐ Do I get headaches when I read?

☐ Do I lose my place when I read?

☐ Do I read very slowly?

☐ Do I mix up *p* and *d or b* and *q*? Do I read *8* for *3*? *5* for *2*?

☐ Do I read *llamas* for *small* or *unclear* for *nuclear*?

☐ Do I hate to read out loud?

☐ Do I omit word endings when I read aloud, reading *row* for *rowing*?

☐ Do I skip or omit words, sentences, or paragraphs?

☐ Do I have to reread material to understand it?

☐ Do I avoid writing whenever possible?

☐ Do I use the telephone rather than write?

☐ Do I spell badly?

☐ Do I have trouble even writing a thank-you note?

☐ Do I have trouble writing a complete sentence?

☐ Am I unable to take notes?

☐ Am I unable to fill out forms?

☐ Does my writing look like chicken scratches? Is it tiny and cramped?

☐ Do I hate using scissors, pasting, or tying knots?

☐ Do I have trouble fixing things with my hands?

☐ Do I have great trouble with math?

☐ Are decimals and fractions very difficult for me?

☐ Is long division really difficult for me?

☐ Do I have problems counting change?

☐ Do I have trouble keeping my bankbook straight?

☐ Am I disorganized?

☐ Are my things always in a mess?

☐ Do I lose everything?

☐ Am I overorganized?

☐ Do I have to have everything in place?

☐ Do I have trouble organizing myself to begin things?

☐ Do I have trouble paying attention?

☐ Am I very distractible?

☐ Do I have trouble staying on task?

☐ Do I forget to bring necessary things to class or to work?

☐ Do I have trouble following spoken instructions?

☐ Do I have trouble following directions when driving?

☐ Do I mix up my left side and my right?

☐ Do I get lost easily?

☐ Do I often wish people would repeat what they asked or said?

☐ Do I have trouble comprehending what is said on the telephone?

☐ Do I hate talking on the telephone?

☐ Do I often miss the point of jokes?

☐ Do I get confused by puns, plays on words, and sarcasm?

☐ Do I have trouble remembering names?

☐ Do I have trouble remembering dates, telephone numbers, and zip codes?

☐ Do I have trouble organizing my thoughts?

☐ Do I forget what I was going to say?

☐ Do I forget words I know well?

☐ Do I tend to stutter?

☐ Do I avoid discussions?

☐ Am I a very visual person rather than a word person?

☐ Am I easily sidetracked?

☐ Do I have trouble sitting still?

☐ Am I restless, always moving my feet, my fingers, or my mouth?

☐ Do I have trouble waiting for things?

☐ Am I usually late to work?

☐ Do I have trouble reading a watch?

☐ Do I have trouble meeting deadlines?

☐ Do I hand my work in late?

☐ Do I have to do one thing at a time to be successful?

☐ Do I have trouble doing several things at once?

☐ Am I inflexible?

☐ Do I hate surprises or changes in routine?

☐ Am I easily overwhelmed?

☐ Do I have trouble breaking things down into manageable chunks so I can begin with one thing, move on to the next, and then on to the next to finish?

☐ Do I have trouble setting priorities?

☐ Do I avoid making decisions?

☐ Do I start things and never finish them?

☐ Do I tend to back out of things, quit, or not show up?

☐ Am I easily frustrated?

☐ Do I tend to explode when frustrated?

☐ Do people tell me that I'm hard on myself?

☐ Do I exhaust myself from working so hard?

☐ Do I plunge into things without thinking them through?

☐ Do I concentrate on details and tend to miss the main issue?

☐ Do I tend to be inconsistent and erratic?

Along with having these characteristics, a person with learning disabilities is likely to have clusters of excellence in the form of artistic talent, academic or athletic gifts, extreme sensitivity, an outgoing personality, high motivation, fierce determination to succeed, or any number of other positive attributes.

2

Feeling Stupid, Acting Smart

"I had been through nine literacy programs before I found I was learning disabled. At last, I'm learning to read."

"I thought when you became an adult it was too late to learn."

"Now that I know what my problems are, I can let others know how to help me. It feels good to be on the move."

"I didn't tell anyone I was going to Night School because I was sure I would drop out, the same as I did at college. But, now, a year later, I'm on my way back to college!"

A person with learning disabilities often carries a heavy burden of loneliness, feeling that he is the only one in the world who has struggled so hard only to experience the pain of failure. Not understanding what is causing his failure, he blames himself and tries to hide it, as if it were a shameful secret. Of course, this only makes the problem worse because it prevents him from asking for help.

In a high-achieving family, a poor achiever feels like a total disgrace. Even when parents don't pressure their child directly, the very way they live often constitutes pressure. This is especially true of educators, scholars, journalists, novelists, or editors, who continually and for the most part happily immerse themselves in the written word. They read books and magazines and cannot imagine what it would be like not to enjoy reading or critiquing what has been read. Their world is filled with quotations, with puns, with notes and letters, with reports and memoranda. The child with learning disabilities feels isolated from the parents' culture and learns to hide her "shameful secret." And, of course, as the child carries this secret into adulthood and begins to face adult responsibilities, the burden of it grows and grows. Surprisingly, when the secret is finally revealed, it turns out not to be shameful at all. Once a person openly acknowledges having a learning disability, she finds it possible to relax and request help and support. Only after openly acknowledging the learning disability is the person free to work on improving her ability to learn.

When a condition has been kept a secret,
then shame is attached to the condition,
and one can be overpowered by shame,
which engenders guilt,
which produces even more dissatisfaction
which produces even more dissatisfaction
with oneself.

THE NIGHT SCHOOL OF
THE LAB SCHOOL OF WASHINGTON

In January 1984, the Night School of The Lab School of Washington opened its doors to adults with learning disabilities. It was one of the first such night schools in the country, if not the first. There, precise teaching methods are geared to the needs of each individual. At this school, adult students working with master teachers find out how they can learn most effectively. And they continually teach their teachers more about learning disabilities. As founder and director of the Lab School, I have had the opportunity to see, firsthand, how people can flower once their learning disabilities are confronted.

To announce the opening of the Night School for adults, we initially circulated a simple brochure. Then we realized that our prospective clients would probably not be able to read the brochure, much less write back. Once we had made this realization, I went on the radio, took part in TV talk shows, and answered telephone queries on the air. Many adults said, "You were describing *me* on that show! How did you know about me?" (Learning-disabled adults typically do a lot of self-diagnosis. They hear somebody talking about learning disabilities and say, "That's me!")

Our first batch of adult students was diverse: an engraver, a foundation executive, a salesman, a furniture mover, a telephone-company worker, a secretary for the FBI, a nursery-school assistant teacher, a restaurant owner, and an athletic coach. As other classes followed, it became clear that most Night School students had not been previously diagnosed as learning disabled. Few had received any special education. Parents, neighbors, friends, and teachers without any background in learning disabilities had tutored them. Most of them had dropped out of college; some had dropped out of high school. Others had completed high school but were stymied in their jobs by their inability to read well or quickly enough, to do math, or to write clearly. Some were college students who were failing in their courses. A few had made it to graduate school but could not meet the writing demands.

Our learning-disabled adult students sometimes wept with joy when assessment showed that they had perfectly normal, often above-average intelligence but had trouble receiving, processing, or expressing information. This news often told them they were not stupid, as they had feared. There was a reason for the difficulties they had confronted all their lives.

Most of the adults in the Night School had been hiding their problems and fears since they were young children, never knowing why they had had so much trouble learning to read, to spell, to write, or to do math. Many of them knew very well that they were disorganized, couldn't tell left from right, forgot appointments, or had a hard time following instructions. Some would get lost on their way to the Night School, thus demonstrating their problems in dealing with space and direction. Others would turn up at the wrong time or on the wrong day, thus showing their problems with time and with timing.

As our adult students came to grips with their learning disabilities, a sense of community, sharing, and mutual support grew among them. Almost all students at the Night School described the appalling isolation and secret shame they felt in the years before they sought help. However, once they found that they were not alone in their struggles, a burden seemed to lift from them, and they were able to move ahead much faster. Here are some examples:

SOME ADULTS WHO CONFRONTED THEIR LEARNING DISABILITIES

Jim is a top official in a bank. He looks distinguished, is well spoken, and relates well to everybody. He is married and has three children, two of whom are learning disabled. Secretly, Jim used to panic whenever he had to write a top-level memorandum because he couldn't spell even simple words and found it impossible to remember names. For years he told no one of his problems except his secretary, who covered for him. He learned to use a computer, and his secretary checked his spelling. Jim was so anxious when put in a situation where he had to remember names that his secretary always called ahead to find out exactly who would be present at each meeting he had to attend. She reviewed the names with him and tried to shield him from surprises. Other institutions complained that she seemed pushy and aggressive with her insistent calls.

Now, at age fifty, Jim feels confident enough about his job and his record of accomplishments to be open about the things he cannot do. He lets people know how he compensates for his disabilities and has often been able to make colleagues into partners who help him develop compensatory strategies.

Beth, a widow who had raised four successful children, felt comfortable explaining her left-right confusion and her clumsiness to them only after they had grown up and were no longer sharply critical of her. From that point on, she learned to make jokes with others about her habit of getting lost and forgetting things. She learned to laugh at herself, and as a result, people laughed with her, not at her. She found that they made allowances for her and did not respect her less.

Alex, who works as a fireman, had the reputation of being the most reliable, sturdy member of the crew. He talked very little; he was an action man. Secretly, he had difficulty expressing himself. He had trouble focusing on a conversation and sticking to the point but no trouble concentrating on a task and following up with a plan of action. Eventually, he told his colleagues that his son was dyslexic and, like himself, was a man of few words, while his daughter, the family chatterbox, could talk them all under the table.

Doreen, though pretty, charming, and verbal, failed in her training session as assistant in a school library. She consistently reversed numbers and could not replace books on the correct shelves. When she told the library committee that she was learning disabled, they put her in a job that built on her strengths, especially on her ability to deal with people. She developed a successful after-school storytelling program.

A popular professor of political science at a western college was known for his energy and for his dynamic teaching style. He paced around the classroom, firing off questions and provoking wide-ranging discussions. One restless student with learning disabilities felt totally frustrated in the class. The professor befriended the student and confessed to also having learning disabilities. The professor had channeled his hyperactivity into a positive, energetic teaching style, he had chosen a field that bypassed his severe difficulties with mathematics, and he had devised numerous strategies to deal with his messiness. He was able to guide his student toward shortcuts and strategies that circumvented the student's disabilities and permitted him to learn. The student ended the course with a solid *B*.

Each of these five people had to struggle to find a way to function effectively, but the most crucial battle in this long struggle was won once they had acknowledged their learning disabilities and could ask others for help.

CELEBRITIES WITH LEARNING DISABILITIES

In 1982 The Lab School of Washington started holding luncheons for the community at large. These luncheons featured eminent speakers who were learning disabled. Parents, teachers, community leaders, legislators, businesspeople, mental-health workers—all kinds of people came. The purpose of these luncheon meetings was to raise public awareness about learning disabilities.

In 1985 the meetings outgrew the luncheon format and turned into annual, daylong celebrations at the Lab School involving students, faculty, parents, and celebrities with learning disabilities. The day culminates in an awards gala for Outstanding Learning-Disabled Achievers in a local hotel ballroom before an audience of eight hundred distinguished Washingtonians and out-of-town guests.

The day of activities is electrifying for both the awardees and the Lab School students. The students ask the celebrities all kinds of questions, and the guests are refreshingly honest, frank, and open with their interrogators. The hundreds of students who cram the school's multipurpose room see, sitting before them, examples of the success that could crown their own lives.

Most of the celebrities who have visited the school were admitting for the first time publicly that they suffered from the hidden handicap of learning disabilities. They spoke of their struggles and shared the strategies that allowed them to succeed, and like the Night School students themselves, they painfully but cathartically revealed the secrets buried deep within them.

These celebrities, like other adults with learning disabilities who confront their problem in public for the first time, frequently found themselves reliving the devastating shame, guilt, and anger they felt during youthful torments and schoolroom humiliations that had not been dredged up in years. Once exposed, these celebrities often had to face questions from reporters uneducated about learning disabilities and often were subjected to prejudice, ridicule, and sensationalism. It took courage and self-confidence for them to speak out.

Headlines in a tabloid newspaper trumpeted that movie star Cher had a "dreaded disease." The article itself, once one got past the blaring headlines, gave a factual account of her dyslexia. Greg Louganis, the Olympic diving champion, said that he felt much more comfortable scantily dressed on a high-diving board than standing in evening dress talking to hundreds of people about how stupid he felt as a child or still feels when he gets lost.

Many deserving people have turned down the Outstanding Learning-Disabled Achiever Award. A banker felt that it would be bad for business. A fashion designer thought that it would ruin a carefully cultivated image. A nationally known TV entertainer dreaded that "the whole world would see me as a dummy, and I don't need an award for being dumb!" A scholar feared that letting out his secret might cost him his tenure at his university. A Cabinet officer was afraid of repercussions from opponents in the press. One author simply did not want to "complicate her life" by having to discuss or think about problems that she had effectively repressed. An athlete was furious when an out-of-town newspaper wrote about his and his children's disabilities. When his manager received a telephone inquiry about these disabilities, there was a confrontation, and the athlete stormed out of the room, shouting at his manager that this matter was nobody's business but his own. Sometimes a husband or wife has not wanted his or her spouse to receive publicity for having a "defect." Occasionally, an agent fears that his client will be hurt.

For some, admitting to learning disabilities is extremely irksome to their own self-image. "I will not let myself be honored for outstanding achievements despite my having learning disabilities," said one Renaissance man who has invented, designed, and sold a host of innovative products, "because I still feel I'm a fake, an imposter, a fraud, that my whole life has been a cheat, with my getting away with it. Maybe someday I'll get over it and feel clean and you can honor me." His friends cannot convince him that he has produced not only wealth for himself but also great good for society at large. Fortunately, he is engaged in therapeutic counseling and so may be able to heal these open wounds.

> Adults who were fat when they were children
> often go on feeling fat when they are adults
> even when they are thin.
> Adults who felt stupid when they were children
> often go on feeling stupid when they are adults
> even when their achievements prove otherwise.

A writer who dictates her novels said that she could not speak out because doing so would be like removing a layer of her skin, and underneath she might find not another layer of healthy skin but an abscess or a pool of blood.

In contrast, King Olav of Norway made public his difficulties in reading and writing when he was eighty-four years old. From that moment on, the phones of the Norwegian Association for Dyslexics have scarcely stopping ringing. People felt it was acceptable to seek help. The king's daughter, Princess Astrid, also dyslexic, chairs the association. Whenever royalty or other national leaders speak out, they exert enormous influence over public opinion and give tacit support to those suffering from the same problems.

Role models are needed by the learning disabled of all ages who are struggling to succeed. Their best role models are, of course, adults with learning disabilities who are functioning well in society in fields that are engaging and satisfying. Plumbers, engravers, policemen, firemen, and day-care workers who have been very successful in their fields despite their learning disabilities have kept our Lab School students enchanted with the stories of their lives.

The dozens of celebrities who have visited the Lab School to receive awards are prominent enough that public knowledge of their struggles with learning disabilities has not done them any harm and in a few cases has actually helped their careers. These celebrities have helped many ordinary citizens to reach for the stars. The following list names celebrities who have received the Lab School's Outstanding Learning-Disabled Achievers Award and gives the primary occupation of each celebrity at the time of the award.

1985

G. Chris Andersen, investment banker

Cher, actress and singer

Tom Cruise, actor

Bruce Jenner, Olympic decathlon champion and gold-medal winner

Robert Rauschenberg, artist

Richard C. Strauss, real-estate financier

1986

Harry Anderson, TV actor

Ann Bancroft, Arctic explorer

Frank Dunkle, director of the U.S. Fish and Wildlife Service

Greg Louganis, Olympic diver

Henry Winkler, actor, director, and producer

1987

Marina B., jewelry designer

Chuck Close, artist

Richard Cohen, syndicated columnist

Mark Torrance, CEO, Musak Corporation

Margaret Whitton, actress

Roger W. Wilkins, scholar and head of the Pulitzer Prize Board

1988

Tracey Gold, actress

Malcolm Goodridge III, senior vice president, American Express

Magic Johnson, basketball player

Thomas H. Kean, governor of New Jersey

Emily Fisher Landau, foundation president

Daniel Stern, actor

1989

Harry Belafonte, singer, actor, and activist

Gaston Caperton, governor of West Virginia

William Doyle, chairman, William Doyle Auction Galleries of New York

Fred Friendly, broadcast journalist and scholar

Dexter Manley, Washington Redskins football player

Paul J. Orfalea, founder and chairman, Kinko's copy shops

1990

Donald S. Coffey, Ph.D., Distinguished Professor of Urology, Oncology, Pharmacology, and Molecular Science

Marc Flanagan, TV writer and producer

John Horner, paleontologist and specialist on dinosaurs

Hugh Newell Jacobsen, F.A.I.A., architect

HOW THE CELEBRITIES DISCOVERED THEIR LEARNING DISABILITIES

Cher recognized her own disabilities when she had her daughter tested: "I found out about myself because of Chastity, who has a learning disability. When I took her to be tested, I said to the lady, 'I know she's intelligent.' Her school was telling me she had psychological problems; they were painting it so bad, really black. So when I took her to be tested, I started talking with the lady. When I was young, they used to say on my report cards, 'She has the ability, but she doesn't apply herself.' And I was busting my—you know. Really working hard. Everything I learned in school was from spoken information because I had such a hard time reading and writing. I can't spell, and if I have to dial the telephone long-distance, it's a hassle."

Richard Cohen, the syndicated columnist, traced a pattern of learning disabilities through three generations of his family: "I was about forty when I found out. I had a son who was not doing particularly well in school. We transferred him to another school, where they realized something was wrong and had him tested. We met with people at the testing center who explained his learning disability, and at one point the psychologist said, 'Your son has a hard time looking up words in the dictionary. For some reason he'll go ahead of the word or behind the word or all over the page.' And at that point my wife looked at me and said, 'That's you!' She had always noticed it, and it was true. When I realized I had approximately the same problems as my son, I called my father. He was seventy. I asked him, 'Dad, can you read your handwriting?' He said, 'No, I've never been able to read my handwriting.' And that's when he realized it, too. So there we were, aged seventy, forty, and, in my son's case, around ten."

Chuck Close, whose colossal photorealist portraits hang in major museums throughout the country, said, "I was in my forties when I found out I had a learning disability. I went to hear a lecture at my daughter's school, because my daughter is learning disabled, very much the same way I am. I always knew there was something wrong, but I just thought I was the only one in the world, so I tried to hide it in order to try and pass. It's very nice to be out of the closet, able to talk about these issues, and know you're not fighting this thing alone."

Marina B., known for the exquisite contemporary jewelry she creates, used her left hand to draw and write. Her school insisted that she change to her right hand, so she stopped drawing because she couldn't draw with her right hand. Schooling was exceedingly painful for her. She felt that she struggled with all her power and saw only poor results. It took many years before she discovered that she had a learning disability. Today, with her left hand, she produces about a thousand sketches a year, and about three hundred of them are translated into earrings, collars, bangles, and ornate evening bags that are treasured by her clients and highly acclaimed by the fashion world.

When Mark Torrance, former chief executive of the Musak Corporation, was invited to receive an Outstanding Learning-Disabled Achiever Award, he felt that he was not learning disabled enough to accept it. In trying to make a telephone call to turn down the award, he misdialed the number three times—at which point he decided that he really was learning disabled enough to come and accept the award!

THE VALUE OF SPEAKING OUT

The awardees report that facing their difficulties and speaking out has brought them many benefits. They especially like the feeling of honesty that they get from proclaiming, "I am what I am, take it or leave it. This is me!"

Ann Bancroft, an explorer who was the first woman to reach the North Pole on foot, said, "I had not discussed this disability with anyone, really, until *People* magazine came. My father was in the yard, and when somebody asked him how I did in school, his face went white. He didn't think he'd ever have to answer that question about me. He stammered and finally said, 'Ann has dyslexia, and she didn't do very well at all. She found other avenues in which to express herself.' Now I have learned to be open about my learning disability, to sort of stand up."

Night School students agree that a certain purity comes from baring the truth. Acceptance of what is brings relief. Acceptance of imperfection is difficult for those who strive hard for perfection. Deciding that what you are doing is good enough can allow you to tolerate and even to like yourself more.

Speaking out allows adults to realize that countless others have experienced similar traumas. There is great relief in not being the only one. And connections are made; mysteries are solved: "Oh, this is why I did that. . . . Now I understand." Sharing the terrible secret helps put the pieces of the puzzle in place and often brightens a whole life.

Some adults with learning disabilities begin to feel a need to serve the learning-disabled population by creating more public awareness. In a panel discussion at the Lab School among adults with learning disabilities, several of them stated that school principals need to have them meet with the teachers. "We can teach them what is going on inside the head of that normal-looking child who is riddled with learning disabilities," said one adult. They wanted to explain the kind of teaching that would work for them—the more concrete and specific the better! They also wanted to talk directly with parents of children with learning disabilities, to explain what had worked for them and what had hurt them and to reassure the parents that their children's learning disabilities could be overcome.

Many in our society think of success as climbing a ladder to the top of an institution, as being a lawyer, a doctor, a political figure. A more multidimensional view is needed in our society, for in fact there are many different ladders, many kinds of success.

Success can be simply doing whatever you love and do well. Success for one person might mean climbing only halfway up a certain ladder. Success for another might mean being happily married, at home with the children, and free to paint in his or her spare time. One Night School adult said that he had worked for twenty years in an office where he felt incompetent even though he was considered successful there. Now he works with his hands as a ceramicist. He makes much less money, but he feels successful and is happy (even though he would like to make more money—wouldn't we all).

Many prominent adults said that they had learned to see their learning disabilities as an advantage, not a handicap, once these disabilities had been identified and understood. Having been forced by their learning disabilities to solve problems in a unique way in order to show the world what they could do, they felt that they had become far more interesting people. Their success did not take away the pain but did give the pain meaning and worth.

Fred Friendly, renowned broadcast journalist and professor in charge of media and society at Columbia University Graduate School of Journalism, said to the Lab School students, "I'm seventy-four years old. I'm so old I was around before there was radio or television. My father came home one night in 1922 and said there was a new invention—the radio . . . and I said I could be a radio announcer because I wouldn't have to learn to read! It turned out I did have to learn to read, and I learned pretty well. But I've become a much better professor than I was a student—all because there were lots of things I couldn't do as a kid. The dyslexia gave me enormous drive and motivation. I wouldn't give up my dyslexia if I had my life to live again!"

A NEW VIEW OF LEARNING DISABILITIES

In the 1990s, more people than ever before are aware that learning disabilities do not simply go away as people grow up. Although many of the associated problems can be overcome, learning disabilities are a lifelong condition that people can learn to manage. Disabilities that have been kept as closely guarded secrets by adults are now beginning to receive proper diagnosis and remedial attention. As people with learning disabilities have become willing to discuss the once-unmentionable subject, several messages have emerged:

- There are lots of adults with learning disabilities who have built successful lives despite, *and sometimes because of,* their disabilities.
- It is never too late to learn. There is a growing recognition that adults can be helped with reading, writing, math, oral language, memory, organization, and study skills; can become able to finish high school or college; and can learn new professions and trades.

There is a lot to learn from those brave and generous adults with learning disabilities who have gone public in order to share their experiences. They have inspired others who felt that there was no way out of the darkness and have provided others a light to guide them on their way.

3
Masking Secret Shame

"My name's Franklin, so they called me Frankenstein from first grade on. My teachers told me the kids would stop teasing, but they didn't."

"I wasn't very good at anything. I was basically a clown."

"Since I couldn't learn anything from books, I learned to lie, cheat, and steal at school. I knew it was wrong."

"I thought I was retarded. When they told me I had a superior IQ, I thought they were crazy."

"I'm a person first. I'm an adult with learning disabilities, and learning disabilities complicate my life, but I'm not a learning-disabled adult."

Many of my students at the Night School resent being called *learning-disabled adults*. They would rather be called *adults who are learning disabled*. There is a crucial difference. The former phrase implies that identifying a person's learning disabilities gets at the essence of who that individual is. The latter phrase, though far from ideal, at least leaves open the possibility that *there is more to a person than his or her learning disabilities*.

Adults with learning disabilities have had a lot of experience with labels, with having other people sum them up in a phrase: "You didn't try hard enough" (that is, "You're *lazy*").

"You're a *bad boy*." "You're *slow*." "You failed" (that is, "You're *a failure*"). And, of course, many have struggled painfully with secret shame because they internalized such labels as children.

Labeling is part of an even more insidious tendency in our culture at large—the tendency of parents, educators, policy makers, and ordinary citizens to judge human intelligence and personality by one uniform standard. In recent years, among at least a few enlightened educators, a new view of personality and intelligence has been emerging—a pluralistic view that celebrates human differences. It has dramatic implications for adults and others who are learning disabled.

GARDNER'S THEORY OF MULTIPLE INTELLIGENCES

Howard Gardner, professor of education at the Harvard University Graduate School of Education, is one of the foremost exponents of a new approach to assessing human intelligence. In his book *Frames of Mind,* Gardner describes seven different types of intelligence, no one of which takes priority over any other. These are:

- musical intelligence, which gives great composers and performers to the world
- spatial intelligence, which produces artists, sculptors, and architects
- bodily-kinesthetic intelligence, which brings forth dancers and athletes
- interpersonal intelligence, drawn upon by all the world's great leaders, from Alexander the Great to Gandhi to Gorbachev
- intrapersonal intelligence, or empathy and insight, which produces psychologists, teachers, and healers

- linguistic intelligence, which gives rise to writers, journalists, and orators
- logical-mathematical intelligence, the intelligence of scientists and mathematicians

Of these, only linguistic and logical-mathematical intelligence are measured by IQ tests, SATs, and the other placement tests widely used in America to categorize children and adults alike. Creative intelligence in the five other areas is discounted or ignored.

Professionals hear a great deal about the IQ scores of the learning disabled and not enough about their approaches to tasks, about what they do when they don't know what to do, about how they manage their lives. Parents, teachers, and adults with learning disabilities often get wrapped up in test scores, quoting them at will, perhaps not understanding the subtleties of the subtests that make up a total score. People may forget their Social Security and telephone numbers, but they rarely forget their IQ scores or those of their children. Many people's self-images are built upon IQ and SAT scores, and so a revolution in thinking will be needed to alter the value that has been placed on those scores.

A new kind of testing has been proposed by Dr. Robert Sternberg, a psychologist at Yale University, who wants to test for qualities that actually succeed in the real world, both the whole range of intelligences as defined by Dr. Gardner and such qualities as *street smarts*—a shrewd awareness of what's going on and how it affects one's own survival. This is a quality that abounds in the learning-disabled population, yet rarely is it defined as intelligence or put to constructive use in schooling.

The growing number of proponents of new testing methods would not abolish current IQ tests. Drs. Gardner, Sternberg, and others want to supplement the traditional tests with assessments that evaluate other kinds of intelligence and ways of functioning in society. Several testing centers and university research groups are currently working to devise such tests, which often defy simple pencil-and-paper or question-and-answer formats.

Dr. Gardner would go even further. He is convinced that a narrow-gauge approach to the mind can mean unfulfilled lives for many people, including the learning disabled. So many talents are overlooked at school, at home, and by society at large that Dr. Gardner would look into such personality traits as character, responsibility, tenacity, purpose, courage, and will. These characteristics, he feels, are needed in the world quite as much as measured intelligence. As many biographies show, they are an important part of the makeup of most creative geniuses.

THE CONSEQUENCES OF UNIFORM THINKING ABOUT PERSONALITY AND INTELLIGENCE

The work of Drs. Gardner, Sternberg, and others reminds us that every human being is an amalgam of many thousands of discrete abilities and character traits. However, as he or she grows up, a person with learning disabilities is often viewed by one standard. Because of a single problem or cluster of problems, he or she is placed into a category that becomes a prison, and his or her potential is ignored. Typically, this sort of categorization happens first in school, where students are separated by the grades they receive into *smart* and *dumb*.

Well-known artist Robert Rauschenberg, often called the Master of Modern Art, summed up his experience in school this way: "It can make your life absolutely miserable when you can't keep up with the other people in school. Your whole social life is based on it, and you know, it took me years to realize that I wasn't stupid. If anyone with learning disabilities can learn that when they are still young, they can be saved an awful lot of pain and disturbing memories."

Children tend to believe what they hear about themselves. If a child becomes convinced that he is lazy or stupid, he has another burden to bear, on top of his learning disabilities.

> *Steeped in FAILURE*
> *after FAILURE*
> > *a soul becomes degraded,*
> > *a spirit becomes flattened.*
> *Some never recover.*
> *Other take years to recover.*
> *Still others find the inner strength*
> *To rise up and triumph, against the odds.*

Artist Chuck Close was one of the latter. "When I was in high school, you had to take this two- or three-day-long battery of tests to predict how well you would do in college in each of a hundred different areas. It was predicted that I was going to get an *F* average in every single area, including art, and the only thing I could get a *D*-minus average in was nursing. You know, that was devastating to me. Absolutely devastating. And I want you to know that I graduated from the University of Washington *summa cum laude,* and I graduated from Yale graduate school as a straight-*A* student. So they don't always know what they're saying!"

School days provide painful memories for most adults with learning disabilities. The ninety adult students of the Lab School's Night School are no exception. Ranging in age from nineteen to sixty, these intelligent, capable people have identified themseles as having trouble with reading, writing, or math, and sometimes all three. They have moved to the District of Columbia from Texas, Virginia, Illinois, New York State, Connecticut, and other areas just to attend the Night

School. Consider the following remarks about what they endured when younger:

> "School was a slow, painful daily torture."
>
> "School was a quicksand of frustration and despair."
>
> "My spirit died little by little, year by year."
>
> "It was like facing a firing squad each day—public humiliation, ridicule, potshots taken at me; the only thing missing was a live bullet."
>
> "I felt like I was being undressed in front of the class, and everybody could see all my pimples and warts."
>
> "School offered me a daily lesson on how inadequate I was."
>
> "I wondered if I had a brain tumor or some frightful brain disease."

Well-known recipients of the Lab School's Outstanding Learning-Disabled Achiever Award could empathize easily with these reactions. Singer-actress Cher told our Lab School children, "I don't have much respect for regular schooling. It shaves off your individuality and makes you fit into a world that's dull. You have to find the place that you can shine if you don't fit in with what everybody else is doing."

Harry Belafonte, singer and actor, told of his own horrifying school days: "I grew up in the school system of the ghettos of New York and of the plantation life in colonial Jamaica, British West Indies, where nobody understood the meaning of *learning disorder*. So, although my outward appearances indicated that I had the intelligence level, no one understood—or even worse, no one cared—that, besides sociological reasons, there may have been a genetic or biological reason for my restlessness and distracted behavior. Perhaps the cruelest experience of all was the punishment that went with all of this. In the West Indies as a student, I was constantly being physically abused, because the whipping of students was permitted, and in America, the degrading way in which I was ostracized and punished for my dysfunction made my childhood a very unhappy experience."

Teasing by other children can be extremely cruel and can leave some of the deepest scars. A child with learning disabilities who has internalized the poor opinion that adults in his life have of him is especially vulnerable to such harm. "I was a victim of name killing," said a Night School student. "I was called *retard, spaz, SpEd, Mr. Weirdo, dork* all through school. I'm relieved to be an adult."

Basketball star Magic Johnson said, "I did feel bad, no question, because you're sitting there, and you hear somebody reading right through the sentence, and you can only read word by word. You do feel bad because everybody's looking at you like you're an outcast. . . . It's a bad feeling, and a lonely feeling as well."

"I would have loved to do better at school," says a successful writer and illustrator, "but I didn't know how. So I just sighed and accepted my learning disabilities as one more fact of life, like brussels sprouts for dinner or having to make my bed. I didn't even know my condition had a name, *learning disability*, until I grew up."

Henry Winkler, executive producer of ABC-TV's *Mac-Gyver*, recalls: "As a child I was called stupid and lazy. People said, 'He is not living up to his potential!' My parents grounded me for weeks at a time because I was in the bottom 3 percent in the country in math. On the SATs I got 159 out of 800 in math. My parents had no idea that I had a learning disability. They never knew such a thing existed."

Of course, it is a dreadful error to think that a person is stupid or lazy simply because something is preventing him or her from succeeding at the linguistic and logical-mathematical tasks set by traditional schooling. Because they have been trained to deal with only one form of personality and intelligence, many teachers don't know what to do or to think when confronted by a child with learning disabilities who has exceptional abilities and yet doesn't function well in a traditional school environment.

The story of Roger Wilkins, now a scholar, journalist, and head of the Pulitzer Prize Board, is instructive in this regard: "I was in an all-white junior high school in Michigan, and not only the students but the teachers had never seen a black kid before. The teachers were impressed by my mastery of the English language, and they began to put me in a category, in their minds, with the smartest kids in school, who happened to be my friends. But it was a catch-22 because, since I didn't read well, they thought of me as the dumb-smart kid. It seems to me they thought I was smart the way black people were smart—that is, dumb-smart. It always came through that way, and it was very difficult to handle."

Being black and learning disabled has been described by one of the Night School students as a double whammy. A group of adult students shared that it is easy to wrap a lot of feelings about being slow and stupid and inadequate around racial slurs.

A woman at the Night School admitted that she really believed that blacks were limited in intelligence because she and her mother could not read. She had absorbed prejudice, and it had become part of her self-definition. It was only after she was tested and discovered that she was of high average intelligence that she began to realize how she had surrendered her opinion of herself to the bigots. Obviously, people who are continually seen and judged from one standard view are destined for trouble in school, in race relations, and in relationships generally.

MASKING THE SECRETS WITHIN

One of the terrible ironies of growing up with a learning disability is that people who are continually labeled or categorized often react to others' rigid view of them by constructing a different but equally rigid and destructive face to present to the world. I call these constructions *masks.*

People with learning disabilities adopt these masks to save what self-esteem they can. The masks deflect attention from their disabilities and let them hide, or avoid performing in, their weak areas. Such masks are destructive because they allow people to avoid coming to terms with their learning disabilities. Two examples will illustrate why these masks are constructed:

Richard Strauss, the Texas real-estate mogul and banker, says, "I was called lazy, willful, manipulative—and I wasn't. I didn't know what was wrong with me. I just knew I was trying hard, and it wasn't working. So then I turned to making mischief because I'd rather be called bad than dumb."

Thomas Kean, former governor of New Jersey and now president of Drew University, said, "I can remember rejecting learning as something I could not do and therefore something that maybe wasn't very good, something I should put away and try something else. I remember a couple of years when I tried to be the class clown. Perhaps as the class clown I found a place of my own that didn't require me to shine in areas where I really didn't feel I had the ability to shine."

Although the need for masks arises primarily from fear of exposure and ridicule, a mask can incidentally bestow a measure of power. Adopting a mask and wearing it constantly can be very manipulative. The mask allows a person to control a situation to some extent. He decides to distract others so they won't focus on his inability to do a task or to read or write. Even a person who disappears behind a passive mask, who pleads helplessness or says, "I don't care," is exerting some control over others, using the ruse to deny the importance of failure.

When manipulating events from behind their masks, people with learning disabilities call on their ingenuity, reasoning, and imagination. Diagnosticians tell us that the more a mask is used for manipulation, the more we need to probe the talents of the person who has constructed the mask. The talents that go into desperate role playing could, if recognized and channeled toward constructive ends, provide a foundation for learning instead of avoidance.

There are all kinds of defense mechanisms that adults with learning disabilities use. Adults describe in detail the lengths to which they went to deflect their parents' and teachers' attention from self-diagnosed incompetencies and failures. The message was, "Look at my antics—not at me!" Sometimes they succeeded in their diversionary tactics, but only at the cost of draining energy from their studying and from their work and pleasure. They lived in fear of being unmasked, of the world discovering their unspeakable secret—that they were really dumb. One adult describes a recurring nightmare in which people were pulling at his face and he was forced to put on a helmet to save himself.

> When we don't want people to see us as we are
> we put on a mask.
> When we want to hide what we're ashamed of
> we put on a mask.
> Then nobody can know the darkness
> of our secrets within.

Here are some of the masks worn by adults with learning disabilities:

The Mask of the Clown

"Isn't that a riot!"

"Ha, ha, ha . . . what a joke!"

Everything is funny when this guy is around. Laughter can obfuscate any issue. Academy Award–winning actress-singer Cher was the class clown at her school because she could not read, write, or do arithmetic, though she was exceedingly verbal and outstanding in the arts. Her teacher said that she was not working hard enough. She felt dumb. She dropped out of school at sixteen and was not tested for learning disabilities until she was over thirty. Another class clown, for the same reasons, was Henry Winkler, the Fonz. Marc Flanagan, steeped in failure in many schools he attended, also used the mask of the clown; today he produces comic TV shows, notably the award-winning *Tracy Ullman Show,* and writes for *The Simpsons.*

The Mask of Outrageousness

"I'm far-out."

"I don't like conformists."

"I believe in individualism to the extreme."

Through a wild choice of clothes, hair color, wigs, glasses, stockings, boots, or neckpieces, this person projects eccentricity and hides what he or she is worried about. Cher, remarkably talented as a singer, dancer, and actress, has drawn attention to herself through her provocative clothing and incredible wigs. Artist Robert Rauschenberg, who is learning disabled, did outrageous, unheard-of things, not only in school but with his painting. His works, treasured all over the world, are in almost every important international collection of contemporary art. Many critics believe he expanded the definition of art for a generation of Americans by daring to innovate.

The Mask of Super-Competence

> "Oh sure. Everyone knows that."
>
> "I know, I know, I know!"
>
> "Good artists don't have to read anyhow! I can do anything I want!"

With a great deal of bravado and a bit of arrogance, this person makes everything look simple. He can talk his way through anything. His logic is impeccable. He's good with people, with numbers, with problem solving, with troubleshooting. General George S. Patton, a dyslexic, assured his daughter that Napoleon couldn't spell either and quoted Jefferson Davis as saying, "A man must have a pretty poor mind not to be able to think of several ways to spell a word."

One person with dyslexia functioned as a leader of his city council and of top civic organizations in his city. Reading on a third-grade level, he never accepted a job as secretary or treasurer. He listened and organized well and he delegated reading and writing tasks to more competent people, though he tended to take credit for their work.

The Mask of Seduction

> "Come here, honey. Sit close and read to your man. Your man's too tired."
>
> "Hey, woman, write this down for me. Men don't write."
>
> "You men are so good at math. Can you help little me?"
>
> "Math is men's work. We girls just can't do it."

The macho man often uses flirting to get a female to do for him what he can't do himself. He hides behind his macho mask, making himself appear completely in charge and sexy. In the same way, a "helpless female" will ask a macho man to do what she can't do, thus hiding behind a mask of dependence that some men find sexy. She puts on a helpless act, bats her eyelashes at him, or leans on his shoulder. Both males and females use sexist stereotypes to hide their academic difficulties from view.

The Mask of the Good Samaritan

"Let me carry that for you."

"What can I do for you? Can I be of help?"

"Let me run your errands. I'll take care of your needs."

This person wants to please at any cost. Frequently, this person is too accommodating. He or she will echo what you say, work long hours, and be obsequiously helpful in order to fill a hidden agenda or to avoid tasks that invite failure. One student spent three years in a choir, though he detested it, because the choir director in his high school decided who was going to graduate.

The Mask of the Con

"My smarts got me by. I could sweet-talk any teacher and be absent for all tests."

"I could convince a teacher of any excuse: my dog died, my brother hid my homework, my mother brutalized me, the hand that I wrote with had been operated on twice."

"I learned to lie looking you straight in the face."

This wheeler-dealer negotiates with his teacher as to how much work is expected of him. G. Chris Andersen, vice-chairman of PaineWebber on Wall Street, has used his gift of gab to talk himself into or out of almost anything. He had a terrible time with every subject except math and used every ruse to get through high school. Even though he didn't know his left hand from his right, had great trouble reading, and couldn't spell, he graduated from the University of Colorado and won a scholarship to obtain his MBA from Northwestern University.

Harry Anderson, TV's Judge Stone on *Night Court,* grew up on the streets learning card games and magic. He conned and charmed his way through school. He was called a superior reader in his early school years when his textbooks had clear pictures to prompt him. He possessed an extraordinary memory and could remember anything he heard. At age sixteen he was valedictorian of his high school, and only *he* knew that he could barely read!

The Mask of Being Bad

> "Don't mess with me. You'll be sorry."
>
> "I don't care if she wants me to sit down. I won't."
>
> "I threw a book at him. So what?"
>
> "I'd rather be seen behaving badly than not learning."

Preferring to be seen as bad rather than dumb, a loser at school often becomes a winner on the street. This person feels stupid, powerless, or useless at school. His anger and frustration are often directed toward his teachers. His peers are likely to enjoy his acting out and encourage it.

A Dallas real-estate magnate, Richard Strauss, changed schools several times, always suffering the humiliation of not having learned to read or write. He compounded his problems by causing disruptions in his classrooms that diverted his teachers' attention away from his poor work. He was a senior in high school before he learned that his problems stemmed from learning disabilities.

The Mask of Not Caring

"It doesn't matter."

"Nobody cares about me. Who cares?"

"Whatever you do, I don't care."

The wearer of this mask is never vulnerable and risks no failure. If he tries to succeed and fails, he says that he wasn't trying and that it doesn't matter ("Those grapes were probably sour."). This mask keeps others as distant from him as possible but makes him feel woefully inadequate as well. If nothing matters, then there is no motivation for change, and it's impossible to get this person to move.

The Mask of the Strong, Silent Type

"I don't need to talk much."

"I believe actions speak much louder than words."

"Everything will work out just fine. We don't need to discuss anything."

Having excellent coordination and skill in sports, this person is revered by many, even idolized. Bruce Jenner, an Olympic decathlon champion who is dyslexic, says sports gave him self-esteem, and that reading aloud in the classroom was much harder and more frightening for him than competing in the Olympics. Sometimes the strong, silent type aches to open up and share his feelings, but he can't. He too frequently creates a wall between himself and those around him.

Sometimes the strong girl hides behind a smile and perfect behavior. Whatever the teacher tells her to do (except read) she does, and rather than admit that she can't understand, she pretends that everything is fine. She can never talk things over.

The Mask of Activity

"Have to make a call now."

"Sorry, I'm in a hurry. I can't talk now."

"I'm late now. I'll take care of it later."

This person is always on the move. Standing still might bring him too revealingly close to others, and so he precludes any intimacy. Constant activity wards away others and keeps him from having to perform. This person frustrates everyone around him. People complain that they cannot get hold of him. He wraps himself up in busy-ness, often smiling all the way. Nobody can catch him.

The Mask of Contempt

"They don't know how to teach here."

"The whole place sucks."

"Nobody in this world wants to help anybody."

Blame and negativity are the defining attitudes of the wearer of this mask. This joyless person has a bad word for everything. He wears out the people around him because nothing is ever good enough, and he takes no pleasure in his small successes. He's angry at the whole world for making him feel stupid, and he feels that the world owes him recompense. He puts everybody else on the defensive. Some prominent people who turned down Outstanding Learning-Disabled

Achiever Awards fit this mask. Hard on others, they were even harder on themselves.

The Mask of Boredom

> "Boy, is this dull!" Yawn, yawn.
>
> "What time is it now?"
>
> "Can I go to the bathroom?"
>
> "You don't really know how to teach, do you?"

With big yawns, loud sighs, tapping fingers and toes, this person lets his teacher know how bored he is. He operates by putting the other person on the defensive. Usually he is not bored but frustrated, unable to do what he's been asked to do. Thomas Edison, who often appeared bored, was kicked out of schools for not following instructions. He probably could not even hear the instructions and could not write down his assignments. Teachers who feel bad when a student acts bored often attempt to improve their presentations, not realizing that the boredom has little to do with their efforts. Frequently the child with learning disabilities makes teachers feel terrible about themselves. Feelings of inadequacy are very contagious.

The Mask of the Victim

> "It's not fair! Everyone picks on me!"
>
> "Why me? There's no justice anywhere."
>
> "Look, she's not calling on the others, just me!"

Often called a jailhouse lawyer because he has an argument for everything, this person collects injustices and takes on a "poor me" attitude. Though aggressive and precipitating arguments continually, he assumes no responsibility for anything. It is always someone else's fault. He angers the people around him and twists their annoyance with him to mean that they have singled him out for abuse.

The Mask of Helplessness

"I don't know. I don't understand."

"I'm such a failure."

"I'm dyslexic. I need help."

Through pity, whining, and sighing, this person gets everyone to help him, to do his work, to take on his responsibilities. This way he never puts himself on the line. He refuses to risk failure; he does not even try. However, he feels worse inside because he knows he did none of the work himself.

The Mask of Frail Health or Vulnerability

"My head!"

"My poor stomach!"

"My side . . . my back . . . my bladder."

To receive extra attention and get out of the work he cannot do, this person constantly pretends to be sick and talks about his frailties. Given something to read, he uses illness or fatigue as an excuse not to do it. He often holds his head, grabs his stomach, or limps along so that little is expected of him. He whines or cries if necessary. Expecting special privileges while avoiding what he cannot do, this person confuses everyone around him and usually gets away with it.

The Mask of Invisibility

> "I would hide in my shell, hold my neck in like a turtle, my eyes bulging out, almost pleading with the teacher not to call upon me."

> "You can get through school by not talking, just repeating when necessary, and taking a low profile—no waves!"

> "When I was in high school, I didn't speak up because the words tended to come out backward. I always sat in the back, and the bell usually rang before the teacher got to me, so I didn't have to embarrass myself."

Through looking frightened, whispering to teachers, or acting terrified with peers, this person, too, has everyone else doing his work for him. Nobody bothers this person sitting quietly for a long time with his head down. Sitting in the back of the classroom, he can melt into the crowd, into nothingness. . . . Teachers realize later that they barely knew he was there.

Frequently, the quiet, compliant child is bumped up from year to year, not learning, feeling dumber and dumber, whereas the child who acts out and who makes the teacher's life unbearable is often quickly referred to special services. The quiet one, who hides from everyone, usually is absent from school a great deal. He manages to keep others from expecting anything from him.

TAKING OFF THE MASKS

The earlier a child can be identified as learning disabled, the less he will be made to feel helpless and stupid or need to hide behind a mask. Parents and teachers must encourage the child to feel OK about himself. They need to let the child be who he is, prizing his talents and working on his areas of need. If a child is not made to feel stupid, he is much more open to being taught and more likely to embrace the support of adults around him.

Masks can be dropped when people understand their condition, have accepted it, and feel comfortable about being learning disabled. Enormous relief comes from learning that a person can be both intelligent and learning disabled.

A Night School student who had for years played the part of a comedienne to mask her many insecurities told a group of fellow adults with learning disabilities, "I feel like a leaden weight has been lifted off my shoulders by not having to pretend to be having a riotous time and not having to think up all those quips. I have energy now for my studies. I still want to have a good laugh from time to time, but the difference is that I'm not entertaining others anymore. I'm having fun!"

When students know which teaching methods work for them and which do not, when they discover how they learn best and what strategies they can use, usually there is no more need for covering up. But adult students confide that it is not that simple, even when they are feeling pretty good about themselves. When they are fatigued or facing major disappointments, they tend to fall back inside their masks. They need to seek refuge in these masks from time to time before they can give them up entirely. As one Night School adult put it, "The frailty of human beings is powerful . . . extraordinarily powerful. If only the world knew."

A WEALTH OF UNTAPPED POTENTIAL

When people view others in only one way, they overlook obvious talents and abilities. As former U.S. Fish and Wildlife Service director Frank Dunkle said, "I graduated from high school 114th out of 114. They referred to me as the little devil. I was condemned to be a person who would never go far. The principal told my folks, 'What you need to do for Frank is to try to find a plumber who will apprentice him and that's about the height of his endeavor.' Had I followed that, I would be a rich man right now. I turned out to be something that they didn't think I would be!" Too often, the world assumes "the pockets are empty."

Of course, no one's pockets, in this sense, are ever empty. When we dig a little deeper, beyond problems that lie at the surface, we discover a wealth of untapped potential. There are many ingredients that contribute to success in life that tests do not measure and that traditional teaching too often does not reward. These include subtle ingredients that have to do with drive and determination, with the setting of goals, with ingenuity and resourcefulness, and with interpersonal skills. To compose a sonata, to choreograph a dance, to photograph with an unconventional eye, to build a beautiful boat, or to ease the last days of someone who is terminally ill—these are the skills that humanize our civilization.

Rare is the adult who as a child could say, "Well, it doesn't matter so much that I can't read and write like other kids, because I'm a whiz at chess, and I'm pretty good at most sports." More common is the adult who said, and often still says, "I'm absolutely no good because I can't read and write properly. Nothing else counts. I'm just no good." That has to change.

Once adults with learning disabilities realize that they are not stupid, or lazy, or bad, or incompetent but are intelligent people with a mass of potential, their masks can gradually drop. Shame can melt away. Slowly, they can begin to prize their differentness and develop their unique talents into something productive.

4
Talent

"If I hadn't been able to escape to the art studio and paint, I think I'd have died!"

"I made the varsity football team, so kids respected me and didn't laugh at me too much when I goofed up in the classroom."

"Photography was what saved me. I couldn't write or spell, but I could compose essays through my pictures and express myself visually in countless ways."

"I loved organizing parties and social events. That success took the sting out of school, where I was a failure in class."

"Once my uncle showed me how to use a hammer and nails, and I found I could make things. That was always the one bright spot in my life."

"When I danced, I was completely happy and forgot that I couldn't read."

"Sometimes I thought my trombone was my only friend."

Each of these students with learning disabilities found escape from the devastation of feeling stupid by exercising a talent that brought satisfaction, respect, or at least some measure of comfort. Adults tell us that a talent or overriding interest does not completely compensate for feelings of failure in academic areas, but it does provide much needed enjoyment and a solid sense of achievement. It can also grow into a career that side-steps the obstacles presented by the learning disabilities. Parents and teachers, as well as the learning disabled themselves, must actively seek out areas of talent and special interests. The nurturing of talents and the remediation of learning disabilities must go hand in hand.

Some obvious talents are often ignored or misguidedly interpreted as annoyances—such as the thinking skills of a nonreader who compensates by manipulating everyone and every situation, or the dramatic flair of a teenaged comedian who embarrasses his family.

OBVIOUS TALENTS

When people have an obvious talent in a sport, in a science, in an art form, in speech, or in social interaction, they usually receive praise from the outside world, which helps to build their wobbly self-esteem and to soothe the sting of failures in school. However, adults with learning disabilities point out that such praise helps only a little; it does not make up for academic defeat.

Several learning-disabled celebrities demonstrated early talent in sports. Bruce Jenner, Magic Johnson, and Dexter Manley made subsequent careers in sports, but many who made careers in other areas also showed athletic talent, including Tom Cruise, Chris Andersen, Ann Bancroft, Malcolm Goodridge, Daniel Stern, Governor Gaston Caperton, Dr. Donald Coffey, and Margaret Whitton. Receiving recognition from others because of their athletic prowess gave these people an extra life, and in some cases the lift that they needed to propel them into successful careers.

Bruce Jenner, an Olympic gold medalist, tells of his own experience: "I just barely got through school. The problem was a learning disability, at a time when there was nowhere to get help. Probably the biggest fear of my life, barring none, was *not* competing in the Olympic Games against the best athletes in the world, but when I was a young boy, it was having to stand up in front of the class and read. It wasn't until later on that I found my niche, and that was in athletics. For the first time in my life, I could hold my head up high. I could go out on the football field and compete against a guy I knew was a real good reader, a real good student, and all of a sudden we were equal, and in most cases I could beat him. It was very important for me."

Adults who were excellent athletes often admit that teachers were more lenient with their grades because of their performance in sports. The athletes counted on these breaks to help them get through high school. Often they would coach their teachers' kids or give them good seats at ball games as a way of sliding by in the classroom.

Some athletes never received the scholastic help they needed because teachers stood in awe of their sports abilities or because schools wanted their teams to win so much that they neglected the academic needs of their athletes. Dexter Manley, the renowned football player, is a perfect example. He was so big and aggressive, even in grade school, and later demonstrated such football talent that he was passed from one grade to another without learning any academic skills. He graduated from high school and ended up at a university on an athletic scholarship, though he was barely able to read at even a second-grade level. For four years he played football at Oklahoma State, but he never graduated. What was the message to Dexter? He was treated as an animal, used, and exploited. Harboring inside himself the secret that he could not read, write, spell, or do math, he carried around a *Wall Street Journal* to project an intellectual image and disguise his shame. He played on the Redskins football team for years, but no one, including his wife, knew that he could not read. He finally learned to read at the Lab School's Night School and with a Lab School tutor.

Actor Daniel Stern credits his drama teacher, who doubled as his English teacher, for getting him through his Maryland high school. Stern says that this man admired his talent and wanted to see it developed. This teacher worked with him on his acting and his English, and when he could, he ignored some of Stern's poor written work. Stern comments, "I had a special talent of talking people into things, or out of things. I'm really lucky in that I have been able to have an artistic career where I actually make a living at it. I can't really imagine doing anything else!"

At age eight, Richard Strauss sold his mother's best jewelry to children in the neighborhood for twenty-five cents apiece. At school, he sold lost pencils back to his fellow students. If parents and teachers had looked for his hidden talents, they would easily have spied his joy in selling things. Not surprisingly, in adult life Strauss sells property. At age twenty-two, he opened his own real-estate firm. All told, he has developed well over a billion dollars' worth of commercial and residential real estate throughout the United States.

Many entrepreneurs with learning disabilities remember how their families complimented them on their salesmanship. "When I ran a lemonade stand, I could get people who weren't even thirsty to buy my stuff," said one Night School adult proudly. He is now working successfully in sales in a department store. Some women with learning disabilities apply their interest in fashion to jobs in boutiques, where they feel very successful helping customers choose outfits that flatter their figures. People with a flair for design, for the mix and blend of colors, for arranging shapes and forms, usually show this propensity at an early age. The lucky ones are encouraged to develop these skills.

Many adults knew from early childhood what their interests were. Dr. Donald Coffey, a noted science researcher and deputy director of the oncology clinic at Johns Hopkins University Hospital and Medical School, said, "I got really fascinated with the outdoors in Tennessee. I didn't read much, but I loved *Huckleberry Finn*. I wanted to build my own raft and go down the river to explore the wild. I got into . . . curiosity about nature and life, and later that led me into science."

Dr. John Horner, curator of paleontology at the Museum of the Rockies at the University of Montana in Bozeman, said that he found his first dinosaur fossil at age eight, at which time he first decided to become a paleontologist. With his father he collected, catalogued, and stored away the fossils he delighted in finding. His love of dinosaurs and fossils kept him attending school because he knew an education would allow him to pursue his great interest: "I thought I was a real idiot, and I'm sure everybody else thought so, too, but I loved digging, and I knew one day I would find the remains of dinosaur life that could tell me how they lived, and I wanted to know that."

Famous architect Hugh Newell Jacobsen has won ninety different awards for design, including six from the American Institute of Architects and twenty Architectural Record Awards for the best house design of the year. Since childhood he was noted for his impeccable eye, his fine taste, his sense of history, and his boundless energy. At the Lab School gala of 1990, Jacobsen said, "It is particularly joyful to stand in front of all of you after this grief, and I really mean grief. I still smell floor wax and feel scared. The hours of agony, of standing at the blackboard, never coming up with the answers, and everybody else sitting down . . . and our fathers knew we were lazy, and schools knew we were dumb, and we knew we were neither. I was terrible at math. I failed math time and time again. I never did pass algebra or geometry. I still can't. As an architect I hire engineers; someone else has done that for me for years."

Jacobsen, like many other artists and architects with

learning disabilities, was a visual thinker in schools that didn't appreciate visual thinking. Unable to conform, such individuals often drop out. Fortunately, Jacobsen was allowed to get through the Graduate School of Architecture at Yale University without meeting the math requirement. Jacobsen's plea to Lab School students was, "It may come late to you, but the cry is to find something that you really love to do. I did about the only thing I really loved to do; it all came out of drawing and imagining what was inside a drawing."

Celebrated artist Robert Rauschenberg, another visual thinker who hated school, immersed himself in nature and sketched instead of wrote. Rauschenberg said, "I think we make fantastic artists because we don't have any past to forget. We don't have to fight history because we can't remember it! We start all over every day, and if one can feel excited about that, it's an advantage, not a handicap. I do lots of print work and . . . I cut right through it because I can see it backward while I'm doing it forward. When I figured out I was dyslexic, I was already a well-established artist. . . . It was a great relief to find out, because there was a reason for it. It wasn't something created by the outside world. It was something created by the inside world. I think if you have difficulty achieving in one area, there's a certain kind of balance that comes out, and you can achieve in another, if you can find your level."

For many children with learning disabilities, talent in music, art, photography, film-making, drama, or dance has a good chance of being noticed and nurtured by a parent or teacher. Applause from an audience helps. So do exhibitions in which the child's artwork is beautifully framed and his or her name is prominently displayed. Exhibitions of beautifully bound books authored by child storytellers and either dictated to adults or written on computers excite children further about the world of books and help them to feel good about their creative abilities.

A person with the hidden handicap of learning disabilities

will often have an artistic talent precisely because he or she has learned unique ways of looking at things. Very often such a person has survived on "radar," by picking up unusual signals, or by developing a special skill that bypasses his or her disabilities. Nineteen-year-old Jerome can create sophisticated animated films, though he cannot write two consecutive English sentences. Many adults with learning disabilities have such a disparity between their potential and their academic performance, between their creativity and their mastery of schoolroom skills.

WHEN TALENTS AREN'T SO OBVIOUS

Often so much attention is focused on a child's disabilities that his or her less-obvious abilities or talents are ignored. Unfortunately, the child is often forced to use his or her abilities to escape from frustration and shame or as an ingenious way to deflect attention from his or her shortcomings. Thus, unique educational opportunities are missed. The treasure troves of hidden talent possessed by people with learning disabilities can lead an educator to new ways of teaching. The unorthodox approaches of a youngster with learning disabilities can often be turned into valuable tools for learning.

Adults are too often prone to see a child's unusual, unique abilities as negative qualities—to criticize a child for drawing instead of keeping his fingers still while listening or to rebuke the child for dramatizing a scene instead of just discussing it factually. The tinkerer who can't keep his hands off anything often turns out to be an engineer or a talented mechanic. One able lawyer says that during his school years he was continually told to stop being so argumentative, but he claims that he kept interested and kept learning by questioning everything, while enjoying the attention he received. The verbal child who provokes arguments may be showing the reasoning and verbal skills that befit a good lawyer. Many children with learning disabilities shine in areas where inventiveness and resourcefulness are prized. A professional puppeteer remembers that as a child he used all kinds of objects to represent dramatic characters. Often a daydreamer has a powerful imagination that could be put to good use—visually, if not verbally.

There's a special aura of wonder that people with learning disabilities often radiate. They don't take everything for granted. They seem to discover anew the smell of freshly cut grass, the feel of the wind caressing the face, the loud gurgle of the last drops going down the bathtub's drain, perhaps because they sometimes do not see the whole picture. Maybe they display a certain guilelessness, but there's a freshness to their perceptions. With maturity most of us lose that freshness and become jaded. The more creative among us seem to hold on to the playfulness of children. Many learning-disabled adults do so.

My point is that many adults with learning disabilities are especially gifted and creative. Sometimes they are impulsive. The more impulsive they are, the more we become aware of their unusual visual responses, tune in to their divergent ways of thinking, and hear their unedited comments. In a very verbal world, people who are language impaired cannot convey their genius through words, so it comes out through computer graphics, mechanical models, architectural renderings, or some other artform. With children, we see examples such as the following:

- Margie, eleven years old, when asked what her father, a doctor, did, drew circles, which confused everyone. Finally she said, "He does rounds."
- Twelve-year-old Alan, when asked what animal he saw in a forest, drew a recognizable fox.

- Teen-aged George, given the date 1812, tapped out a drumbeat with his hands and then was able to put into words various features of the War of 1812.

There are many adults who, rather than describe something to you, prefer to say, "Let me show you" or "I can demonstrate it." Our society tends to characterize these people as boring because they don't use language well. However, a good demonstration is far from boring, and skill at giving demonstrations is an extremely marketable ability.

Sometimes talents are recognized and prized at school, but at other times, especially when the inability to read, write, or do math is looked upon as willful laziness, children are punished by being kept from the very activities in which they excel. A teacher might say, for example, "Carol is so far ahead in music that she should skip music and work on her spelling." A remedial period of spelling then replaces Carol's beloved music class, which is equivalent to removing a life preserver from a drowning swimmer.

Bruce Jenner, talking to Lab School students, put it this way: "Your parents are trying to do their best; they love you. But they may say that until you get your reading skills up, you can't go out for sports or you won't be in music class. That's unfortunate because it is so important that everybody gets a pat on the back and knows they're doing a good job. I found sports, and I could hold my head up with all my friends and feel good about myself. And that gave me confidence that I could lick the reading problem or at least cope with it. You've got to have your activities that you can do well in and feel good about yourself. But you also have to continue to work on the problems you have."

Often the talents of people with learning disabilities are developed as coping mechanisms. What the general public tends not to recognize is how many things the learning disabled have to do consciously. Most people don't have to think about screening out noise or to devise methods to focus their attention on what's being said. They don't continually have to invent ways to remember things, and they don't explicitly have to organize everything that they do. They don't have to create visual ways to remember passages of time so that they can hand papers in on time or arrive somewhere promptly. They don't have to rely on landmarks to find their way around. They don't have to think about how not to bump into a wall, knock everything off their desks, or spill the coffee. Most people simply do these things.

The effort that adults with learning disabilities must expend just to live is unbelievable, and then they must do even more to keep paying attention, to organize themselves in a society regimented by space and time, and to become productive. It is amazing that they have the energy to be competitive with others when just getting through daily life and school is so overwhelming. Non-celebrities with learning disabilities have not been recognized for their incredible achievements, but they deserve profound respect from their families and communities. They have worked ten times harder than the rest of us for their successes, and they have had to reach deep within themselves to find all the resourcefulness they can muster.

They have had to take many risks to succeed, and they have had to ask continually, "Why not?" Not able to follow the proper rules in folk dancing, they have designed exciting dance patterns of their own. Unable to create neatly ordered scrapbooks, they have produced magnificent collages. Unable to retrieve the exact words they need, they have coined beautifully evocative phrases such as "It makes the heart in a person expand when they play that music" or "The powerful hot sun was patting my back."

Dr. Donald Coffey said, "In my field [medicine] a learning disability can be a blessing because it forces you to think. I say, 'If this is true, what does it imply?' I start thinking about it. I don't read about it. You can have straight *A*s from Harvard and not really think. Many of the people who come through my lab cannot think. And I'm running around all the time thinking, 'What does this mean? How can we test? How can we prove this?' By overcoming the fact that I cannot read and write well and I misplace things, it has actually strengthened me in this other direction, because now I really think."

Other, subtler abilities that the person with learning disabilities may not be aware of need to be recognized and cultivated. These include perceptiveness in interpersonal relationships, insight, the ability to disregard details and go to the core of a question, empathy for others, and street smarts. Many adults with learning disabilities have succeeded because of their interpersonal skills. The child who was a genial host may be the maitre d' in a fine restaurant. The gregarious child who made everyone feel good about himself may well become your representative on the city council, in the state legislature, or in Congress. The diplomatic youngster may go into the State Department.

Some adults with learning disabilities are very direct: they go to the core of a question with no beating around the bush, maybe because they speak impulsively, without thinking through the consequences of what they will say. Nevertheless, it can be refreshing to hear: "The truth is that we are destroying our own environment and poisoning it, and the world's future depends upon our activities now to preserve it." Sometimes the comments pinpoint a friend's or relative's flaws, with more unpleasant consequences.

Some adults with learning disabilities are so literal and concrete that they have no sense of humor; others learned to laugh at their disabilities and to make comedy from them. Architect Hugh Newell Jacobsen said, "It's the peer group that used to get to me harder than anyone else, the kids my own age. There's smoke one puts up: you get to be funny; you get to be very funny!"

Comedy writer and producer Marc Flanagan built a career of comedy writing and producing comic TV shows. He claims it all began with a disaster he experienced as a boy. He said, "I wanted desperately to get on the Catholic Youth Organization baseball team. I wasn't a very good athlete, but perhaps as a by-product of dyslexia, I became real crafty. I asked my father to coach the baseball team so I would have a place on the roster. But I was cut. I was stunned. While I was still reeling from the defeat, some other parents put together a sort of B league for kids who failed to make the CYO peewee team—a kind of cut squad. I practiced and I practiced, and then this coach cut me, too. I walked down the road feeling sorry for myself and sort of banging my head with my autographed glove and thinking, 'Oh, this is so terrible! I got *cut from the cut squad!*' And then I just started to laugh, and I continued to find the humor in it all."

One Night School adult shared that his parents saw him as devious, able to get out of or around anything, but not as clever and pragmatic. Today he invents and develops children's toys. "The most manipulative child I've ever seen" frequently turns out to be a most talented youngster who anticipates defeat and failure, tries to save face, and uses his excellent brain to sidestep humiliation. Many successful adults were "terrible" children. A school principal, like many teachers, says, "These learning-disabled youngsters are a bunch of con artists." The mask of conning demonstrates quick intelligence and excellent problem-solving abilities. Many adults with learning disabilities have "conned" themselves into high-level management jobs where they have succeeded.

A successful actress recalls that she first found her dramatic flair as "a con artist and a cheat" at school, where she would do anything to hide her disability and to avoid failure: "I was always acting to cover up the fact that I wasn't doing the work the way everybody else was doing it. I'd make up stories and act them out. And I'd act like my teachers, too, to make sure they wouldn't find out that I didn't know what I was doing! The only subject I couldn't cheat in was math, because I couldn't understand enough of it to cheat."

SPURRING INTERESTS AND TALENTS

Many disabilities that produce failure in traditional schools might be seen as abilities in life's rough waters. Thomas Edison, Auguste Rodin, and Hans Christian Andersen were disasters at school but learned to use their abilities to compensate for or circumvent their disabilities. When this point was raised at a meeting for parents whose children have learning disabilities, one father bellowed, "My kid will never be Einstein or Woodrow Wilson or Nelson Rockefeller or any other great guy. I don't want to hear about them! All I want is for him to live a decent life and hold a job." Another father, who himself had learning disabilities, shot back, "Tell us what your son *can* do. Tell us what you *like* about him!" The second father's message was to look at the whole person, not at just the student; to look at his strengths, not just at his bundle of problems.

"Well, none of us asked for a dyslexic child. The Einsteins, the Pattons, the Edisons did not ask for one, either, nor did they realize that God was giving them a genius, a hero, a great inventor. But all of us will learn, in time, that what we have been given is a very special gift for which, in ignorance, we did not ask," said Mrs. James Totten, daughter of General George S. Patton and grandmother of a Lab School student who is now en route to graduating from college. She was speaking at a Lab School luncheon honoring her in 1984 in Washington, D.C.

Special interests can be turned into a life's work. Judy, a biologist, tripped over everything, was totally disorganized, didn't look carefully at anything or listen well to directions, and expressed herself poorly. As a child, in one of her class-rooms, she became intrigued with tadpoles. Her parents helped her raise tadpoles until the tadpoles became frogs. There followed many trips to the library to learn about frogs, and her parents introduced her to a scientist who showed her around his laboratory. By the time Judy reached junior high school, she was a walking encyclopedia, not only on frogs but on all amphibians, and in high school she was the star of her biology class.

Another adult, Martin, got hooked on cars. In his youth, his father took him to every car show for miles around and encouraged him to build up a collection of model cars. He, too, went to the library, to see picture books on cars, and then became interested in Henry Ford and the development of the first cars in America. This language-impaired youngster, diffident and isolated, spoke with enthusiasm and knowledge about automobiles. He made a best friend who loved cars, and they worked in a garage as teenagers. This opened up a whole new interest in manufacturing, the business he is in today.

The learning disabled seem to fall into two extremes—those who are guileless and naive, and those who are street smart and shrewd. The street-smart people employ on the streets all the problem-solving ingenuity that has not been uncorked in schools. Sometimes the street activity turns into crime. A lot of criminal activity, if turned into positive actions, could lead to inventions, success in business, investigative work, or detective stories. Channeling negativism into productive activity demands careful analysis of what tasks a person has done successfully or has simply enjoyed. Then those tasks must be combined into challenging activities appropriate to the person's own learning style.

All of us seem to prefer a particular way of learning. Some of us need to see things to learn. Others need to see and touch. Some need to see and hear. Others require a demonstration. Some can learn only by hearing what to do. Others need to write something down to learn it. Many people learn best by doing—by seeing, touching, hearing, and discussing. How do you learn best? What means do most schools and colleges employ? Usually educators use lectures and reading. We lose many learning-disabled people that way, because we are not looking for their talents or deep interests. As author Elizabeth D. Squire has said, "Because my three sons, my three grandchildren, and I were all able to read in a limited way and talk like crazy, no school ever diagnosed even one of us. I shiver to think how many people there are out there who continue to think they must be dumb or lazy or jinxed because they can't learn in the 'right' way."

5
Drive

"My whole life has been work, interspersed with a little play from time to time."

"I worked ten times harder than anyone I knew, and still my school results were not exactly great."

"I felt—I'm going to show the world I can amount to something."

"All life seemed to be about was sitting at a desk, working, trying, getting help with the assignments, eating, sleeping, and more working."

"I nearly killed myself with hard work."

The adversities faced by people with learning disabilities often give them enormous drive. Called stubborn and inflexible because of their single-mindedness, they sometimes reach their goals through sheer, dogged tenacity, at a cost that is almost beyond belief. Those who succeed know that the struggle was worthwhile, and many of them are glad to extend a helping hand to others with learning disabilities who are coming after them.

People with this fierce drive exhibit high energy, perseverance, and a great deal of willpower. Once they have settled on an objective, nothing will stop them. Almost invariably, they mention the support they received early in life from parents or teachers or both as a vital ingredient of their final success. But the drive itself comes from within.

What ignites this fierce determination to succeed? Here's what some people with learning disabilities have said:

> "My mother worked so hard to help me succeed, I'm not going to let her down."

> "My uncle's dyslexic, but he made it, so I can, too."

> "Anger motivated me. I was angry that I was stuck with this problem, and I was going to show the world that I could do it!"

> "I managed to squeak through college out of sheer meanness and because creative thinking was 'in' then."

> "I felt so rotten inside that I just had to keep trying to prove I was a good guy."

> "I wanted to show my friends I wasn't all bluff."

> "I had to make up for a lot of lost time."

> "I sometimes talked out loud to myself, saying things like 'Hang in there, you'll get it' or 'You're going to get there.'"

> "I did what I had to do to get through school. So what if it took much longer for me than anyone else!"

STUBBORNNESS

Everybody fails at something at some time in life. Some of us just quit and give up. Others return to the task with renewed vigor and zeal, determined to lick it. Perhaps the fighters feel a need to prove that they are competent, to show their worth to other people, and perhaps that is part of what creates the unbelievable drive and stick-to-itiveness demonstrated by many people with learning disabilities. Their tenacity, perseverance, and massive determination must be witnessed to be fully comprehended. It is awesome!

Many adults with learning disabilities appear incredibly stubborn. Parents complain about this stubborn streak in their children with learning disabilities. They say their child refuses to be flexible, will not give in. Sometimes the child will not stop doing what he has been told not to do, will not stop defending himself, and continues to argue, going on and on, driving parents and teachers to distraction.

Maybe we need to look at stubbornness in a more positive light and see it as the grit that contributes to later success. This stubborn child who will not give up easily will pursue his vital interests to the nth degree. He falls down, gets up, meets more obstacles, teeters, falls, and gets back into the fray.

Malcolm Goodridge, a top manager with American Express, tells how he got started: "I was running a hotel in Pennsylvania when a job opened up. The person who was picking the individual for this particular job had three contenders to deal with, and I was probably the last one of the three. I got in my car at eight o'clock at night and drove for three and a half hours and banged on his door at 11:30 at night and said, 'I want this job. What do I have to do to get this job?' He was so impressed with the idea that I drove down to his house and woke him up that he said, 'You've got the job, so I can go back to sleep!'"

The almost naive directness of Goodridge's approach is typical of people with learning disabilities. He went straight to the man who could give him the job he wanted and demanded to know how he could get it. A more sophisticated person might have used a more subtle stratagem, such as calling on influential contacts, to gain the same objective. Goodridge barged straight to the heart of the matter with sincerity and trust. And it worked!

One adult with learning disabilities who was at the Lab School as a child had the nickname "Mule" because of his stubbornness. He wanted a job at a graphic-arts studio. However, he could not have filled out an application, and he tensed up when talking about himself. Therefore, he sent the studio a videotape of himself working on various art projects. This brilliant strategy landed him the job!

ENERGY FUELS THE MOTOR

Often described as very energetic and hardworking, some of the learning disabled have what is today often called ADHD (Attention Deficit Hyperactivity Disorder). Their relentless energy often seems purposeless and scattered, but in an adult such energy can lead to great productivity.

Dr. Donald Coffey, a distinguished professor in three departments at Johns Hopkins University Medical School, told our Lab School children, "You cannot become a professor in three different fields if you've only read three books in your life, and that's been my problem. One of the things I have trouble doing is focusing on something. And so my mind sort of jumps around. I cannot pay attention to things, but once I sort of lock in on it, I'm sort of like a bulldog. . . . I just stay right on it until it almost becomes absurd. I'm scatterbrained about things. I get into everything. Yet I am tenacious—the bulldog—once I am involved in something."

Another clinical condition that we often see in the learning disabled is *perseveration*. This means the mindless repetition of an action, such as drawing the same picture over and over again or relentlessly making the same remark beyond the point at which most people will stop. A person who perseverates seems to have been taken over by an activity. The perseveration is organic. Organic behavior resulting from neurological dysfunction or immaturity may thus contribute to the dogged pursuit of a single goal. As one adult at Night School said, "When I am involved in something, nothing else matters. I will proceed there at all costs, not looking around me at anything else. It's like something inside me is driving me."

An innovative junior-high-school teacher constructed an intriguing maze for his students, all of whom had learning disabilities. The class attacked the puzzle with enthusiasm. As the students got more involved, the teacher suddenly realized, to his dismay, that the maze lacked an exit! It could not be solved until he made corrections in it. He asked the students to stop, but they simply would not give up, despite his explanations. It was as though their racing motors could not be turned off.

Fred Friendly, a professor in charge of media and society at Columbia University Graduate School of Journalism, was equally persistent. "In high school I took geometry, which I never should have taken. The teacher said that nobody in all the history of mathematics, from Archimedes on down, had ever trisected a triangle and proved it. So I set about for three months to try to trisect a triangle and prove it. When I came in with a half-baked version, the teacher, who was also the football coach, bawled me out, "How do you like this kid having the arrogance to try to do what nobody has ever done in 2,500 years?" He made an absolute fool of me, and I never did another piece of homework in geometry ever again. The kids razzed me and called me Aristotle. That turned me off math for the rest of my life."

One leading American paleontologist, Dr. John R. Horner, who has greatly expanded the world's knowledge of dinosaurs, described his dogged determination to get an education despite his rather severe learning disabilities. He barely made it through high school. "I read real slow. If there were difficult concepts in a conversation, it took me a long time to understand what was being said. It was much worse in college," he said. Horner flunked out in 1967, served with the Marines in Vietnam, and then returned to America to try college again. He pursued courses in paleontology for seven years without earning a degree. But he learned a great deal, and his work earned him an honorary doctorate in paleontology many years later from the University of Montana.

Horner said, "I took only courses that applied to paleontology. Every once in a while I tried to sneak into an English class, but I was just too far gone by then. At the end of every quarter, they'd kick me out, and I'd just reapply. One quarter they wouldn't let me in, so I just went and sat in on the classes. . . . I think that if kids are really dyslexic and they want to do something, they are going to do it. I figured if it came to the point where I was starving, I could always drive a truck. But it worked out. And it wasn't anything insurmountable." When asked by Lab School children to explain his single-mindedness, he said, "I like to dig holes in the ground. I like to be outside. And I like to find things that nobody else has found. . . . A dinosaur egg that has an embryo inside—well, there are thirty-six of them in the world, and I found thirty-five."

SINGLE-MINDEDNESS

Successful people with learning disabilities are frequently characterized as persons of great energy, as more enthusiastic than others, as able to work longer and harder hours, and as being obsessed with being successful.

Gaston Caperton is a man with a passion for excellence. He gets up to read at 6:00 A.M. every day, just as his father had done when reading to him. In almost no time, through drive, zeal, and a competitive spirit, Caperton turned his father's small insurance company, which had five or six employees, into one of the largest independent insurance companies in America, with five hundred employees. He had never been in politics when he decided to run for governor of West Virginia.

Like everything else he did, he went for it just as hard as he could. And he won, against the odds. He said, "I think I'd have had a much different career without a learning disability. One of the things it did for me was give me a lot of energy. I'm always trying to prove myself; so I was probably an overachiever and overworked."

Actor, director, and producer Henry Winkler would not settle for mediocrity: "It is not easy to compete when you have a learning disability, but it is possible. When you *will* something, it is no longer a dream. I wanted to do what I'm doing today. People told me I'd never make it. . . . They told me I'd never get into school. . . . They were responding to who they thought I was, not to who I really was."

Many adults with learning disabilities tell us how single-minded they were about mastering some special skill. Some remember being bedeviled by tying their shoes; they conquered the problem by working for hours on it. Others remember how difficult reading a clock was and how many contortions and hours of work they had to go through to do it.

Enrico had the problem of speaking English as a second language added to his learning disabilities, but his poor eye-hand coordination was the problem that distressed him most. He could not catch a ball. Unable to play baseball or tennis in junior high school, he went out for soccer. The school coach let him play, though he was by far the worst member of his team, but when the coach was absent, his teammates relegated him to the bench. He was teased by his peers both for his poor English and his bad soccer. Enrico was absolutely determined to succeed. He got his parents to send him to summer soccer camp. He practiced kicking at home for several hours each day. As he slowly improved, his determination won the admiration of his school friends. In his sophomore year in high school he made the varsity team. By his senior year he was the team's highest scorer. He still lacked agility and precision, but he learned to wait for his opponents' mistakes and then to move in aggressively, with dogged tenacity. He became a school hero.

The positive side of this sort of single-mindedness is that it gets the job done. However, there is a negative side as well. Often the job is completed at a terrible personal cost, and sometimes the tenacity of adults with learning disabilities makes them rigid and unbending. Frequently they see only one way to do things. They don't like to try anything new or different, shy away from the unfamiliar, and cannot tolerate substitutions or changes in plans. Frequently, their rigidity turns off acquaintances, and they have trouble making friends. Sometimes such a person tends to be obnoxious in his insistence that there is only one correct way. He may take the same route to work every day, eat the same breakfast and lunch every day, use only one brand of pen, or make an incontrovertible rule of calling the weather report on the telephone every morning before he brushes his teeth.

Some students with learning disabilities outgrow this one-way inclination by adulthood. Others do not. Students in the latter group must be helped to select vocations or colleges in which the demands on them are not too varied at one time. At some colleges, only two subjects are studied in depth every minisemester; some students can do their best in such an environment.

Nonnie Star, a social worker and director of a reading program for adults with learning disabilities in Woodmere, New York, is herself learning disabled and spent hundreds of hours at college taping classroom lectures, listening to taped textbooks, and then transcribing the tapes into notes. Her handwriting, spelling, and organization were so bad that she often could not decipher the notes once they were finished—but there was no other way for her to learn. She often thought of quitting college and graduate school. However, she says, "If I had quit I would have had nothing, and nothing is what I felt like most of my life." She persevered single-mindedly and succeeded.

Cathy, a college junior who has great trouble with auditory memory, tapes every two-and-a-half-hour class she takes at the local university and then recopies the lectures word for word to get them fixed in her brain. Subsequently, she highlights the most important points with a yellow marker. It takes Cathy at least five to six hours to copy every tape and at least an hour more to highlight the critical issues. And then she studies the material! She does not question the incredibly hard work involved. She simply says that it is necessary in order for her to pass a course.

Neurological immaturity or dysfunction can make it difficult for a person to integrate several things at once. Many people with learning disabilities can do only one thing at a time if they want to do it well. Milton, aged twenty, said, "Please don't talk to me when I'm putting mustard on my roll." His friends laughed and thought he was either joking or being ridiculous, but Milton was in fact saying that he could do only one thing at a time.

Joe confided that he can do several operations at once when he is sitting in front of a computer: "It's all framed for me and I just burrow in." But Joe had failed at a summer job serving at a lunch counter, where customers typically made several different, urgent demands on him at the same time. He understood each separate order as it came to him but could not integrate requests from so many directions at once and grew frantic in the attempt. He is now successfully employed by the military as a computer specialist.

HIGH-POWERED WILLPOWER

Most of us habitually function on automatic drive, screening out noise and distractions. We don't need to think through everything we do, step-by-step. We take much of our daily life for granted, brushing our teeth or dialing a long-distance telephone number without a thought. We have an internal sense of time. We proceed without pause to a nearby destination. We can describe events or remember people's names and addresses without strain.

Many people with learning disabilities can perform these same tasks only with supreme effort, if at all. It can be humbling to watch a jaunty, wide-eyed young person try, try, and try again to pack a suitcase neatly or to carry a tray in a cafeteria without spilling everything or to write down a telephone message. Getting ready for school often taxes such a person's energy for work in the classroom. Yet he or she usually manages to put out 100 percent anyway. One teacher of an adult with learning disabilities said, "He's an extremely slow reader, but he will sit until he gets through whatever he has to read. It's mind-boggling. I would never be able to work as hard as he does!"

Malcolm Goodridge of American Express recalls, "In 1958, I had to take a botany examination. This meant walking through the woods with a professor and identifying some 100 to 150 plants, bushes, and trees by their Latin names. The night before the exam . . . I broke a lot of pencils. I almost broke my hand hitting it against the wall. I cried a lot. And I said to myself, 'Goodridge, you gotta do it now, because if you don't, you're never gonna do it.' So I buckled down for fourteen hours and learned every letter in the Latin alphabet and the American alphabet, a couple of times, and I pulled through and passed the exam with an eighty-three the next day."

Frank Dunkle, former director of the U.S. Fish and Wildlife Service, said he "memorized, memorized, memorized" to obtain a master's degree in wildlife biology, which would allow him to be employed by the Montana Fish and Game Department—his first goal in a memorable career.

Achievers like Dunkle and Goodridge are so engrossed in their efforts that they seldom realize how immensely hard they are working. They almost take it for granted that a person has to work that hard to make something of himself.

People with learning disabilities who are driven to succeed rarely look at their watches. Often they estimate time poorly and, when focused on a task, like studying for an exam, cannot evaluate how long they have been at it. One college freshman worked so hard that she became seriously exhausted; her worried parents had her tested repeatedly for mononucleosis. Another student, having collapsed at the end of her first year of college, took off the next year and worked. After another year of college, she became so ill that she had to take off another semester. She completed college by taking only two or three courses a semester until graduation.

The learning disabled aim for high goals as if to prove once and for all that they are as capable as others. They work as if to make up for lost time. Sometimes they exude a single-minded, ferocious intensity of which people meeting them for the first time are uncomfortably and acutely aware.

When adult students come to the Lab School's Night School determined to achieve and to go to college, there is no stopping them. They are not distracted by dating or cars. In the past they may have had drug episodes, bouts with alcohol, or wanderlust, but now they are consumed by high-powered willpower to reach their goals. "I have never seen so much raw ambition," said a visiting specialist in vocational rehabilitation. And yet these students are continually hard on themselves, insisting that they should have worked harder or done more. They tend to berate themselves for being lazy and not going all out. It's as though the voices of others in their past continue to harry them, telling them to try harder.

Tracey Gold, a teenaged TV star with learning disabilities, asserted, "You have to fight harder to succeed. But it makes you a stronger person. I never thought of myself as disabled or inferior in any way. Sure, it took me a little longer to read something and memorize lines, but I could do it. It was tough sometimes, and frustrating, but eventually I realized that the only person who could stop me from achieving what I wanted was me. I wasn't going to let anything stop me. I know it's a cliché, but if you believe in yourself, you really can do anything."

A young man with learning disabilities who repeated the tenth and eleventh grades twice and barely graduated from high school had a passionate interest in marine biology. He found a job at a marine-biology center in Woods Hole, Massachusetts, and eventually was able to go on to the University of Florida to claim his degree in the subject.

A boy who had very severe learning disabilities during his nine years at the Lab School pursued his love of plants and gardens when he grew up. First he worked for a florist. When he decided to branch out on his own as a landscape gardener, he stood outside a supermarket and handed out fliers to everyone, giving them the broad, friendly grin that had kept his teachers working hard with him as a child. Today he is head of a successful landscaping business with five employees. An accountant, a secretary, and a lawyer handle the tasks that he cannot do, while he concentrates on the areas where he can excel. This business is built on his personality and on his good relations with his clients.

Out of sheer willpower and a desire to be on the same level as their friends, two young men who took eight years each to get through college are now in graduate school. Another young person spent nine years at a community college and went on to obtain a college degree so that she could teach art at a local school.

Two American University students who are learning disabled have audited several courses before registering to take them for grades to make sure they will be able to pass. One of them pulled out of a course halfway through so that he could spend the extra half year building up the skills he would need to pass it the following year. Neither one was afraid of the extra work and effort but, on the contrary, welcomed it.

The words
    stubborn
    recalcitrant
    intractable
    unmovable
    impossible
can often mean
    tenacious
    single-minded
    indomitable
    fiercely determined
    driven
and can point
toward success.

Many people with learning disabilities see movies twice. The second time, they claim, they can pick up the subtleties. Many an adult with learning disabilities will see a film ten times if it contains something he wants to master that he hasn't yet learned.

Magic Johnson, basketball star, said, "I was big and tall enough so they didn't really tease me, but the looks, the stares, and the giggles—that was enough to embarrass me in itself. I wanted to work hard when I did go to reading classes. I wanted to show everybody that I could do better and also that I could read."

Part of these people's willingness to drive themselves relentlessly may derive from deep frustration and anger. But perhaps part of this willingness results from all the attention and support these hardworking people have received for their passionate efforts. Having seen how their parents, teachers, and mentors have had to fight for them, perhaps they continue that fight for themselves. There is control to be gained—over oneself and others—by achieving what the world thought was impossible, against all odds.

When drivenness is combined with rebelliousness, a need to prove oneself, and a desire to do as well as one's friends and family, the result can be a relentless drive toward success. American Express executive Malcolm Goodridge said, "Being dyslexic is like Avis—you try harder. I'm not sure I'd be as far along in life if I was just a normal guy."

MAKING IT TO THE TOP

It took scholar Roger Wilkins so long to read anything that it was years before he realized that the speed of reading had nothing to do with absorbing the content. Since he loved words and content, he decided to put in a herculean effort and became a voracious reader. In 1980 he was elected to the Pulitzer Prize Board and later became its chairman; he must read, read, read, and then judge the quality of what he has read.

When celebrities like Roger Wilkins, Tom Cruise, and Governor Gaston Caperton of West Virginia reveal their long battles with learning disabilities and tell how they made it to the top, they serve as beacons to many struggling youngsters, lighting the way ahead and infusing hope into the struggle.

The energy, drive, and ambition of achievers with learning disabilities inspire awe; the cost to themselves in time and effort deserves the deepest respect. Most of the achievers do not make headlines or earn public awards. There are probably several of them in your neighborhood. Their successes are measured by satisfaction in a job, by stable family lives, and by the many contributions that functional lives make to the fabric of society.

"If I could make a Faustian deal today, age seventy-four," said Fred Friendly, "if I could make a deal that I didn't have to be dyslexic and have my whole life to live again, I would take dyslexia. Because it gave me, when I was fourteen years old, forty years old, sixty years old—all my life—the drive and motivation that made me somebody to whom someone would say many years later, 'If you can make it, anybody can make it!'"

Drive is one of the personal characteristics required for success, and many people with learning disabilities have this characteristic in spades. However, drive, by itself, is not always enough. A person with learning disabilities must also learn to organize, to learn by doing, and to become responsible for himself or herself. These topics will be explored in the next three chapters.

6

The Need for Order

"My belongings are all over the place."

"Someone told me I looked like an unmade bed."

"I get lost trying to find new places, and I'm not good at reading maps. Then I need landmarks to find my way home again."

"Managing time is the hardest thing for me. I'm always late; my college papers are late. It's like I'm late getting up and I stay late all day."

"My boss reprimands me constantly, saying, 'Get your act together!'"

*D*isorganization is the subtle cause of much of the failure experienced by people with learning disabilities. Disorganization causes the gifted and the well motivated to fail. It causes students to drop out of college and employees to lose their jobs. It takes many forms and invades every aspect of daily life. It is pernicious. It is self-perpetuating. It builds on itself, and it dooms fine minds to menial work. This chapter examines those aspects of daily life most affected by disorganization stemming from learning disabilities. It also looks at how some people with learning disabilities learn to structure their lives for success.

GETTING RID OF THE MESS

Some people with learning disabilities live in such messiness and disorder that they can function only at a minimal level. They may be personally clean, but their clothes are all over the floor; grocery bags stand around still filled with food, and papers are strewn everywhere. When they can't get into the piled-up bed anymore, they move to the couch. When all the dishes are dirty and stacked in the sink, they use paper plates or the same dish over and over. Their clothing is often messy, washed but not pressed, and either strewn about or hung in a disordered way.

Gus, a student at the Night School, lives with three cats, whom he loves dearly. He always remembers to buy cat food and to feed his pets. However, empty cat-food cans litter his floor, attracting cockroaches. Sometimes he picks up the cans and puts them in the trash, but then he doesn't remember to take the trash out for the garbage collector. He likes cleanliness and order and is grateful if someone else cleans and organizes for him, but he can't organize himself well enough even to maintain such conditions once they are established by someone else.

Totally disorganized with respect to his belongings, Manuel, another Night School student, complained that he lost everything. Soon he started to appear at school with a garbage bag filled with his schoolwork, mail, clothes, pens, pencils, and glasses. This did not elicit great praise from his peers. What for Manuel was a coping strategy could be perceived by others as messiness.

Employers sometimes complain about how messy employees with learning disabilities look. Part of the problem may be due to poor planning—to not thinking ahead about what clothes are clean, what the weather is going to be like, or how visible one is going to be to the public. Poor visual-spatial perception may also be a contributing factor to ill-fitting clothes. An unkempt appearance sometimes reflects feelings: if a person looks like trash, often he or she feels like trash. When the person feels better, his or her appearance usually gets better. People can have real trouble keeping jobs if they consistently look messy.

Many people go through a stage of extreme messiness in late adolescence but grow out of it. Some people with learning disabilities get stuck there. They become so defeated by the mess in their room or apartment that they simply give in and add to it. They don't try to change it because they don't know where to begin. Another person, with a fresh eye, needs to come in from the outside to start the cleanup, to establish routines, and to get the place functioning.

However, this other person must act as a facilitator, not as a drill sergeant. There is an eternal and largely fruitless hassle between parents and young people with learning disabilities over the messiness of their clothing and their rooms. People who can't visualize letters and numbers often can't visualize what is in bureau drawers. They don't need lectures. They need coping strategies. Shelves work better than drawers. They need to *see* where to put things, where to stack things, where to put things back. Their spaces need to be set up so that there is a visible place for everything.

ORGANIZING TIME

Lacking internal monitors to provide an accurate sense of time, a person with learning disabilities is likely to race through each day helter-skelter, feeling out of control. He may wake up late, miss breakfast, rush out without gathering the papers he needs for work, and arrive at his job late and rattled. Also, intense concentration on a single activity sometimes causes people with learning disabilities to lose track of time. This may be a necessary trade-off. To succeed at a task, they have to focus on it exclusively. One successful graduate of the Lab School Day School said, "I can only do one thing at a time. If I take on too much, I get frustrated to the point that I become depressed. Then I'll sleep for three days."

Adults with learning disabilities will tell you that, as scatterbrained and disorganized as they are, they can lock in on something in the midst of chaos and be oblivious to everything going on around them. One mother described how she got so absorbed in her computer that she didn't notice that her children were not around. About an hour later, to her chagrin, she found that they had been locked in the bathroom all that time. Such compulsive attention to tasks wreaks havoc on internal monitors that tell us, "About half an hour has passed" or "It's about dinnertime."

Procrastination is another time-related pitfall for the disorganized. A graduate of the Lab School, now in college, would always put off writing a term paper until a few days before its deadline, when it would appear too big to tackle. In desperation, she would persuade someone to help her break the task down into small steps that she could deal with. Typically, she had to slog through three sleepless nights but then could hand the paper in on time. In one class a fellow student, also severely learning disabled and prone to procrastination, came to feel such defeat that he failed to reach out for help. Instead, he simply disappeared from class and added another *F* to his record.

This second student's pattern is typical. Masses of young people with learning disabilities start but do not finish classes, projects, hobbies, and jobs. They fear failure because they have tasted too much of it, yet they actually set themselves up for failure by quitting, by not asking for help, and by letting tasks victimize them. The learning disabled of all ages are easily overwhelmed. They cannot break down a task into manageable chunks or steps. They can't fathom how to begin wrestling with a problem, so they postpone dealing with the problem, which causes it to loom ever larger and larger. At a certain point, frustration takes over, and they become seriously stressed. The result is further disorganization and inability to function.

Some people with learning disabilities deal with the temptation to procrastinate by adopting a strategy of immediate action. Dr. Florence P. Haseltine is director of the Center for Population Research of the National Institute of Child Health and Human Development. She is also a person with learning disabilities. She says, "I lose everything. I have trouble remembering. . . . I do things as quickly as they are assigned to me, so I won't forget them. I have portable phones, so instead of writing notes, I call people the minute I think of what needs to be done."

Time regulates all our waking hours with tyrannical force. The alarm clock must wake us up at a precise time, so that we can get to work on time. We schedule meetings and appointments throughout the day and calculate how long they will last so that we can still find time for lunch. We leave work at a given time to catch a bus. The person with learning disabilities who gets lost in time has life disrupted even more severely than does a person who gets lost in space.

Time is an abstract concept, and persons with neurological dysfunctions often have trouble with abstractions. They understand the world in very concrete terms. Symbols baffle them. They need to see something to believe it. But time is invisible. They are stumped by having to estimate how long fifteen minutes is and what they can get done in fifteen minutes. "How long is fifteen minutes?" *Long* refers to space and distance, but minutes cannot be seen as they go by. A watch is marked with numbers that are symbols, not minutes, and clock hands are symbols, too.

When the Night School opened in 1984, many applicants failed to show up. They were apt to get lost, to leave their homes or jobs at the time they were expected to arrive at the school, or to arrive on the wrong day or in the wrong week. The Night School director told them to write down the date and time on their calendars, which they may have done, but they obviously never looked at their calendars again.

Now newly enrolled Night School students are asked to telephone the director or a staff member before they leave home to go over the directions before proceeding and to take part in a joint estimate of when they will arrive. If this is not done, the staff member may wait day and night, losing valuable time.

Leaving is another matter. One student always telephoned her boyfriend at 10:00 P.M. to pick her up at 10:05, although he lived forty-five minutes away. She needed to look at a map of the city and to calculate how long it took to drive each section of the route between the friend's home and the school before she could understand the problem and begin timing her phone calls correctly.

College students with learning disabilities often find that it is harder to manage their time and to organize their priorities for studying than it is to deal with the subject matter itself. A student must decide how much time should be allotted to one subject as compared to another. Which subject should have priority? Which requires the most reading? Which is more important as a foundation for future courses? The way a student handles these questions affects his performance and his grades.

A college student must also estimate the time needed to accomplish written work. In order to produce a research paper, a student must:

- use a library
- read numerous articles and books

- take notes in some form
- prepare an outline
- write one or more rough drafts
- edit the rough draft(s)
- write the final draft and put it into an acceptable form
- proofread the finished paper

Each step takes a certain amount of time, and the steps cannot all be taken the night before the paper is due. The student needs a monthly calendar he or she can look at every day. Time slots on the calendar, perhaps color coded, have to be marked for doing research, outlining, and then writing the paper.

Most any project involves such discrete steps. The whole must be broken down into chunks to be completed within specific time spans. Learning how to break down and organize tasks cuts down on the degrees of stress suffered by the learning disabled.

ORGANIZING SPACE

Many people with learning disabilities have difficulties in the area of spatial organization. They have trouble distinguishing left from right. They have a poor sense of direction. They misread maps. They tend to get lost even in their own neighborhoods. They lack landmark-based internal maps to guide them and often make wild guesses and just keep going until a street sign or some familiar object comes into sight. Helpless frustration overtakes a person with learning disabilities who stands at a crossroads, bewildered about which road might lead to his or her destination.

"When I get lost, which is frequently, I use my portable car phone," says Dr. Florence P. Haseltine. "I write down instructions wrong, and inevitably get lost. I always try to park in the same parking lot and use the same two rows; otherwise, I never can find my car when I come back. And I'm quite apt to lose my parking-lot ticket, too!"

Night School students report that they get into a lot of minor car accidents because they forget they are moving through space. While they are driving, they start thinking about their jobs, their families, their schoolwork, or some other topic and fail to keep their full attention on the road and the traffic. Several fender benders have alerted them to this danger, and so they try to monitor themselves while driving. Dr. Haseltine says that she drives as little as possible because she tends to space out and to forget that she's behind the wheel of the car.

Difficulties in organizing space can show up in many activities. Richard Cohen, now a syndicated newspaper columnist, said about his elementary mathematics classes, "I couldn't even keep columns and numbers straight, so in school I would get lost doing long division." Many people with learning disabilities require graph paper when they deal with numbers.

Occupational therapists, often known as sensory-integration specialists, can help disorganized people learn to plan their movements, and organizing the body helps to organize the mind. Therapists find that stroke victims need to learn how to organize such simple activities as brushing their hair, feeding themselves, and writing words and numbers. Some adults with severe learning disabilities, ones who have not had strokes but who confuse left and right, need the same help in planning their movements in space and in organizing space on paper.

Organizational difficulties are easily demonstrated in movement activities, from walking to sports to ballroom dancing. Some people with learning disabilities exhibit excellent coordination and move gracefully; others trip over everything, bang into doors, and knock things off tables.

In adult life a person has to provide himself with the borders and parameters he feels he is lacking internally. A child with learning disabilities depends on parents and teachers to provide the spatial organization he is lacking. Sometimes this will mean a secure, quiet corner at home, inviolably set aside for a distractible child to do his homework in, or a square of masking tape laid on the floor around the desk of a hyperactive child to define his personal space at school. The same people may crave their own private spaces after they grow up. "I can't stand sitting in somebody else's seat in the classroom," said a college history major with learning disabilities. "I can't listen to what the professor is saying if I'm not in my usual place."

MEMORY

Memory is often compared to a filing system in the brain. If it is well organized, associations are made quickly and effortlessly, and information is retrieved at will. Most people slot new data automatically into their memory filing systems. Many people with learning disabilities cannot depend on their memories to do anything automatically. The files in their brains seem to be random, inconsistent, out of order. A well-organized person easily remembers dates, distant relatives, appointments, duties, ancient history, and this morning's news, whereas many people with learning disabilities suffer from both short-term and long-term memory problems, largely because something is wrong with their storage system. Information goes in but is not filed correctly, and when an attempt is made at retrieval, the wrong thing, or nothing, comes out.

Everybody struggles with memory problems to some extent as he or she grows older, suddenly forgetting a name, unable to recall the title of a book or movie. The learning disabled have these same difficulties, but from a very early age. For them, information retrieval can be a slow, painful process. Students with erratic memories often find their academic work unfulfilling and unwittingly create the impression that they are poorly motivated or lazy.

Famous modern artist Robert Rauschenberg said, "Memory and memorizing are very difficult for me. My mother is always surprised I can remember things she said, things she did. But bad memory doesn't mean you are without that kind of past. You just don't have an *organized* past to carry around."

A former Lab School student says, "I have a great memory. I've really worked hard on it. It helps if things are tightly organized for me to remember them. Otherwise, I have to use every trick in the trade—create mental images, use key words to trigger recall, make up mnemonic devices, the whole bit. I've become a first-rate listener." He listens well in his college classes, but he can't write anything down. He can do only one thing at a time, so he relies on his strong memory.

Richard Strauss, the Texas real-estate magnate, is also a good listener with a strong memory. He believes that most dyslexics have better verbal retention than nondyslexics because it compensates for their main disability. Though they can't read, they *can* listen and remember. In a sense they take notes in their heads. Memory is a muscle, and they work it harder than most people. Cher, the actress-singer, says of her memory, "If you are not able to work in one area, then something else usually kicks in. I read scripts. I read very, very slowly, but if I read something once, I pretty much have it memorized. I don't really have to look at it again."

Reggie is not a good listener but can remember everything he sees in minute detail. He knows immediately when something is missing in a room; he knows where everything is

stored. He's a whiz on computers and produces brilliantly creative graphics for a living.

LANGUAGE

Poor listeners, like Reggie, have severe language problems.
First of all, although their hearing is fine, the way they process
incoming information is very disorganized. They have difficulty following directions. They hear the voice of a lecturer
but do not absorb what is said. Conversation swirls around
them, but the topic eludes them. Telephone calls produce ago-
nies of misunderstanding.

Lillian, who has learning disabilities, always sits in the
front row of her college classrooms because she has trouble
processing information from a distance. She easily loses the
delicate thread of what is said in a crowded room or in a noisy
shopping mall. To organize incoming information, she really
needs to see the people who are talking to her.

Some adults with learning disabilities process and organize information well; their disability lies in expressing it.
A graduate of the Lab School sometimes talks about her
lapses, by which she means her trouble in saying exactly what
she wants to say. "I say to myself, 'Stop, Joanie. Think about
what you're trying to say!' But when I'm going out on a date
with a new guy, he just doesn't understand what's going on
with me."

This bright student has trouble retrieving the precise
words she is seeking. Her disorganization in formulating sentences slows her down. Some people with learning disabilities
have fluent speech and syntax, but many, no matter how advanced their vocabularies, have disorganized language and use
clumsy sentences that obscure their meaning.

Some students speak clearly but have trouble putting their
ideas down on paper in a well-organized way. If the physical

act of writing is difficult and slow and gets delayed by problems of spelling or punctuation, thoughts may far outrun fingers, resulting in a scrambled mess on the page. It requires an immense effort for these students to produce an acceptable paper or report, even though they know what they need to say.

Richard Cohen, a syndicated columnist with the *Washington Post,* told our Lab School children, "I had enormous difficulty writing and keeping things organized. I write everything on a word processor and before that on a typewriter. I can't even write a thank-you note. I mean, I can, but nobody could read it, so I type everything." As a young reporter in the early seventies, Cohen had to write notes covering the alleged corruption of Vice President Spiro Agnew. Agnew later tried to prove that the Justice Department had leaked all the information appearing in Cohen's columns and so subpoenaed Cohen's notes. The publisher of the *Washington Post* was prepared to go to jail over this issue. Little did the publisher know that Cohen's notes were so illegible that neither the lawyers, the judge, Spiro Agnew, nor Cohen himself could have read them!

One college student with learning disabilities never takes notes in class because his handwriting is so illegible that he cannot always decipher it. But he also says, "I can't listen carefully and take notes because then I can't get what I hear organized inside my head, and I lose it all!" He borrows notes from a fellow student, types them in exchange for the loan, and spends hours organizing them into categories that will help him remember them.

Sometimes it takes people with learning disabilities so long to organize their ideas into sentences that effective communication becomes very difficult. Melissa, a Night School student, interrupts other people's conversations, unaware of the irritation she causes. When asked about this, she says, "But I can't get it organized again! If I don't say it now, I've lost it!"

Disorganization in a person's language is often connected to other types of disorganization. For example, to take a test successfully, you must look at its structure and then create a plan for taking it. You must organize both your time and your sentences. A Night School student says, "My anxiety is so high that I can't even read the instructions and make sense of them. Under the stress, my reading ability and thinking disappear, and I just freeze up."

Language disorders can be very subtle. People who have grown up in highly verbal families may pick up phrases without really understanding what they are saying. When sophisticated people respond in kind and try to continue with verbal play, people with learning disabilities may go to pieces. Difficulty with words in their own language prevents many bright students from learning a foreign language. Even if they can learn to master speaking a foreign language, rarely can they learn to spell or write it.

OVERORGANIZING

Because of their need to be very well organized to function at all, many adults with learning disabilities lean toward overplanning and rigidity. They cannot tolerate surprises, which for them are booby traps and embarrassments. To deal with their learning disabilities, some businesspeople create an extreme degree of order in their offices. They train their assistants to protect them by going over every schedule in minute detail, checking and rechecking schedules and agendas, accounting for every moment, reconfirming appointments, listing every person who will be present at a meeting, and finding out exactly how long each part of a meeting, appointment, or conference will take.

"I can't function when there is a mess. When I have plates

on my coffee table or unwashed dishes in the sink, I get out of cycle. I get so overwhelmed, I won't even answer the phone," says a free-lance designer who works at home.

Some people with learning disabilities fear disorganization as much as they fear failure. They are like the homemaker who makes you feel that you are messing up the house by sitting down on the sofa. They become obsessed with making lists of everything they have to do. Frequently they live so completely by the rules that they infuriate other people. They stymie their own efforts, and their inflexibility makes them unproductive.

To counteract their inner disorder and to meet the demands of their studies, some college students with learning disabilities also become rigidly overorganized. In essence, their study skills take over their lives. They are ruled by lists. They check off each single accomplishment and then print up new lists of things to do. Their notes have boxes around them saying, "To do by Wednesday" or "Finish by Saturday," and everything is rigidly ordered. Every paper they have ever written is in a folder; every note they have ever taken is carefully saved. The overorganized leave themselves no time for the joy of living.

FATIGUE

People with learning disabilities exhaust themselves just by getting organized. Every part of their day needs organization. Organizing their thoughts, figuring out how to begin, and sustaining a thought process long enough to complete a task consume masses of energy. A college student explained: "Just getting ready for class is a major feat for me. I have to remember which class to go to, what time it meets, and where, find the right notebook, lay out the materials I'll need for class, find the classroom, and get there on time!" All this overwork exhausts the student. Fatigue caused by disorganization—or by efforts to overcome it—allows disorganization to reign. The disorganization and fatigue positively reinforce each other, leading to an escalation of both.

STRUCTURING FOR SUCCESS

What can be done to combat or to compensate for the disorganization experienced by people with learning disabilities? My experience suggests several applicable strategies but no easy answers.

Structure Imposed from Without

One strategy is for other people to provide the disorganized with structure that they can use in their lives. Adults with learning disabilities learn at an early age that they need structure. Parents and teachers can provide a child with boundaries within which to work or play when the child has little innate sense of limits. Such structure will give the child the order he or she so distinctly needs but does not have. Regular routines, definite procedures, well-defined sequences of steps, and clear limits and expectations can help the child with learning disabilities to feel able to succeed and accomplish tasks. Parents and teachers can help children to organize situations and assignments, one step at a time, so that failure and depression are less likely. As the child grows older, he or she can begin to operate under fewer outside controls and to develop more internal discipline. However, many of the learning disabled continue to need tight structure up to and sometimes during adulthood.

Thus the people who really need to be highly organized

are the teachers, parents, and friends of people with learning disabilities. They need to be especially well organized themselves in order to create the necessary structure in their charges' lives. At the start of every term, the director of the Night School presents each student with a schedule, and each teacher gives the students ring-binder notebooks, folders for papers, and assignment books. The organization of these adult students is so precarious that there has to be silence in the Night School. Hubbub distracts the students and makes them lose their place so badly that they may have to start a piece of work all over again. Often they say, "What am I supposed to do? I forget," when they are pushed off their track. If a teacher has to talk to one student, he will often take the student outside so that the others can continue their work undisturbed.

On the other hand, some gifted students with learning disabilities fail at college not because of their inability to read or write well, but because they *cannot* organize information and activities or meet deadlines for papers. A specialist in learning disabilities at a large state university reports that her main job is to provide the structure that will allow her students to succeed. She claims that organization is the key element in the success of a college student with learning disabilities.

Important tasks that require organization include meeting with a professor before the course starts, arranging to see a tutor, obtaining a syllabus as early as possible in order to obtain books and tapes early, and making sure that one's tape recorder is in good working order so that lessons can be recorded and played. Planning is needed for the use of computers, typists, and photocopying machines.

Arranging summer job interviews also requires organization. A highly motivated Night School student worked hard on writing his résumé. He sent it out to several prospective employers and then waited. No answers came.

"Didn't you telephone to follow up and ask for appointments?" asked his teacher.

"How could I?" replied the student. He had kept no record of the people to whom he had sent his résumé!

To organize his complex life at college or to apply for a summer job, a student has to focus on the main task, break it down into its component parts, and then sequence those parts in terms of what is more or less important. Often these skills can be directly taught.

Structure through Organizational Aids

For those who can learn to use it, a computer can automatically organize material, so can visual materials—for example, videotapes, drawings, and photographs.

A student who gradually acquired methods of organizing himself during almost eight years at the Lab School went on to regular high school for three years and matriculated at Oberlin College, where he graduated Phi Beta Kappa. He has gone on to law school with his portable computer on his lap. The organizing systems that he has developed for himself are working.

This strategy is also used by Dr. Florence Haseltine: "I carry with me my little Casio computer, and I put everything in it—my schedule, names of people, because I don't remember names, and I label them by what they do, like *demographer* or *anthropologist*. I paint the little computer in bright colors with nail polish, and I write the word *reward*, along with my name and phone number, all over it. I keep a backup memory of the computer, so if it gets lost I might only lose a week's information."

Structure through Alternative Action

A disorganized person can sometimes find alternatives that bypass his worst areas of disorganization. Frank is one of the few who eventually learned to spell and read well; he had mild difficulty with math. His nemesis in adult life was driving a car. He could not coordinate his feet, hands, and eyes. After six serious car accidents, he tried riding a motorcycle, then a bicycle, but experienced the same difficulties. He now uses public transportation.

Chuck Close, a master of contemporary art, paints a portrait by dividing a photographic image of his subject into a grid of small squares, which he then paints one by one. He explained, "I think accomplishment is figuring out your own idiosyncratic solution. I've always had to chop things up into little, bite-size pieces in order to understand them. My work looks very mathematical, you know, with lots of little, incremental squares, but I couldn't even tell you what six and seven make without counting on my fingers. So I end up folding little pieces of paper, and I slide them along the canvas and make marks, and if it comes out the right number, OK. But if not, I fold the little pieces of paper smaller and do it again. You can get done what you want to get done, even if you have to take a circuitous route."

Tanya can organize her thoughts well but can't get them down on paper in an organized fashion. As a college student, she had to write a fifty-page paper on China's Cultural Revolution from 1968 to 1978. She spent two entire weeks in her university library, researching the subject in books, periodicals, and newspaper files and taking notes on cards color coded to indicate the main topics. But when the time came to start writing, she could not produce the written language and could not get her topics into sequence. Her solution was to work with a tutor. She talked over her ideas, explained the conclusions she had reached, and showed him her note cards. With tutorial help, she wrote the paper. Tanya got an *A* on it, with the professor's two-word comment "Excellent research!" The paper *was* all her own thinking. For her, using help in writing was like using a computer or a TDD (telephone for the deaf) to record her ideas. "Hey, I'm going to be an idea person, TV producer, or a director anyway; that's what I'm going to do with my life," she said.

Wayne had the same problem as Tanya. Wayne talked Marisa into editing his writing while, in exchange, he computerized Marisa's history notes for her master's-degree thesis.

Many adults with learning disabilities find colleagues who will do pieces of their jobs in exchange for their helping these colleagues in other ways. Through cooperation with others, such adults manage to meet what would otherwise be quite daunting challenges. Of course, the person on top can to a large degree create his or her own order and thus control the challenges to be faced. When Frank Dunkle was appointed director of the U.S. Fish and Wildlife Service in 1986, he had the courage to announce to his seven hundred employees that he was dyslexic and that instead of long briefing papers, he needed clear, one-page summaries that he could read quickly and act on: "Nobody really believed me when I told the staff they had a new and different kind of director. I could not cope with the acronyms . . . *ADC, BIA,* etc., so I asked them please to say the words for the letters. I needed to develop my own method of organization to do the best job possible!"

Richard Strauss, the real-estate tycoon, organizes a paid staff to do the things he cannot do himself. He has a dynamic secretary to whom he dictates whatever he wants to write. He uses the telephone extensively and has specialists on hand who read and explain contracts and financial statements to him.

Mark Torrence, former CEO of the Muzak Corporation, when asked how other people deal with his learning disabilities, said, "Let's see. . . . My secretary, my staff, they all work around me, and they don't let me do certain things that they know I'm poor at, and somehow they all manage to keep me out of trouble. My wife puts up with all kinds of crazy things.

My secretary won't let me dial the phone because if it's long-distance, I get the wrong number all the time."

Dr. Florence Haseltine says, "My motto is *Find out what you cannot do, and discard it. Find another way.*" People have to organize their lives to match their particular strengths and disabilities. And as the next chapter points out, they seem to learn best from doing.

7
Learning by Doing

"I have to see it, hear it, touch it, do it, be a part of it, in order to learn it."

"When my parents showed me how to do things, I learned quickly. If they just told me what to do, I failed."

"My friend can remember anything you tell him, and he gives it right back to you the way he heard it. I can't repeat anything exactly. I was always terrible on tests. But I'm really good at analyzing what's wrong with electronic things and fixing them."

"My mother used to read me stories, and then we acted them out. They have stayed with me forever."

What do you remember best from high school? Is it the classroom lectures or the school activities—the play you were in, the exhibit of insects you helped to mount, the model UN Assembly you participated in, the song you wrote, or the project you did on the planets? Most adults remember the school activities that touched their lives and that gave them pleasure. Night School adults remember attending or participating in sports events, being in the choir, playing in the orchestra, winning a prize for best poster, or enjoying the company of specific friends.

Adults and children alike seem to remember information more clearly when that information has been structured into a concrete activity. Thirty-year-old Jane still sings the alphabet to herself to remember it. Twenty-two-year-old Meyer remembers multiplication tables through tricks he learned when training as an acrobat at a circus training school. For most of the learning disabled, learning information in a concrete way helps them to file it in their brains.

A FILING SYSTEM IN THE BRAIN

Concrete experiences are the key to early learning. They form the foundation of all later reasoning. Think for a moment about how we acquire information and then organize and remember it. To acquire information, we have experiences. Then we slot them into the filing compartments of the mind. That is what preschoolers do through their play. And that is why we must let them play and not push academic work upon them too early. Preschool learning is all about sorting things—objects, pictures, sounds, animals, people, toys—and about classifying them. As the child plays, he or she begins to notice similarities and differences among things and so to group things in categories. A child draws a circle on the ground. An orange is a circle, and so is a ball. They are all round. So by age six, when the child's first-grade teacher uses the word *round,* she can picture it in her mind by drawing on her experience with round things. I am convinced that her experiences have been categorized and classified into a mental filing system, to be retrieved at will.

Our minds have been compared to highly sophisticated reference libraries. Usually, by school age the filing system in a child's mind is in good working order, and the reference library is well stocked with basic concepts that will provide the basis for abstract learning. Connections have been made. Relationships make sense. By age eight, the foundations for higher-level learning tend to be in place. However, such is not the case for someone with learning disabilities. In the mind of such a person, because of neurological dysfunctions or immaturity, the basic systems for gathering, processing, ordering, storing, or retrieving concepts and information are not functioning properly. Smatterings of information come in, and dislocated pieces are retrieved.

How frustrating it is to know something and not be able to come up with the correct term or body of information! What looks like poor memory is often really disorganization. We have found at the Lab School that some children and some adults need to build their filing and reference systems anew. In sophisticated ways, they must be presented with preschool experiences so that they can begin to categorize incoming information correctly. The rationale for our approach derives from discoveries in developmental psychology.

DEVELOPMENTAL LEARNING

The number of years that a child has lived denotes only his or her chronological age. More important to educators is a child's developmental age, which is determined by the stage that the child has reached in his or her physical and mental development. *Educators need to teach children and adults at their developmental levels but to use materials appropriate to their chronological ages.* An adult who needs to learn vowels should have them presented in an adult fashion, preferably in a way that relates to his or her adult interests or vocation. The teacher who treats an adult like a six-year-old will inevitably fail.

The Swiss psychologist Jean Piaget (1896–1980) established that thinking develops in four stages. Children progress from one stage to the next on their own timetables. In each stage, a distinct mode of thought determines what mode of learning will work. The four stages have a prescribed sequence. A person cannot be moved into the next stage without the equipment to do the job.

Stage 1: The Sensory-Motor Stage (ages 0–2). In this stage the child develops the basic physiological systems that compare and coordinate what is perceived through the senses with what is done by the motor apparatus of the body—the muscles. Sensory-motor development through observing, touching, pushing, pulling, handling, and testing things is an essential preamble to the formulation of concepts.

Stage 2: The Preoperational or Preliteral Stage (ages 2–7). In this stage the child's mental life is dominated by appearances, by what *seems to be* rather than *what logically must be.* The child is, however, capable of letting one thing stand for another, as is demonstrated by the rapid development of language.

Stage 3: The Concrete Operational Stage (ages 7–11). Thought is still limited to concrete experiences. The child is thinking but is not yet able to deal with abstractions unless they are represented concretely.

Stage 4: The Formal Operational Phase (ages 11 and on). The child can perform logical operations in which no objects are required, can form abstract ideas about objects that are out of sight, and thus can make inferences of all kinds, including inductions (generalizations) and deductions (conclusions based on general, abstract principles).

The implications of stages 1 through 3 for teaching are enormous. When the central nervous system is delayed in development, the child remains in the concrete stages. Some eleven-year-olds are on a preoperational level; some adults are on a concrete operational level. They must be taught by methods appropriate to their developmental levels, not their chronological ages. The child needs to see the material he is taught, to hear it, to touch it, to smell it, to feel it, to move it, to "be" it. He needs to have enough experience with it to know it well. For a word to have meaning, he must associate it with an object, a picture, or an experience. When asked to copy the word *hill,* twelve-year-old Patrick first had to give meaning to the word by drawing a picture of a hill next to the letters. Only then could he copy it correctly.

Piaget's work suggests that teaching at levels higher than those appropriate to a child's cognitive development is an exercise in futility. Yet this is the kind of teaching to which the learning disabled are frequently subjected.

The learning disabled often beg, "Let me see it" or "Let me do it," as if they know how they can learn best. This urge underlines the importance of listening keenly to the learning disabled for information on how they learn. Another revealing source of information about intellectual development, as the work of Piaget shows, is the mistakes, misunderstandings, and inconsistencies of learners.

Forming concepts has to do with making connections, establishing relationships, reorganizing ideas, and pulling them together. A person's capacity for learning allows him or her to group things and thus to deal in patterns and systems. In the absence of this capacity, each situation is unique and has no relation to anything else. Each issue or situation has to be dealt with separately, in a manner that is both immature and inefficient. Adults with severe learning disabilities often operate in this way.

Dr. Jerome Bruner, of Harvard, who has also explored the nature of intellectual growth, believes that a child can learn most anything if it is presented in a highly organized, simple way. In keeping with this idea, educators need to figure out how an adult with learning disabilities is thinking, how well this adult can form patterns and systems, and tailor teaching to suit him or her. Eleanor cannot remember and dial telephone numbers like the rest of us. Touch-tone telephones have saved her. The knowledge is in her fingertips, which remember the correct configurations. Ben, on the other hand, *sees* telephone numbers as visual patterns on the buttons of the touch-tone phone—as squares, triangles, and rectangles. The keys to teaching Eleanor and Ben lie in understanding their approaches to memory.

The great theorist of education John Dewey (1859–1952) believed that concrete materials familiar to children in their daily lives should be used to teach all subjects in school, whether arithmetic, history, geography, or the natural sciences. He vigorously opposed the application of adult methods to children and pleaded with educators to deal with children on the children's own level. Above all, he recommended that teachers let children *learn by doing.* Immersed in the learning process, the child discovers relationships, makes connections, and draws conclusions, Dewey believed. For a learning-disabled or very young child, adults need to structure each situation, providing materials that will evoke the discovery of relationships and connections.

Theodore Sizer, formerly dean of the Harvard University Graduate School of Education, suggests that teachers give their students what they need to start studying a subject and then, especially with older children, step aside and let the students follow their own instincts, using trial and error. The teacher should coach and give suggestions and encouragement but leave the student free to develop his or her own thoughts and ideas so that as the student masters the subject, he or she comes to see this mastery as a private, personal possession, not as something imposed from the outside. Dr. Sizer recommends that in place of term papers, students be encouraged to display their knowledge and mastery of subjects through projects, models, exhibitions, maps, dioramas, and in as many other ways as their imaginations can conceive of. At the Lab School book reports can be done in three-dimensional forms, such as dioramas, flip books, or storyboards, as well as in traditional form.

The masterful artist Robert Rauschenberg said, "I went to school in Texas, and it was particularly difficult, at least it certainly was for me. The schools were ignorant of dyslexia and so insensitive. They never tried to engage a student who seemed slow to learn, through imaginative ways, like teaching math through objects or colors. It was just miserable going to school. Every day I got further behind, and everybody said, 'He's just stupid.' That's the cruelest thing that can happen. But you can't blame anybody for that, the way that education is set up. It hasn't changed, I think, in thousands of years."

One Night School student, Rob, said, "I have always been quick to understand ideas, great ideas, and I read people very well. I express what I know through my drawings and my projects but never through written essays. Why couldn't teachers tap what I know in other ways where I could express myself? A command of knowledge has to be tested in different ways for different people. Why can't schools do this?"

The body, the mind, and all the senses of a concrete child, adolescent, or young adult must come alive in order for that person to learn. Subtleties, nuances, inferences, and multiple meanings often escape them, adversely affecting their academic progress, their social growth, and even their sense of humor. Yet such literal-minded people see many realities in the concrete world, make many connections, and can discover great and complex ideas, often through experiences in the arts.

All children think concretely when they are very young. It's how long the concreteness lasts that separates one child from another. Bennett, aged eight, understands concepts of equality, truth, and honesty because of his parents' and teachers' discussion of them, and because of his own reading. However, Ricky, aged ten, has come to understand these concepts only through playing with objects, playing games and talking about them, and seeing pictures and films. When Ricky is asked to fold a paper so that it has three parts of the same size, and he sees that his neighbor folds his differently but also has three equal parts, and that Harry folds his differently from both of these, he can see that the folded papers are all the same and yet are different: they are equal. That discovery can lead Ricky to understand that Socrates, Aristotle, and Plato were all different philosophers but were all the same in that they were seeking truth. Bennett enjoys hearing the concept of equality explained in that way but doesn't need the experiential approach to understand the concept. Ricky cannot understand it otherwise.

THE LAB SCHOOL APPROACH

The premise on which I based the Lab School in 1967 was that children with learning disabilities are immature neurologically and need individualized, hands-on experiences and activity learning wherever possible. I designed experiential teaching methods to help them make sense of their environment. They didn't study abstract material from textbooks. To explore the word *justice,* the children became the characters in a minidrama: someone in the room stole their snacks, and they discussed *honesty, integrity,* and *justice* in relation to this theft.

While studying Native Americans, Lab School children were moved out of their familiar, spacious classroom into a smaller, darker room. This happened not once but three times, always to worse quarters. The class experienced what Native Americans felt as they lost their land. The children were incensed. They wrote a petition to the director of the school to give them back their territory. Years later, members of that class continue to refer to that experience in discussions and in written compositions.

Involvement is the key. Lab School students with moderate to severe learning disabilities were frequently not involved in previous learning. Most of them cannot read. Often they have difficulty learning from listening. Sometimes they cannot find ways to organize the material they are given in order to make sense of it. Usually they struggle to express what they mean in spoken words and in writing. Often they feel incompetent, insignificant, and powerless. They have come to think of school as a place where things are done *to* them and *for* them. They have become passive learners because more active attempts at learning in a traditional classroom resulted in failure.

The Lab School classrooms promote active learning. They are filled with teacher-made, diagnostic-prescriptive games designed to teach specific facts and concepts. Children are in classrooms half the day and in art classes and science labs the rest of the day. They are also in academic clubs. I designed what I call the Academic Club Method in 1966 (before the Lab School was founded) so that each child can feel himself or herself to be an intimate part of the history being studied. The clubs supply an important sense of belonging and privilege. There are passwords, routines, and rituals that help students focus and pay attention and that bind them together in vivid reenactments. They see participating in the clubs as a source of fun and excitement, while, in fact, they are learning sophisticated academic material. The teacher of the Middle Ages Club, under the name Lord Don, leads Knight Hal, Lady Rachelle, and eight others through the Battle of Hastings, then on to creating the 231-foot Bayeux tapestry in paper and paint, followed by writing the Domesday Book. This is learning for a lifetime.

A ten-year-old who has experienced a period of history with his whole being and imagination has the peg on which to hang textbook readings in the future. Most of our students have gone on to college and many to graduate schools. I am convinced that this is because they have gained, through experiential teaching, large storehouses of information to apply to later learning.

Many adults with learning disabilities say that their formal education just washed over them and didn't stick. Some of them built up storehouses of information outside of school. Others who had absorbed little information often felt bereft of intellectual interests, as well as inadequate at reading, writing, spelling, and arithmetic.

Tony, a graduate of the Lab School, once said, "You know, I used to think the Lab School was a little like a summer camp. It wasn't like the schools my friends went to, where you sat in rows and worked with books and textbooks all day. But I found that I knew lots more about life and things than my friends did. They were always asking me for information and ideas, and strategies too!" The Lab School has produced a lot of Tonys who function well in adult life. Educators need to *use* play to teach intellectual content. They should never belittle it. Play helps children understand relationships: they think, compare, analyze, generalize, and solve problems. Through play a child makes things happen. Often he is surprised by the results and filled with wonder and awe. Plato believed that the beginning of learning is wonder.

LEARNING WITH THE WHOLE BODY

Even today, thirty-five-year-old Glenn finds that when someone tells him to turn left, he automatically reaches with his right hand to grasp his left hand—the one with the watch. Then he turns. Twenty-five-year-old Anna, who works as a nursery-school aide, was always putting the children's sneakers on the wrong feet. Eventually she learned to stand behind the child to do it correctly. Matthew still remembers learning the phrase *vibration of sound* from touching his neck and then looking at musical instruments and touching them. Maria learned the words *above* and *below* by referring to the top half and bottom half of her body.

Mystery writer Elizabeth Daniels Squire grew exasperated when her husband discussed alternatives for placing the furniture in their house. She could not make an intelligent decision until she had seen the furniture in place in each of the ways under discussion. It was time-consuming to do this, and nerves were frayed, but the house is now arranged in a way that suits them both.

If adults are asked to repeat a series of numbers backward, they realize that it takes much more organizing, visualizing, and focus than repeating them forward. A child who has difficulty moving his body backward in space in a dance class may have trouble with academic subjects requiring a backward organization, such as subtraction and division or use of the past tense in English. When there is a breakthrough in body movement, very often at the Lab School there is a parallel breakthrough in some of the other areas as well.

A child who has a weak sense of time can be helped by a red line painted on the floor to divide *past* from *future*. By physically jumping over the line, the student can be in a physical relationship parallel to time relationships. Then she can decide where to place *fossil* and where to put *supersonic jet*, or she can sit on the *past* side when discussing history and on the *future* side when planning next week's field trip.

A child who is delayed in language development often suffers terrible frustration in trying to speak but can communicate clearly through an art form. If it is a dance, the child's dance teacher must work closely with him, explaining what he has succeeded in doing, showing him how he did it—what he did first, second, and last—so that he can do it again with confidence. Finally, that child must teach another student to do something similar, and use language carefully to explain it.

At the Lab School, students are not allowed to take home their woodwork projects until they can teach other students how to make the same objects. It usually takes a long time for the children's first projects to go home, because at first they can't remember what they did. But soon, *they begin to pay attention to the process, not just to the product.* It helps to have a tangible, enticing object that they want to take home and show off. But the purpose of the exercise is to make them think about what they are doing with their bodies and with the wood. Students who have trouble with order and sequence need to remember what they did first, next, and last, and *why* they did what they did.

LIVING GREAT IDEAS

Thomas Edison claimed that he could learn only from experience, that he had to observe and do things and make things in order to understand a process or a theory. General George S. Patton provides a parallel example.

Patton seemed to learn best from hearing stories and then acting them out. Before he himself could read (which was at around age twelve), his mother and father read to him for about an hour each day, and his spinster Aunt Nannie read to him at least two hours a day, sometimes three. His father read him the *Iliad* and the *Odyssey.* His mother read to him about George Washington and Admiral Nelson. History was his mentor, his constant companion. Aunt Nannie read him the history of Herodotus and of Alexander the Great, *Beowulf,* many books on Napoleon, and again and again she read to him about Julius Caesar.

When George Patton first went to Europe, he walked the routes of Julius Caesar, which he remembered perfectly from listening to Caesar's *Commentaries.* Without knowing it, Aunt

Nannie helped the Third Army in World War II make its dash across Europe. She helped the Allies win the war.

General Patton, according to his daughter, Mrs. James Totten, must have realized that he learned most from doing, because he had his own wife and children act out events from history: "For example, he was a Civil War buff, and when we were stationed in the Washington area, he would read to us about a certain battle or military action, give us roles to play, and then we would drive to the scene and fight it out on foot. Mother was always the Yankees, because she was from Lowell, Massachusetts."

Patton had total recall and could remember history as if he had been there. Mrs. Totten recounts how her father rounded up his numerous boy cousins and sisters to play with him. He was always in command, but nobody minded because he thought up such enchanting games. However, on one disastrous day "he decided to be John the Blind of Bohemia . . . credited with being the Father of Armored Warfare because in one of his endless wars with his neighbors he had the shields of his knights lashed onto the sides of his supply wagons, filled the wagons with archers, and gave them a push downhill into the enemy. The archers kept shooting through the cracks between the shields, which the enemy's arrows bounced off. So this day Georgie nailed barrel heads to the sides of the farm wagon, put six of his cousins inside armed with homemade bows and arrows, and pushed the wagon downhill into the flock of family turkeys, shouting war cries and encouragement. The cousins jumped out just before the wagon turned over in the ditch, but my aunt said everyone ate turkey for weeks, and she never cared for it again."

Mrs. Totten tells of another incident in which young Patton "decided that he was Achilles, dragging the body of dead Prince Hector around the walls of Troy behind his chariot. The cousins were all at school, so the only way my aunt escaped being Hector was by finding the body of a huge dead rat, which George tied behind his pony, Peachblossom, and dragged around the cow barn, while she covered her head to wait, as Hecuba, queen of Troy, for the dead rat, Hector."

Like the young George Patton, people with learning disabilities need to have their intellects challenged at every point. The adults around the learning disabled need to seek out the ways in which these people can best soak in the information and then enable them to learn in those ways.

Patton re-created the events of history so intensely that they became a part of his own experience. This approach is at the core of the Lab School curriculum and the Academic Club Method. Through reenactments, such as pretending to be cavemen making their own Lascaux cave drawings, or being ancient Egyptians irrigating the Nile Valley, or Michelangelo painting the Sistine Chapel, the children at the Lab School develop personal memories of historical experiences. These experiences become a part of their being.

USING THE SENSES TO ANCHOR MEMORY

One adult with learning disabilities who has trouble visualizing anything in geography has always been able to remember Boston Harbor and all its inlets. Why? In her second-grade classroom at a private school, the class used clay to make the whole classroom into Boston Harbor; then they made a boat to ride in and out of the inlets. She has integrated that information into her memory bank and can pull it out at any time.

Another adult with a learning disability was able to learn all the states in the United States because when he was ten, his teacher had the states drawn all over the floor of his fourth-grade classroom, and the children spent the year "traveling around America." Each child was assigned two states in one region and, by having his or her desk and chair placed upon them, literally sat in those states every day. The teacher gave different assignments to students in the northeastern section of the country than to students in the Northwest or the South. She always spoke of regions. Some days she had the desks and chairs removed, and then the class traveled around the whole classroom floor, visiting other states, naming the capitals, seeing and touching the states' products, such as corn, cotton, peanuts, toy cars, or oil.

Geography offers many wonderful opportunities for learning. Some adults with learning disabilities use children's wooden puzzles to learn the geography of the United States or even of the world. One adult found place mats with geographic regions that he uses all the time. Many adults cannot see the difference between the shapes of the continents of Africa and South America on the map, nor do they understand the relationship of one of them to the other on the globe. They were not taught concretely.

At the Lab School, geography is taught by doing. Many of our students think that the city they live in is a state or a nation. "Washington, D.C., is a continent!" announced ten-year-old Harry. "No," said a classmate smugly, "it is a country. So is New York."

To deal with this confusion, their Lab School teacher provided the students with small boxes called City Boxes, and they put cards on them labeled *New York City, Pittsburgh, Birmingham,* and so forth. Then they had to find bigger boxes, called the State Boxes, to put the City Boxes into. Birmingham, for example, went into the State Box identified as Alabama. Then they searched for a huge American Nation Box to put the State Boxes into. Finally they found the behemoth Continent Box. They took the city boxes that were in their state boxes, and state boxes that were in the nation box, and put them all into the North American Continent Box. The act of putting each city box into a state box into a nation box into a continent box made it viscerally clear to the children. It integrated the parts into a whole, and gave the children a concrete concept of geography. Part-whole relationships are difficult for the learning disabled. This kind of activity clarifies these relationships for them and establishes clear patterns of thinking.

Annie Sullivan taught Helen Keller geography at an old tumbledown wharf on the Tennessee River. "I built dams of pebbles, made islands and lakes, and dug river beds, all for fun, and never dreamed that I was learning a lesson," wrote Helen. Sullivan made raised maps for Helen on which the child could feel mountain ridges and valleys and follow river courses with her fingers. The same method works for children with learning disabilities. Adults with learning disabilities often use it when they think nobody is watching. Louise uses this method in her work as an architect. She builds models, as many adults with learning disabilities need to. They need to use their hands or to build something they can see so they can learn something abstract in a specific way.

In a Lab School high-school class, a few students with learning disabilities stood on an outline of North America in eastern cities such as Boston, New York, Washington, and Atlanta. On the other side of the room, students stood on an outline of Europe in the cities of Athens, Rome, and Paris. A teacher brought a big bucket of water and placed it between them. He labeled it the Atlantic Ocean. Then he brought a bowl of water labeled the Mediterranean Sea. It created a picture in the students' minds of something they had not understood in all their years of geography. In the same high school, a pumpkin was used to teach latitude and longitude. Additional lines of longitude were added, as were lines of latitude. The students made a map to scale by using their drawn lines of latitude and longitude on the pumpkin.

Some students in a Lab School junior-high-school science class had difficulty understanding how an amoeba moves across the ocean floor. They grasped the concept easily when presented with a plastic bag filled with basic cooking dough, which, when they flattened it in the middle, reached out extensions and could be made to move.

When a math class had trouble visualizing the concept of volume, the Lab School teacher cut up tennis balls so the students could see volume—how much a ball could hold inside it. They could understand area, but not volume, until they put sand in the balls and could see and measure how much would go in.

A high-school class studying geological eras could not imagine the amount of time involved. The Precambrian Era, for example, lasted about 4 billion years. The teacher had each student make a deck of "geological era" cards from index cards. Four title cards were made—one for each era. Between the title cards were inserted an appropriate number of blank cards, each representing 10 million years. By flipping through the deck, a student could see the amount of time each era took up and compare the eras.

Seniors at the Lab School learn about deadline management and study skills. In September they are given the assignment of interviewing ten prominent artists and craftsmen in the Washington, D.C., metropolitan area, photographing them, writing up their approaches to art, describing the medium they use, and cataloguing the galleries that show their art. By mid-May they need to have a published copy of this brochure on the school director's desk, with advertisements in the booklet to defray all costs. In its fourth year, this project was written up in a local arts magazine, and the annual brochures are now sold at $5 apiece by several galleries in the Washington area.

USING SCHEMA THEORY

Students with learning disabilities often forget what they have learned. Experience has shown that sensory input—the taste, smell, feel, sight, and sound of an object—especially when paired with an explanation, makes that object meaningful to a child. It becomes an established *schema,* or total context. One is able to learn a new bit of information more quickly and to store it more permanently if the information fits into a preexisting mental context, or schema; and if such an internal schema does not already exist, the teacher needs to create it through a "total sensory experience." Reading comprehension flourishes and writing becomes more organized when the student is allowed to experience a subject with his whole being. The concept of internal schema, introduced to psychology by F. C. Bartlett, explains why concreteness can help trigger memory.

Today, many specialists in the field of reading comprehension subscribe to the schema theory. Schemata, those organized structures of knowledge or "memory banks" in which new facts and experiences find a home, hooked firmly to memories of previous knowledge and events, are what makes learning possible. A schema supplies a solid system for memory retrieval and allows us to make inferences about life as it occurs around us. Memory is not just a matter of recalling by rote. New information interacts with prior knowledge and so takes on meaning.

Students of all ages who have difficulty with writing need to talk about their encounters with real objects and real people in real situations. The senses can be tapped to encourage writing. Bringing in a few fragrant roses, or cooking bacon in a microwave in class, can evoke associations and spur writing. Words from real experiences well up from a much deeper source than paraphrases, and the process of re-creating experiences in writing can become much more meaningful if the student draws upon that deeper source.

Mystery writer Elizabeth Daniels Squire, who is moderately learning disabled, writes vividly from her own experiences. If the book she is writing requires a scene that lies outside her experience, she goes and gets the experience that she needs. Recently, she asked the curator of reptiles at her local zoo to allow her to watch rattlesnakes striking so that she would be able to write about it. When a character in her book needed to take a motorcycle ride, she persuaded a young friend to give her a long ride on his motorcycle.

At the Lab School, the Writer's Lab for young children uses a sand tray that a child can fill with miniatures to re-create a situation; the child then tells a story based on that situation and discusses it in the classroom. Then the child either dictates the story to the teacher or enters it on a computer and draws accompanying pictures and adds sound effects. Successes in writing need not be delayed or held up by failure in one or two particular areas of the craft. A student who feels defeated by handwriting or spelling can often forge ahead at the higher level of composition if the mechanics of writing are made possible with help from a computer.

WHAT COMPUTERS CAN AND CANNOT DO FOR THE LEARNING DISABLED

The use of word processors can greatly simplify and speed up the process of writing for people with learning disabilities. A light laptop computer can become almost an extra arm for students, professional writers, or executives with learning disabilities. The clear display of text on the screen and the ease with which text can be revised are the two main reasons word processing works so well. Mental energy can be concentrated on the thoughts to be conveyed, not on the often agonizing task of handwriting. Computer spell-checking programs and electronic dictionaries and thesauruses can be a godsend to writers with learning disabilities, as can desktop-publishing programs, such as PageMaker, Quark Xpress, or Ventura Publisher, with which they can turn out finished, professional-looking documents.

Outlining programs, which are similar in operation to word-processing programs, allow adults and older students to plan projects with clear, flexible structures. Ideas can be moved, joined, or subordinated with one or two keystrokes. Hypercard and other hypertext or multimedia programs extend the possibilities of expression for people with learning disabilities by combining text with drawings, photographs, sound effects, voice-overs, and animation. The effects can approximate their own inner worlds with incredible intensity. Hypertext programs created by teachers can also address the inner world in many different, compelling ways.

At the opposite end of the scale from the programs that give free rein to imagination are the drill-and-practice programs widely used in classrooms throughout the country. Though less useful for the learning disabled in general, such programs do have the advantage of being emotionally neutral. Sometimes, it is easier for a person with learning disabilities to accept correction for mistakes from a neutral machine than from a tutor whose feelings may get hurt or whom the student is afraid of letting down. Sophisticated drill-and-practice programs are a clear improvement over drill books that do not individualize. The best of these programs determine the academic level of each user and adjust themselves accordingly.

Although computers are a boon for most people with learning disabilities, they do not work for all. Some people find the screens visually confusing. Others cannot coordinate their hands and eyes well enough to perform the required functions.

Nonetheless, computers are very useful tools for most people with learning disabilities. A computer cannot do the thinking for a student. A word processor does not organize a composition or suggest the subject. A spell checker can identify misspelled words that are not in its dictionary but cannot spot the error when *way* has been written instead of *weigh*. Even the relatively simple, user-friendly Macintosh demands a certain amount of knowledge and sophistication to be used independently. The active involvement and knowledge of the teacher is as important as that of the student in making the computer a powerful tool for learning. Computers and other technological innovations are becoming what pencils were to older Americans, so teacher-training institutions must be sure that future teachers are comfortable with computers and can use them competently as teaching devices in the classroom.

TEACHING TEACHERS CONCRETELY

To make sure that teachers of children and adults with learning disabilities teach in a concrete way, teacher-training institutions must initiate classes that use various senses and that introduce different styles of learning. We need to teach teachers in the ways that we want them to teach students.

In my special-education classes at The American University in Washington, D.C., future teachers experience what it is like to be learning disabled. While radios are blasting, papers are being passed out, and lights are flicking on and off, they are taught a number of words beginning with the letters X and Z. Naturally, they have difficulty doing the task. "Were you paying attention?" they are asked, sternly. "Try harder!" they are admonished.

They are given a long paragraph to read with words and letters reversed, some of them written upside down. There are questions at the bottom of the page and a loud timer ticking to add pressure. They are asked to listen to a long, complicated, largely incomprehensible series of sentences that they must summarize orally. The experiences make them feel stupid, incompetent, and sometimes resentful; some of them quit trying, just as the learning disabled do.

To gain understanding of visual-motor or eye-hand difficulties, the students wear heavy gardening gloves as they attempt to thread a needle, to open an envelope, or to cut out a pattern with scissors and paste it on a piece of paper. Wearing outsized boots helps them simulate some gross motor difficulties. A Walkman radio playing jazz in their ears while they are listening to a teacher giving detailed instructions can imitate some auditory difficulties. Teachers need to know the learning-disabled world!

Task analysis is one crucial skill that would-be teachers of the learning disabled must acquire. These teachers need to break tasks down into minute detail to understand fully what the task requires and to create an effective learning plan.

What do you need to know in order to be able to perform a motor skill such as skipping? Graduate students have to figure out what prior skills are needed in order to skip, to hop, and so on. What skills do you need in order to learn a nursery rhyme, or to play pick-up-sticks, bingo, or checkers?

To teach these skills, as well as the more obviously academic tasks such as writing book reports and doing research, a teacher needs to know how many steps are involved in each part of the process. In their training teachers need to do each task themselves in order to break it down into its smallest components.

If teachers are taught primarily through textbooks and mimeographed handouts, they will teach their students in that way. Yet adult-education literature today is filled with articles stating that adults learn best by doing, the learning disabled even more so.

LEARNING FROM FAILURE

Many adults say they have to learn from their own failures. They conclude that their parents, teachers, and other adults who give wise counsel cannot get across to them what they themselves learn from failing a course, losing a job, or losing a friend. Isn't that a pretty cruel way to learn? One adult with learning disabilities said, "Cruel it may be, but I didn't select college courses by thinking through which teacher and what methods would work, and God forbid I should ask for advice. So I failed. Eventually, I turned to Special Services at the university for counseling to help me succeed, but I needed to fail a few times first." Another adult said that she lost seven jobs before she tried to analyze what was not working. "On the other hand," she insisted, "it was through losing those jobs that I realized I needed more education and that my classes should be in an art-related field!"

Over and over again, educators who work with the learning disabled say of their clients that they are their own worst enemies: if there's a difficult route and an easy one, they always trek along the difficult path! Their stubbornness, or fierce determination, prevents other from helping them be kinder to themselves. They seem to have to learn from doing, even if the doing is counterproductive.

Tess was determined to live alone in an apartment. Her parents thought it was a good idea but felt that she needed to save up money before attempting it. Tess insisted and moved. Then she learned that she could not pay the rent or meet the costs of transportation and food on the salary she earned. She nearly killed herself working two jobs trying to support herself. Finally, she reassessed the situation and moved to a group house where four young people each had a large room and shared a kitchen and a living room. At last she could work one job and meet her expenses.

Phillip, aged twenty-five, had no friends. His family encouraged him to join a church group, a social group at a nearby community center, a club, or even a spa. Phillip adamantly refused. It took three years of extreme loneliness before Phillip decided to join a chess club. He made friends through an activity that he loved and at which he excelled.

ADULT LEARNERS

Concrete learning can be very intellectual at its base. Too many people worry that if they engage in what looks like play or games, they will be called childish. Yet, done well, concrete teaching is mind building and concept forming and provides a base for extraordinary critical thinking and language development.

We have observed at the Night School that adults will not enroll in classes that teach applied math through woodworking, or language expression through drama. They believe they have invested their money for three one-hour academic classes and a seminar; most of them will not tolerate learning through an art form. Nevertheless, in groups of five, a master teacher can teach them reading through an individualized prescription involving some arts or project learning.

The Night School uses life experiences as a vital teaching tool for these adults. One man was an excellent driver, and his interests were focused on his car. Since he was a nonreader and couldn't do math, all his instruction was based on his experiences with his car—how different parts make up a whole, what it means to be in the driver's seat, how to recognize a stop sign, and why rules are necessary in grammar as in driving. His quick grasp of this extended metaphor carried over into other academic situations.

Another adult in the class was totally wrapped up in football. His math problems and his reading assignments were centered on football. His teacher even explained complex concepts and a higher level of vocabulary in terms of football. The young man didn't understand the word *inference,* so the teacher asked him to suppose that his coach was starting to pay a lot of attention to his rival on the team. "What's going on in your mind?" asked the instructor. "That the coach might let him play in my place." "Aha! You inferred that! That is an inference!"

Actors Tom Cruise, Cher, and Margaret Whitton, all learning disabled, agree that they learn best through experiential education. Whitton described what she learned from acting: "I like what I'm doing because it allows me to teach myself. If you're really into acting, you have to know about the period of history you're working on, what the art was like, what people were wearing. So it gives me permission to teach myself. It's like being a perpetual student."

For many adults with learning disabilities, taking some time off to work between high school and college, or as a break during college, can be extremely beneficial. By trying out jobs, they frequently find out what they are good at and discover the formal qualifications needed, which they can then set about obtaining. On-the-job training is excellent for many dyslexics, who can go back and read all the theory afterward, when it can be placed in a meaningful context (schemata, again). Unfortunately, parents often do not see the value of interrupting the educational process with work experience. They fear that, having left the academic structure, the child will not return to it. Frequently, the job experience gives the necessary impetus to acquire more education.

Richard Strauss, the real-estate specialist, did just that. He didn't find out until his senior year in high school that he was learning disabled. He tried college and found that it wasn't right for him: "As a messenger in a real-estate brokerage firm, at nineteen years of age, I was able to sell a million-dollar office building, only I had to get someone else to deposit the money in the bank for me because I had not passed my real-estate test. I had to study some more in order to pass the test. I worked harder than the people next to me. I put in a few more hours and went around with different people and listened and watched what they were doing. I learned from experiences rather than from the textbook."

William Doyle, a well-known antique dealer and auctioneer, discovered a rare profession through his concreteness, his curiosity, and his sensitivity to concrete objects. When he was a child, his favorite day was Wednesday, the garbage day, when people set out large, bulky objects on the sidewalk to be picked up. It was like a treasure hunt for him, and he had a collector's penchant for squirreling away his finds. Soon he formally apprenticed himself to an antique dealer after school and quickly mastered the complex details of the trade, even though he was doing poorly in his courses at school. He told the Lab School students: "I fell in love with objects, and I became an antique dealer. And now I've become an auctioneer, and for me it's the most exciting business. It's like theater. It's like a treasure hunt every day. I still want to succeed. I still want to do better. If I had all the complete learning abilities, I would have been successful and done a normal job, but I never would have had the life I've had today!"

Concreteness can produce greatness. It can also cause problems in schooling as well as in social relationships. The learning disabled pay a terrible price emotionally. Often it takes years for them to feel OK about themselves, as we will see in the next section.

8
Responsibility: Preparing for Adulthood

"Before I go to bed, I decide on a good plan for the next day, and then I oversleep."

"I make lists and lose them."

"When I count on my internal alarm clock, I'm in real trouble—I mean, real *trouble."*

"For years I just followed my urges. I did what I felt like doing or what I could get away with. Now I force myself to meet schedules."

"I never seem to get to places on time. It's cost me some jobs."

"The hardest part of growing up is showing up regularly and sticking to schedules and following through on everything."

Learning to take responsibility for one's own actions is an essential part of growing into adulthood. An adult must assume responsibility in countless areas of life—for his or her own money and credit, for keeping clean, for eating, for showing up at a job when he or she doesn't feel like it, and so on. Too often, people with learning disabilities fall behind their peers in their readiness to assume responsibility. By the time they are physically mature, they still do not have control over their own behavior. Their inner disorganization prevents them from regulating themselves to meet the demands of the adult world.

Young people with learning disabilities need to be taught many subtle skills and abilities that will prepare them for responsible adulthood. They need to learn how to regulate and monitor their own behavior, how to set goals for themselves, how to plan ahead with care, and how to think critically and then make their own choices and decisions. Caring adults who work with such youths in school, in recreational settings, and in social-service programs, as well as in their own families, can intervene in many ways to help them acquire necessary skills for responsible adult living and so ease their transition into adulthood. And, of course, learning to be responsible for themselves gives the learning disabled power over their own lives.

SELF-REGULATION

Though he was almost thirty years old, Sandy could not discipline himself to rise at an appointed hour, to study several hours a day, or to be ready on time to go somewhere or do something. Neither could Myra, who was twenty-five, nor Bruce, who was thirty-five. Their parents feared they would never learn.

Many young people with learning disabilities are in a similar situation: they cannot count on themselves, and no one can count on them. Their central nervous systems are disregulated, and so are their lives. Some adults with learning disabilities lose track of time at night when they are watching TV or reading. They fall asleep four hours late and wake up four hours late, thereby sleeping through classes, job interviews, and jobs. Oversleeping can also be a sign of depression. Many a mother has found herself screaming at the top of her lungs at "a big lump" in a bed, "How could you sleep through your class [or game/job/appointment/meeting]?" There's probably an excuse, a mumble, and a sense of defeat felt by "the lump" and usually by the mother, too.

Infants and children, because they process sensory information poorly, need parents to regulate their worlds. *But adolescents and adults with irregular central nervous systems need to be taught how to regulate their own worlds.*

A parent of one of these young adults will tell you that teaching him or her self-regulation is easier said than done. It's as though the young adult's internal alarm clock is broken or works only in spasms. How confusing this is to the young adult, and how infuriating to his or her parents and teachers! One parent said, "God makes these kids charming because otherwise we'd kill them!" Of course, when such a young person feels passionate about going to a soccer clinic or on a fishing expedition, he or she is up and out of the house by 7:00 A.M.! But rarely can the young adult with learning disabilities sustain such enthusiasm every day, in ordinary situations involving regular routines. Instead, his or her reaction to the struggle becomes a reactive depression, and he or she becomes a huge, snoring lump in the bed.

I have said that young adults who exhibit such irresponsible behaviors as staying up late and oversleeping need to be taught how to regulate their lives. However, this does not mean that some adults should continually assume responsibility and enforce regulation from outside. Quite the contrary. Adolescents and young adults have to solve such problems themselves. Only by doing so can they learn to be responsible. Parents can only buy them the loudest alarm clocks available, talk to them about the problem, and try to help figure out strategies that will work. As one parent said, "I have to make it *his* problem, not mine, and keep myself emotionally distant from it."

"How do you teach responsibility?" asked Rob, who was concerned about his brother Roger being so irresponsible.

Marcie, a Lab School graduate, said, "It's something you've got to feel inside. It's got to become yours and really matter! It's a little like moving into your own apartment (as distinct from living with your parents) and wanting the place to look clean and nice (as distinct from not caring how the place looked at your parents' house)."

SELF-MONITORING

One step that can be taken toward teaching self-regulation is to encourage self-monitoring, a crucial prerequisite for responsible action. For example, being able to read and do math at grade level are not enough for success in regular school. A student with weak self-monitoring skills cannot do independent work without a teacher near him and will probably fail in the mainstream.

Sixteen-year-old Mickey's reading and math scores were at a high ninth-grade level, his writing skills were at a fifth-grade level, and his family wanted him to enter tenth grade at a small, private alternative school. The Lab School faculty was convinced that he should spend another year at the Lab School, concentrating on self-monitoring skills in order to assure success. So, he stayed. Suddenly, around his seventeenth birthday, Mickey's ability to organize his external and internal worlds took an incredible leap, as did his achievement scores, and he enrolled in the new school's eleventh grade the following year, with great success.

To function independently as adults, the learning disabled have to take charge of themselves. The impulsive outbursts, the opinions better left unsaid, have to be regulated by the young adult himself or herself. Paying attention, being able to be quiet, putting others' needs ahead of one's own, being solicitous of others, lowering one's voice, and other ways of being aware of others' needs are part of the self-control skills one needs for holding a job and for being an adult, a mate, and a parent in our society.

SETTING GOALS

Encouraging a child to set simple goals from an early age is another good way to prepare him or her for responsible adulthood. Goal setting establishes self-directedness: "This is what I want to accomplish." Meeting a goal requires thinking ahead and monitoring one's progress toward the goal. Thus, learning to think in terms of goals both encourages self-monitoring and becomes the basis for planning.

One way in which the Lab School encourages goal-oriented behavior is through our apprenticeship program. Eleventh-grade students with learning disabilities are placed in apprenticeships for over three hours a day. The apprenticeships, which usually don't pay, expose students to several different career possibilities and to the people in the community who choose to work in such places as hospitals, frame shops, radio stations, and boutiques.

Most of these students become more motivated to achieve academically after their apprenticeships because they then know more about what they want to do later in life. In addition, they develop good work habits and learn how to get around a city by bus or subway, how to socialize with people of different ages, how to speak to a boss, and how to joke with a fellow worker.

To make this whole process meaningful, however, they need careful adult monitoring, individual conferences, and group seminars to help them evaluate their experiences. They don't learn much from just going out and getting jobs.

The director of the internship program works very closely with both employers and students. She encourages employers to be frank with the student apprentices, to give them feedback when they do well, and to tell them where they must improve.

"Let's pick one goal that we're going to work on for a while, John," said Perry, who was John's supervisor on the job. "It can be your lateness, your follow-through on activities, or your overreacting. Of course, none of these really describes you, but I think we need to improve these areas." John chose overreacting, and they came up with a battle plan that included rewards for not overreacting (such as being able to do more work on the computer) and consequences for overreacting (such as having to stay late). John's improved self-control carried over to his school behavior. So far, almost every Lab School student apprentice has been offered a summer job or after-school paid employment by his or her employer.

PLANNING

As almost every chapter of this book has emphasized, planning is an essential key to success. For many people with learning disabilities, poor planning results from their general disorganization, their not seeing what belongs and what doesn't, and their difficulty with sequences—what comes first, next, and last. Poor planning is responsible for the failure of many bright college students.

A student with learning disabilities studied four hours a day for ten days before his examination in economics. He studied every word of his notes, every word from his books, and every question from the midterm test. He had no study plan. He didn't organize the material into categories. He didn't figure out what the examination would cover. His reward for all that inefficient studying was to have to repeat the course, and unless he learned how to study, he was doomed to failure again. A similar lack of planning on the job, for example, or a lack of anticipation of sales slumps or of cash-flow problems, could cause a person to lose a job.

Important logistics in socializing include planning when to be at a particular place, what needs to be done, what equipment or materials are required, and how long it takes to get there. Dan, because he comes late all the time, misses a lot of fun. Jason, who forgets what he is supposed to bring, gets criticized or ridiculed. Meg's messiness and clumsiness spoil the projects of other members in the groups to which she belongs. Chuck never has the correct change for the bus and waits until the last minute to beg for change, which irritates his friends.

Most people plan when to get up and how to allow time for breakfast. They plan how to get to work or school on time, when to schedule lunch and to come home, what time to set aside for recreation, and when to turn in. Many people with learning disabilities just let these things happen to them. Waves of time wash over them; sometimes they make it on time, but often they don't. They don't plan for tomorrow and barely plan for the next five minutes.

Time and space are the two basic organizing systems in our lives. They must be structured effectively if our lives are to function smoothly. Parents, teachers, and friends must show people with learning disabilities how to break a task down into its separate parts, and then how to plot, in a visual way, the time required for each step. A large wall calendar can show exactly how long it will take to do each part.

The learning disabled need to be taught explicitly how to organize projects and how to plan to accomplish specific goals. Since adolescents with learning disabilities tend to be more immature and less organized than people in the general population, it helps them most to simulate real-life situations. They should spend as much time as possible working on projects that need to be planned in great detail.

Art projects are good examples of ones that require such planning. All art forms require adolescents to organize and plan their worlds. Making an animated or video film, choreographing a dance, creating a mural, building a go-cart, acting in a play, making puppets, putting on a puppet show, playing a guitar, sculpting life forms—all such activities demand organization and planning. They cannot be accomplished without careful analysis of the parts that make up the whole, sequencing of the steps, and allocation of time.

Many people consider art activities to be frills. Yet an untraditional learner can frequently learn basic skills through an art form. Youths with learning disabilities can develop their planning skills and a sense of responsibility by running a school store, a message center, a dance, a refreshment stand, or a mock credit union. They need to be encouraged to plan parties and ceremonies and then to evaluate the results. Lab School students run the school store—taking inventory and working on spreadsheets on the computer. Putting together a yearbook is an excellent exercise in planning, as is working on a literary journal or a student newspaper.

Often parents of adolescents with severe learning disabilities do too much for them. Such parents try to keep their kids very busy in structured activities and to rescue them when problems occur. As a result, these adolescents have no experience in planning for themselves. Adults who work with such adolescents must be willing to stand back and let them experience the consequences of poor planning. Then the adult can talk over where errors could have been avoided, help them replan, and give them a chance to learn how to ensure success in another venture. Remember, all people learn best from experience! That is, they learn by doing.

CLIMBING BEHIND THE WHEEL

Responsibility for oneself is never more keenly felt than from behind the wheel of a car. It is a sobering experience for many young people to have so much power and independence in their hands. For youths with learning disabilities, it's not just the reading of signs that causes problems. They may have difficulty:

- in judging space
- in knowing how close they are to another car
- in paying attention to how fast they are going
- in inhibiting their impulses
- in making their feet work the pedals while their hands are busy doing something else with the steering wheel

For some, there is too much to do all at once with the body, the senses, and the mind. Adults with learning disabilities tell us that the greatest difficulty in driving comes at an intersection, where the driver must look left, then right, and then judge the time and the space needed to make a turn. Difficulty in integrating several things at once is at the core of the problems of the learning disabled.

Parents' legitimate concern about their children's readiness to drive is a major conflict area between parents and adolescents. Some young people with learning disabilities wait a few years until their nervous systems are more mature before attempting to get a license, and some responsible youths do not drive at all. On the other hand, there are many youths whose learning disabilities consist mainly of auditory and language deficiencies, and their problems do not interfere at all with their prowess in driving. In fact, they excel as drivers.

MAKING CHOICES AND DECISIONS

Many people with learning disabilities tend to appear irresponsible because of their inability to make choices and decisions. For such people, making choices is very difficult because they have too much to deal with at once: they have trouble sticking to the main issue and often get lost in the details. They cannot assign greater or lesser values to situations or outcomes and thus establish priorities. They may try memorizing *all* the information relevant to a choice or decision rather than extracting the most important data. They may try to give equal study time to all courses, leaving no room to consider the difficulty of a course, the different demands of each course, and their own talents in dealing with these.

One girl who had been in special classes through most of her schooling had felt good about her progress and realistic about not yet having the skills needed for college; so she plunged into the working world. After several months in her job, she simply wanted to hole up in her room and listen endlessly to music. She stated, in awe, "It's a fast world out there! I wish I had received some advice about which jobs I could succeed at and which ones to avoid. There are so many options and choices to make that I don't know where to turn! I don't know how to begin!"

Career decisions need to be based on strengths and weaknesses, on knowing which career will call upon one's best and which will minimize what one cannot do. The choice of a college requires the same care. A student's interests and needs, strengths and deficiencies, must be weighed against the facilities, attitudes, and philosophy of each college. Does this student need much or little help? Does she learn better going strictly by a textbook, or is she a hands-on, concrete type? Is he sloppy and untidy, or a compulsive perfectionist? Thoughtful, prescriptive career and college counseling can match a student to a career or university in which he or she has a good chance of success.

Of course, young adults should help to solve the problems in their own lives. They make wonderful coinvestigators and coworkers in plotting their future courses of action. That's why they, even more than other students, need direct training in problem solving and critical thinking.

Schools can and should provide youngsters with learning disabilities more formal problem-solving opportunities. Such youngsters need logic labs, invention fairs, cause-and-effect games, chances to unravel mysteries, and opportunities to devise strategies to stamp out infectious diseases or to address environmental dilemmas.

Often teachers spend too much time presenting facts to students. In most schools, students are not asked whether something is working or allowed to anticipate problems and predict outcomes. *It is far more important to teach students with learning disabilities how to approach a task than it is to teach them how to do the task itself.* Hence playing games that require planning (like checkers, chess, Clue, or Stratego) is very important. Helping the learning disabled to look at patterns, groupings, and relationships is vital. They need help in developing systems for learning new material, for remembering names, for memorizing directions, for sticking to tasks. They need to make choices and evaluate consequences.

Teacher-training institutes must demand more problem solving, ingenuity, critical thinking, and development of original materials from teachers in training. Teachers will then weave these processes into the whole curriculum. Divergent thinking will be prized, and students with learning disabilities will learn how to attack problems through their best modes of learning.

BEING ACCOUNTABLE

Being accountable, accepting responsibility, not rationalizing or making excuses, following through—these are all important parts of adult life. Young people need to be taught to assume responsibility, and they can be taught in many ways: by being asked to put away the basketballs, to wash the dishes every night, to make their beds, or to do tasks that the whole family depends on them to do. Learning to clean up after a party, to straighten up the house, to take responsibility for how things look, and to assume the responsibility of being considerate of others—these are essential parts of growing up.

Many adults with learning disabilities will sign up for a meeting, an exhibition, or a party and never show up. They forget. They become distracted. They feel bad about themselves. Most of all, they do not feel accountable and never let anyone know of their changes in plans. Sometimes, juniors and seniors in high school don't feel accountable to remain in school. Curt left three weeks before graduating because he failed a big test and simply assumed that the school would not let him graduate. Cindy left two weeks before the end of her junior year because she didn't like one of her teachers and because she had been offered a job at $10 an hour. Cher said, "I left school at sixteen because I thought, This holds nothing for me." These people didn't feel accountable.

COMBAT READINESS

Night School students coined the phrase *combat readiness,* which describes, they say, a pervasive feeling that begins in elementary school and that takes form in junior high school as a strong defense mechanism. It's their way of taking control of their lives. Some people with learning disabilities live in a constant state of combat readiness caused by fear of embarrassment and failure. They anticipate problems in order not to look stupid.

Some people's form of combat readiness is to overregulate themselves. Always early, constantly referring to schedules, they are so rigid, tense, and joyless that people around them want to teach them relaxation techniques and yoga.

Many adolescents with learning disabilities plague adults

by asking, "Exactly what is supposed to happen next?" or "What is the whole procedure, from beginning to end?" The intensity of their questioning can be annoying to people in charge (parents, teachers, employers). As one adult with learning disabilities put it, "I was embarrassed enough at school, and that will never happen again in my life if I can help it!"

9
The Emotional Toll

"I was angry at the world for inflicting learning disabilities on me."

"I felt there was no hope for me, real despair."

"There were times when I wished I had never been born."

"It took years before I felt that I was okay."

"Here we are, perfectly competent people, feeling so yucky, when we have a lot to feel good about."

"I can read pain in others better than words."

The emotional effects of their learning disabilities cause far more harm to children and adults than their academic deficiencies do. In this chapter some of the general emotional consequences of learning disabilities will be explored. The following two chapters will examine emotional issues as they relate to family life and to social relationships.

SELF-ESTEEM

Normally, a child grows up knowing that she is pleasing almost everybody around her. This makes her feel good about herself. Then, as she finds she can accomplish various tasks, she develops a sense of competence, which creates more feelings of self-worth. These feelings become self-fulfilling. Increased self-esteem creates a "can do" attitude. Success feeds self-esteem, and self-esteem feeds success.

Imagine what it is like to grow up in a world of constant criticism, reprimand, negative feedback, and punishment. What does that do to a person's sense of self-worth? Unable to please the people who matter most to them, people who grew up under these circumstances develop an all-pervasive feeling of not being OK, a feeling expressed by many adults with learning disabilities. This sense of inadequacy is nailed down by subsequent defeats and failures. As one adult with learning disabilities said in a seminar, "I'm just a screw-up. I have always been one."

Finding the inner strength to refuse to feel negative toward oneself can pave the way to success. "Nobody can make you feel bad unless you let them, and I do not let people make me feel bad," said Dr. Donald Coffey of Johns Hopkins University Medical School, speaking to Lab School children. "Everybody has something wrong with them. Some people are, like me, too fat, or they are too thin, too tall, or too short, and everyone else makes fun of that, and if you let that get to you, then you start believing it yourself. But the worst person who can make fun of you is yourself. Just don't let anybody strike you out, particularly the person in the mirror. That's you! You strike yourself out, you get into real trouble."

Actor Harry Anderson, Judge Stone on TV's *Night Court*, makes the same point in a different way: "When they held up cue cards and asked me to read them on *Saturday Night Live*, I had to tell them that I was very embarrassed, but I couldn't do it without sitting down and reading them first with no pressure. I thought that he was going to laugh in my face, and his comment was: 'We've had lots of guys like you.' I mean, it was no surprise to them. That problem was really in me."

Once people with learning disabilities learn to accept their own shortcomings and to believe in themselves in spite of these, they can accomplish remarkable things. Actor, director, and producer Henry Winkler told the Lab School children, "When I was growing up, dyslexia was not even in the vocabulary. I went to an all-boys private school in New York, very chic, and all the guys were going on to these great colleges. I applied to twenty-three schools before getting into Emerson College in Boston." Then, as he says, "all of a sudden, in my sophomore year, I began to do very well. Something clicked! It's important to understand that you are not stupid," Winkler told children at the Lab School. "The feeling of feeling stupid when you are not is terrible. Your person, your personality, your inner song is a lot more important than the speed at which you get things done!"

Speaking at the 1987 Lab School gala, Olympic diver Greg Louganis concurred: "You have to have a strong belief in yourself to overcome a lot of obstacles, especially when things are a lot more difficult than you'd like them to be. . . . Maybe these children's scars won't be as deep as ours have been."

What can be done to improve the self-esteem of children with learning disabilities? As has been pointed out in previous chapters, one must give them opportunities to build on their strengths and interests, to find and develop their particular talents. Consider businessman Richard Strauss, who built a real-estate empire. Speaking of his own experience with overcoming low self-esteem, Strauss said, "Learning disabilities cause a tremendous amount of inferiority problems. If you're not the fastest on the track or the biggest on the football team or tall enough to play basketball or good in your studies, what happens is you become a juvenile delinquent. I was the number-one juvenile delinquent I knew! . . . Finally, I got into an area where I could compete. You don't have to be a genius at reading and writing in my business."

STRESS

Stress is a constant companion of many people with learning disabilities. As one graduate of the Lab School confided, "I sprinkled anxiety wherever I went. Calm people became nervous and nervous people fell apart. I couldn't get out the right words. I trembled and my insides writhed."

Stress is prevalent among people with learning disabilities because such disabilities are often life disabilities. People with learning disabilities encounter constant frustrations. They become consumed by fears of being inadequate, by anger at being born learning disabled, and by guilt over their own inabilities and over the problems that they cause for those around them.

All this stress is intensified by the additional stress caused by fatigue resulting from the energy put into defense mechanisms. Some people put all their energy into hiding their difficulties. When people rely on their defense mechanisms to handle stress, they may:

- withdraw or quit
- regress to an earlier stage of development
- displace responsibility for their failure
- blame others or objects or situations
- become passive-aggressive (silent and dawdling but subtly manipulative)
- become aggressive and hurtful
- become dependent and helpless
- distract or clown

People with learning disabilities can learn to anticipate situations that will cause them anxiety and they prepare themselves. None of us can anticipate all stress; but once a frustrating situation occurs, strategies can be forged that will work the next time.

In her autobiography, the severely dyslexic British actress Susan Hampshire says that she knew she had to be very clear about left and right during the filming of *Living Free* in Africa, because she was working with lions. However, under stress, her confusion grew worse. When the director yelled, "Run to your right!" she ran to the left and nearly collided head-on with a full-grown lioness. Fortunately, it made a good take, but thereafter Susan wrote a big *R* on her right palm, and an *L* on her left and kept looking at them throughout the shooting of the film.

A prominent illustrator of children's books tells story after story about her left-right confusion and all the embarrassments and stress the confusion has caused her. She has missed appointments, lost jobs, and angered friends because she turned the wrong way and became lost. Now, she literally touches her chest to feel where her heart is beating every time she is told to turn left.

A former Lab School student said, "Stress forced me into action. I could not live with so much anxiety and get things done. I wanted to be a creative writer. I needed to enjoy life as well as suffer. So I came to grips with my problems. I stopped hiding them. I let others help me, and a whole bunch of us figured out ways I could manage. You know, I would start to stutter when I had trouble organizing my thoughts, and then I'd get frustrated. Now I take my time. I take a deep breath if I need to and grip the chair if it helps. We can invent ways to make it all work!"

"PASSING FOR NORMAL"

Success can frighten a person with learning disabilities: if he succeeded once, he is expected to succeed again. A person with learning disabilities may be so afraid of failure that he will avoid any situation where he is expected to do well. Others put themselves in the situation but feel like frauds; they do not feel successful, despite their obvious success.

I am appalled when I hear successful adults with learning disabilities say, "Well, I passed for normal!" It's like hearing a black talk about passing for white or a Jew talk about passing as a Christian. When a bright, attractive, gregarious, articulate person takes part in a social event, the casual observer is shocked if told that that person has learning disabilities. This paradox has given rise to the term *invisible handicap*. Since the person looks so normal, she is expected to achieve like everyone else. But she is ambivalent: she likes being thought of as regular but believes that she isn't. She feels dishonest and terribly insecure.

Many people get to college before their learning disabilities are diagnosed, because they worked hard throughout high school to pass for normal. Often it is a fast-paced, intense, college-level foreign-language class that forces the issue. They find they cannot keep up. They cannot handle a second language orally or in written form (or both), and so they fail completely. Sometimes it is the amount of reading and the number of papers to be written that first brings the student in to be tested for learning disabilities.

Eileen Simpson, in her captivating autobiography *Reversals,* describes all of her efforts and subterfuges in high school, where she struggled with unrecognized learning problems and tried to pass for normal. She succeeded so well that, to her astonishment, she was elected class president in her freshman year at Hunter College. When she was first attracted to the poet John Berryman, she tried to tell him that she had something wrong with her, but he did not believe it. Only after he received a hand-scrawled, misspelled, nearly illegible letter from her did he grasp the extent of her difficulties, and then he introduced her to the word *dyslexia*.

DEPRESSION

The learning disabled often do not feel safe in the world. Their alarm systems have to be on all the time, on the alert to mobilize whatever resources they need to make them feel safe, and this drains their energy. Chronic anxiety predisposes a person to depression and being drained beyond the ability to mobilize into action.

Most adults who attend the Night School talk about how depressed they feel, and some have had a clinical depression that required therapy or even hospitalization. One adult asked, "Why do we always get it? It's bad enough to have dyslexia and dysgraphia and allergies and asthma, but then I have to get depressed as well! It's not fair!" That's right, it isn't fair!

Therapy conducted by a professional who understands the nature of learning disabilities can be enormously helpful. Successful therapy allows pent-up feelings of anger, guilt, fear, and stress to be released. To be successful with people who are often concrete and literal, however, therapy needs to be carefully directed, not free flowing. The therapeutic process needs to interpret reactions and actions back to patients in an understandable way. Therapy must aim at bolstering their egos, empowering them to take charge of their own lives and tackle their own problems. If adults can't afford therapy and no free counseling is available, pastoral counseling or adult support groups can help. The learning disabled need to know the behavior they are projecting.

For the child with learning disabilities, early intervention by a team would be ideal. The team would include parents, teachers, tutors, mental-health counselors, occupational therapists, and speech and language therapists who could draw on the child's hidden talents and engage them as part of the healing process. Prevention in the early years seems the best way to forestall major problems and to prepare for a productive life. According to adults at the Night School, the two times of greatest danger for most of them were the junior-high-school years and the period right after high school or college. "I was zapped by depression, man. It took me over and I couldn't fight it by myself. I needed to get help," said one Night School student.

The adults shared common experiences in which emotional nightmares started to take the place of academic horrors. Many of them had been so busy with their climb to achievement in school that they had not learned to identify the strong feelings within themselves, nor had they learned to express the profound anger they felt. Depression is often anger turned inward. People with learning disabilities justifiably have a lot of anger. They have frequently been treated callously, accused wrongly, and expected to perform in ways they cannot. When that anger is turned outward, against the offending people or situations, even against the learning disability itself, the person becomes healthier and the depression subsides.

EMOTIONAL RELIEF THROUGH SUBSTANCE ABUSE

Some people with learning disabilities can be extremely vulnerable to suggestion and influence. In order to feel "in" with a cool crowd, they may begin drinking too much alcohol or taking drugs. Friendless people who are learning disabled can be lured by false hopes of friendship; the more guileless they are, the more easily they are fooled. Impulsive people are quick to try anything and can then get hooked.

Not all the learning disabled turn to drugs or alcohol. Most do not. Many consciously avoid even experimenting with drugs and alcohol. Yet for some, drugs and alcohol offer a seductive journey into a world of pleasure and self-indulgence, an escape from negativism, devastating criticism, ridicule, and humiliation. People who don't feel safe in an overwhelming world naturally look for relief. They need to obliterate some of their anxiety, to reduce some of their pain. Drugs and alcohol don't do it, but these people need something. Their foray into the substance-abuse world demonstrates that they are in pain and are trying to medicate themselves. There is responsible pharmacology available for these states of being. Psychiatrists usually know how to provide the necessary relief.

"Chemical dependence," said one adult, "seemed to cure my restlessness, my tension, my moodiness, and my being out of sorts with the world, but it didn't really cure them. I just wanted more and more until I lost my soul. It took years of rehab to put me back together, and now I'm back to remedying the original problem—the learning disabilities." The following are some of the effects of substance abuse:

- poor attention span
- disorganized thought
- restlessness
- listlessness
- impulsivity
- irritability
- aggressive behavior
- argumentativeness
- memory loss
- word-retrieval problems
- confusion in time and space

Some of the same symptoms are displayed by people with learning disabilities. Substance-abuse specialists refer to this list as *the signals of distress in drug users*. Some substance-abuse specialists have come to the Lab School to ask how these signals differ when a person is simply learning disabled and not on drugs. Like learning disabilities, drugs and alcohol interfere with the "computer circuits" of the brain. When adults with learning disabilities make the mistake of using drugs and alcohol, it is hard to tell the chicken from the egg.

Sometimes it is Alcoholics Anonymous or a drug rehabilitation and treatment program that first forces a person to confront his own history of learning disabilities. So many wasted years! People need to start learning about the dangers of chemical dependency in elementary school.

EMPATHY

With what seems to be a special kind of radar, people with learning disabilities can be unusually sensitive to the feelings of others. They can tune in to the feelings that lie dormant in the people around them. "How did you know that I was under a lot of stress?" a teacher asked a student who had surprised her by saying he was sorry to see her so worried. She thought she had kept her feelings well hidden.

Some young people with learning disabilities seem to have a special kind of ESP that responds to pain in others. This may be why many of them are extraordinarily capable in medical emergencies and are able to give genuine comfort to the ill and dying. It is as though the people who can't anticipate and plan for their own needs in daily activities can anticipate and sense what is needed in life-and-death situations.

Actress Margaret Whitton told how some of her empathy helped in her profession: "One of the abilities a learning-disabled person often gets is that you can read people emotionally really well, and I think that helps an actor in terms of creating a character."

The same empathy can be used negatively. Some people who are learning disabled know precisely how to go for the jugular. They know intuitively which buttons to press to make other people furious, to upset them, to worry them, or to make them question themselves. Some adults with learning disabilities are so self-centered that they cannot become close to others; they cannot share or cannot enjoy mutuality. Others are so self-absorbed that they cannot put themselves in another person's shoes. If they attempt to be social, they literally have to remind themselves to be aware of others. Patrick lived a fairly isolated life with his car and his TV, spending only a little time with his family. He didn't have any friends. "You know, sometimes when I'm talking with a person I have to tell myself to try and think how he's feeling," Patrick said. He has socialization problems, along with deficiencies in mathematics, writing, and listening skills.

The amazing thing is how people who, unlike Patrick, can adroitly recognize pain and know how to nurture someone in pain can also, just like Patrick, be clumsy socially and unable to function effectively in most group situations. They seem to need help with the fourth R—relationships.

10
Family Tensions

"My brothers called me retard."

"My sister used to yell, 'Come here, dummy'."

"My being learning disabled put the whole family on edge."

"They fought about me all the time."

"I caused the divorce."

"I wonder if I caused my father's heart attack."

"As much as they picked on me at home, they were my greatest defenders outside."

One person's problem, especially a problem as broad in its ramifications as a learning disability, inevitably affects the people closest to him or her—siblings, parents, spouses, and significant others.

BROTHERS AND SISTERS

Brothers and sisters, craving acceptance by their peers, often are mortified by the antics of a sibling who is learning disabled, who says inappropriate and embarrassing things. He may overreact when they wish he would remain passive, or he may underreact when they wish he would be enthusiastic. The sister who can't concentrate well, who forgets what she has just been told and can't follow directions, may elicit the dreaded questions, "What's the matter with her? Is your sister stupid or retarded or what?" Or a brother with learning disabilities may have a catastrophic reaction that looks like a full-blown tantrum, while a sought-after friend asks, "What's with your brother? Is he crazy or something?"

Many adults with learning disabilities witnessed argument after argument between their parents and siblings who did not want to take them along to some event. What they heard was the shame that their siblings felt, which, one adult said, "made me want to vomit, I felt so rotten. Then I would say that I didn't feel well and didn't want to go along anyway. I would then take to bed." Absorbing the shame felt by brothers and sisters merely contributed to their feelings of worthlessness.

Frank Dunkle, former director of the U.S. Fish and Wildlife Service, said, "I had a very bright older brother and younger sister who did very well in school, and it was continually called to my attention that I wasn't as smart as they were. I was the troublemaker, unruly, and they hoped that I might find a job as a plumber or somewhere else where I wouldn't be embarrassing to them."

Parents are continually being told by their other children that they are spoiling the one who is learning disabled, that he would not be half as bad off if the parents would hold him to higher standards: "Why should *he* get all the attention?" "How come you let *her* get away with that? You never let *us* do that. You've changed your standards!" Sometimes parents need to explain again why the child with learning disabilities genuinely cannot do something. But there are times when, just to have some peace and quiet, a parent will let the child who is learning disabled watch TV or have something he wants. Inevitably, this brings out the sibling rivalry in full force.

Siblings at times demand more from the one who is learning disabled than parents are willing to demand. The sibling who is learning disabled may in turn rise to the challenge, striving harder than ever to please a brother or sister. Usually it's a superhuman effort that can achieve success once; rarely can the energy required to sustain the achievement be found every day.

When a psychiatrist from Georgetown Medical School and I ran a Saturday-morning workshop for siblings of the learning disabled, we discovered that younger siblings generally like the older brother or sister who is learning disabled and are often afraid of achieving too much academically for fear of making the one who is disabled feel bad. Sometimes they copy the older one, and adults treat them as learning disabled also when they are not. *There is clearly a dire need for siblings to be informed, in as much detail as they can understand, about the strengths and weaknesses of the sibling with learning disabilities. They need to be brought in as problem solvers and helpers, with ample opportunity to talk. Never discussing or laughing about the foibles of behavior related to having a learning disability makes it that much more shameful.*

Football player Dexter Manley said, "I never thought that I would ever be able to read and write because I thought God dealt me a bad hand, because I felt like I was the black sheep of the family because I could not read and write. I couldn't even say the ABCs, and I just didn't really know what was wrong. I was told I was retarded and all those sort of things, and the negative began to grow with me; I have to overcome all the negative things that I heard because now I can feel good about who I am. . . . My life demands more than what I was doing for myself."

Brothers and sisters can help the sibling with learning disabilities to recover. Some Night School adults, though not all, felt that the approval of their brothers and sisters was more important to them than the approval of their parents.

For many children with learning disabilities, grandparents offered a safe refuge. Grandparents told enthralling tales of their own childhoods. They shared information about the childhood and growing up of their children. They taught skills that the parents didn't have time to teach. They listened, listened, listened. Sometimes they offered wise counsel. Often it was the grandparents who rescued the child who was learning disabled from his siblings or who took his siblings away so that he could have time alone with his parents.

SEPARATING FROM PARENTS

The hidden handicap of learning disabilities is a multiple handicap because so many areas of a person's life are affected. As a result, people with learning disabilities have had to depend on their parents for longer periods of time than others and have had to rely upon their parents emotionally in ways that others did not. Sometimes parents come to rely on that dependence for their own fulfillment. Caring for the child who is learning disabled has become their main work and the center of their lives. Such parents have to learn to wrest themselves away from their child, just as the child has to carve out her own identity and establish an independent life.

As painful as it is, parents of children with learning disabilities frequently must watch them being teased and not take action. The job of parents is to help them find the tools to handle such situations *themselves*. Parents have to watch their children fall and fail and pick themselves up again. If parents absorb too many of the bumps and bruises, their children do not learn the skills that allow them to grapple with adversity.

Some parents become so angry with the school system, and battle it and the personnel in it with such vehemence, that their child suffers. The personnel that they batter tend to take it out on the child. These parents overreact so much that they defeat their own purposes. On the other hand, there are times when parental militancy gives a child enormous support. The child knows that his parents know him well, better than the school authorities, and is pleased that his parents are willing to go to bat for him.

In an attempt to rescue their child and "put an end to his torture at school," wealthy parents sometimes arrange for their child to graduate early without fulfilling all the requirements. They do this by using political clout, by making financial donations, or by using their own status. Unfortunately, this scenario confirms the student's sense of his own worthlessness, the feeling that he could never have done it on his own.

What parents need to do is to listen carefully, to keep lines of communication open, to feel their child's feelings of rejection, humiliation, failure, and despair without absorbing them. Part of separating from one's children is becoming detached from their anxieties and hurts. Parents hurt when their child hurts, but that must not become the parents' problem. It must become and remain the child's problem. Parents and teachers need to help empower the child with learning disabilities to confront his problems and to seek ways to grapple with all the bumps and bruises effectively.

One adult commented that he hated his parents at times for not just taking care of some of his problems, instead of always asking him what *he* was going to do about them: "In retrospect, I see that they were trying to help me feel that I could cope, but it was incredibly painful. I was always stumbling. But even so, you know, they were always there, listening, cheering me on like good coaches, and giving suggestions. It was probably better that they did not take care of a lot of things for me, because then I would have known that I was a total nonentity."

THE HEALTH OF THE WHOLE FAMILY

A child who is severely learning disabled, with or without attention-span difficulties, hyperactivity, and/or impulsivity, strains the whole family. It is difficult to live with a child who taps into the insecurities and frailties of everyone around, particularly when learning disabilities are not fully understood. Profound emotions are aroused. Confusion takes over, and anxiety prevails. These are just a few of the negative possibilities:

- Grandparents criticize the worried parents for spoiling the child with learning disabilities.
- Neighbors complain to the parents.
- Teachers often blame the parents.
- The other children get angry at their parents.
- The parents blame each other, accusing each other's families of having bad genes.
- The parents undermine each other.
- The parents discredit each other's methods.
- The whole family suffers.

The whole family needs to know and talk about learning disabilities. They need to know where to turn for help. They need to be able to define their problems, and they need to take part in solving them.

The world of people who are learning disabled is very fragile. Battles tear them apart, and losses leave them more vulnerable than ever. If the family is in crisis over, say, a grandparent's illness, an older child in trouble with the law, an uncle dying, or a relative who reveals his homosexuality, the child who is learning disabled may become paralyzed emotionally, unable to function. Often the child wrongly assumes that he caused the crisis. Either his huge insecurity or his egocentricity makes him feel that everything bad that happens is his fault.

Divorce happens frequently when one of the mates decides there must be an easier way than living with such stress. The mate usually couches it in terms of no longer being in love with his or her spouse. He or she claims to feel unfulfilled and unhappy in the relationship. The relationship frequently *is* burdened by the stresses and strains of parenting the child with learning disabilities. But discord often can be ironed out with help from a therapist, in parent groups, or by two people, as partners, sharing their worries and their problems.

An adult in the Night School described the hyperactivity (ADHD) that prevented him from sleeping much as a child. He would get up in the small hours of the night and wander around the house. One time he found a pair of scissors and, without reflecting on what it would do to the beauty of the house or on how his mother would react, cut out squares and triangles from the living-room curtain; he had cut out shapes at school the day before and liked it. Another time, he found a jar of peanut butter and left smears all over the living-room furniture, unaware that his parents were having guests for dinner the next day. "When my parents woke up," he recalled, "there was an uproar like you wouldn't believe, and each time I got whipped." Several of the Lab School's Outstanding Learning-Disabled Achievers referred to punishments they received at school—whippings, having their hands slapped, being stood in the corner for seemingly interminable periods of time. Many of them told of their parents getting frantic with them and spanking them. Abuse of the more hyperactive, impulsive children who don't sleep well or of children who are very irritable is, unfortunately, common.

Some children cannot tell the difference between a hard touch and a soft, gentle touch. They react to any touch by pulling away, by acting as if it were a blow. They may even jump up and run away. The parents feel rejected and angry—imagine not being able to cuddle or pat your own baby! In a discussion group of adults with learning disabilities, some said that it took them many years to find out why they hated to be touched. They did not know that they suffered from *tactile defensiveness,* a disorder of the sensory system. "I made my father furious because he felt I rejected him every time he touched me," said one group member. "I pulled away because any touch made my whole system feel dreadful, inside and out. And then I'd get a spanking. I truly felt abused." Others in the group who had the same problem said that it affected their sex lives.

SEX, LOVE, AND MARRIAGE

Social worker Nonnie Star, who is learning disabled herself, has been a leader since 1980 in researching sex, love, marriage, and parenting among people with learning disabilities. Teamed with an occupational therapist who is well trained in disorders of the sensory system and their remediation, Star has explored the effects of tactile defensiveness on a normal sex life. Obviously, it makes a loving relationship much more difficult. Star's mission as a social worker is to teach other mental-health professionals to recognize clues and cues in order not to misdiagnose adults with learning disabilities as emotionally disturbed, especially in the area of sensory defensiveness.

Many young people with learning disabilities do not have this predicament and enjoy normal sex lives. In fact, one adult stated, "My impulsivity has helped me. I reach out and start relationships easily, and everyone is kind to me." Some other, very intense, single-minded adults search seriously for mates, but their very fervor and drivenness frighten away possible partners. One woman said that she had become promiscuous to gain a lot of attention. "It took me a year or so before I realized I was being used," she said. A mature man summed it up by saying, "For the most part, the learning disabled struggle like everyone else to find a suitable mate. We don't have to read guidebooks or take written tests or do algebra to marry, and so most of us are quite successful at it!"

Others felt that the deeper insecurities associated with being learning disabled—always anticipating defeat, disapproval, and rejection—made it harder to find a mate. "We feel so lousy about ourselves, usually, that we ought to clear that away first and try not to bring it as baggage into a marriage," said an older woman who is happily married.

Still others say that not enough is done to help the learning disabled learn courtship skills. Typically the learning disabled fail to pick up social clues and either don't read the signals or read them wrong. "When I think a woman is really after me, it turns out she's just being friendly and is appalled that I thought she was coming on to me," said a Night School student. Some adolescents and young adults with learning disabilities are delayed in developing and accepting their sexuality, as they are delayed in most other areas. Some, with raging hormones, simply do not know what is going on.

Women in the same Night School group were not aware of the ways in which their clothes gave out signals. They did not know that an unkempt appearance could prevent them from obtaining a job for which they are qualified or that provocative clothing could evoke a reaction that could have unpleasant results. Others of these women concentrated solely on their image and neglected their sense of values. "People look at my style; they don't care what I say or do," said one Night School adult who was taken to task on this by the group.

Personal hygiene is a problem for some people with learning disabilities who have not developed routines for bathing, brushing their teeth, fixing their hair, or shaving. A certain measure of cleanliness is essential in intimate relationships.

Many adults shared fears of intimacy that harked back to

their old feelings of worthlessness and their fears that potential mates would discover that they were failures. One graduate of the Lab School confided that it took him longer than most people to become close to others, to trust, and to bond. "Perhaps it was because I spent so many years hiding the real me. I was embarrassed by all my problems, and I was afraid of intimacy." Another adult with learning disabilities said, "I never felt good enough. I could hardly believe that this girl wanted to marry me. I was really scared I wasn't good enough, but I turned out to be rather good."

II

Socialization

"Something I do turns people off. I'm trying to find out what it is."

"I don't have friends my age. They're much older or much younger."

"I'm doing fine on my job, except they told me I have to work more on my relationships with my coworkers."

"I cuddle up with my music and turn off the world. Sometimes that's necessary."

"I was working so hard all the time, I had no friends up until I went to college. But, man, I made a point of discovering how great friendships were in college!"

In 1987 the University of Kansas did an extensive national survey in which adults with learning disabilities were asked to name the most important skills they had needed to acquire. The top five skills they listed were related to social development:

1. self-confidence
2. effective communication
3. decision making
4. making friends
5. getting along with family and in close relationships

This should come as no surprise. Our lives center around our relationships, our families (our mates, our children, our parents), our friends, our coworkers, and our acquaintances. So much of our living is dependent upon our relationships that the parents and professionals who work and live with the learning disabled must consider relationships to be the fourth R, a subject meriting at least as much systematic study as reading, writing, and arithmetic.

SOCIALIZATION AND THE LEARNING DISABLED

For many adults with learning disabilities, their social skills are their strong suit. In fact, many develop strong social skills precisely because they are learning disabled, as a way of compensating for (and sometimes saving themselves from) failure in school or on the job. They learn how to make good friends and develop active social lives.

However, other people with learning disabilities falter socially. Their timing is off. They put their feet into their mouths. They produce one malapropism or faux pas after another. They say whatever comes to mind, without any screening whatsoever. They embarrass and bewilder their families and friends as well as themselves.

Problems with relationships plague them throughout their lives, leading to feelings of loneliness, low self-esteem, and low productivity on the job. Night School adults frequently describe how hard they have struggled with relationships. They believe that the pain of bad relationships has blighted their lives far more than have academic difficulties. Some of them have received help with reading, writing, and arithmetic, but rarely with relationships.

What causes a person with learning disabilities to have socialization problems? As is often the case in the field of learning disabilities, there are many possible answers to this question:

1. A learning disability may cause a person to be unable to read gestures and facial expressions.

2. A learning disability may cause a person to be unable to hear voice tones, making it difficult for them to react.

3. A learning disability may directly affect a person's ability to communicate. ("I can't find words when I want them." "Speaking is hard for me." "I couldn't write, so I couldn't write notes to my friends or even take messages.")

4. A learning disability may cause egocentricity ("me, me, me"), which makes it difficult for a person to evaluate the impact of his behavior on others.

5. A learning disability may cause a person to become so concrete and literal that others find his or her comments inappropriate. ("But you said I was stifling your fun, and I haven't put my hands near you!")

6. A learning disability accompanied by hyperactivity, distractibility, and impulsivity affects social relations. ("I gave away the family secrets. Whatever the family did not want the world to know, I blurted out. I told my friends' secrets also.")

7. A learning disability may cause disorganization to the extent that peers cannot tolerate it. ("I was always late, got lost, forgot what I was supposed to bring.")

8. A learning disability may make a person unable to participate in ordinary activities that develop social skills. ("I was such a klutz, I couldn't go out for sports." "I got all mixed up when I played Monopoly or even a simple game like Uno and ruined it for everybody.")

9. A learning disability may cause a person to be ostracized. ("I was called *space cadet.*") "I was teased all through school for the awkward way I walked." "I went to the basement of our public school for classes with the 'Cootie' group. I'm relieved to be an adult now because it has finally stopped!")

10. A learning disability may cause a person to feel stupid and rotten and to withdraw from social interaction. ("Books became my best friends. I buried myself in them, once I could read.")

11. Misguided teachers and parents may subject the person with learning disabilities to intensive remedial studies that steal all time away from social interactions. ("The worst part of my youth was that I spent so much time with grown-ups. I had no friends.")

In addition, specific cognitive problems of people with learning disabilities can cause them to act immaturely and so hinder their social development. Often nursery-school and kindergarten teachers are concerned over immature social behavior long before any specific academic deficiencies appear. The records of children who transfer to the Lab School in elementary grades often include comments by former teachers on their inappropriate behavior, such as asking silly questions and telling pointless stories.

An inability to socialize appropriately may reflect, to a large extent, the same neurological immaturity that is at the root of other problems of the learning disabled. For example, a person with a faulty judgment of space, who trips because he doesn't notice what is close and what is far away, may have trouble looking at others and relating to them. A person who doesn't understand concepts such as *the same as, different from,* and *equal to* may fail in socialization because he cannot distinguish situations that call for variations in behavior. He cannot size up social situations or tune in to other people's feelings. He says the right thing to the wrong person at the wrong time. At a dinner party he makes a big fuss over nothing or just sits there like a bump on a log. He wanders aimlessly around at a picnic or lights on one person to whom he talks for too long a time and with an intensity out of proportion to the situation. In short, social failure can be due to problems in more general cognitive areas—to problems in such areas as estimating, differentiating, making inferences, and understanding proportion.

ADDRESSING UNDERLYING COGNITIVE SKILLS

Learning How to Switch Gears

People with neurological dysfunctions often want to do things in one way—in the way that they did them yesterday and the day before. This is a normal stage of development for a young child, but if it lingers on, it can become a big social problem. "I've always been thrown out of whack by sudden changes. I like to eat at a regular time every day and follow my routines exactly," said one Night School adult. "But when I went to work, my routines got interrupted, and I couldn't cope. I lost a lot of jobs that way. Couldn't they have helped me at school or at home with this?"

"I'm having a real problem at college," reports another, "because when I have three classes one day and only one the next day, it gets me off balance, and I don't know where I am. It was much easier at high school, where the schedule kept steady—every day the same."

Adults who are inflexible are often extremely concrete and literal. When asked a question, Jeffrey always answers literally. Somebody asked him if he had found that beautiful rock he had in his hand in a stream near his house. "I did not find a beautiful rock," retorted Jeffrey. "But look at it," said Anthony, "it's beautiful." Jeffrey grunted, "It is a porous rock, not a beautiful rock." Eventually he could agree that the porous rock could be beautiful, too.

Sometimes this literalness and precision can be an asset. Author Elizabeth D. Squire is an extraordinary interviewer. She said, "I take every vague or abstract thought the interviewee utters, and get him to translate it into simple concrete examples. And, of course, that is what fiction is: life presented in concrete examples."

The literalness of children can be enchanting. Some of the best descriptive writing is produced by very concrete youngsters. However, the same precision that produces fine writing can turn into hairsplitting. Then the person can sound carping and unreasonable when he is merely seeking literal explanations.

Schools can actively help a child who is severely learning disabled to accept change with more equanimity. *A concrete, literal, inflexible elementary-school child needs to be taught by means of concrete activities that there is more than one way to do things.* Literature chosen for storytelling can be helpful. Once learning occurs through concrete strategies, discussion is useful. Teenagers need the same basic approach—one involving visuals, role-playing, literature, and discussion.

Learning the skills of negotiation and compromise is difficult for the "one-way" person because there is much back and forth that must go on. Learning that certain compromises have to be made is part of job readiness. Working on strategies for adapting to change and for compromising should become part of high-school curricula. In fact, the whole topic of negotiations would make an excellent teaching unit. Career counseling can also address the needs of the "one-way" student, who should be advised to head for military service or for other occupations that involve highly structured, rarely changing routines.

Classroom learning and relationships may present insuperable difficulties to rigidly single-minded adolescents. Disorganized children have difficulty with transitions. Children who are learning disabled tend to learn how to switch gears as neurological maturation occurs. At the Lab School we see striking changes in children around ages eleven, fourteen, seventeen, and nineteen, when they suddenly become much more organized and able to do several things at once. Often, at the same time, they advance several grade levels in reading.

Among adults at the Night School, we sometimes see the same thing happen in the late twenties and middle thirties. All of a sudden, they look much more put together. If the central nervous systems of these dysfunctioning children and adults are the culprits, then making these people aware of their problem in dealing with change may be the best approach. By learning to identify the problem, students become aware that they need to learn strategies for dealing with their resistance to change.

The concreteness that makes it difficult for them to face change is also responsible, in part, for the problems they have with generalizing and relating cause to effect.

Learning How to Relate Cause and Effect

Thinking through the consequences of one's remarks and actions is a mark of a mature adult, who knows that there is no such thing as a free lunch, that we pay for what is given to us in one way or another. The people with whom we associate, the events that we participate in, and the actions we take are usually the results of our own choices. These choices determine how we are to live, and we must accept their consequences.

Immature adults often say or do things on impulse, without thought as to what may happen as a result. Many a family gathering has become tense and unpleasant because of the thoughtlessness of an adult or child with learning disabilities. The egocentric need for instant gratification (" I want . . . I need") drives out any thought for the welfare of others.

As a means for controlling such impulsive, egocentric behavior, cause-and-effect relationships need to be taught to children with learning disabilities, both at home and at school, starting with concrete objects and direct experience. Simple lessons with objects (for example, if you press too hard, objects will fall apart; if you don't press hard enough, nothing will happen) can be applied to human interaction (for example, if you are too aggressive, relationships may fail; if you are too shy and withdrawn, nothing will happen).

Seeing pictures of real occurrences and discussing the probable causes can establish a foundation for a child's eventual analysis of a personal experience. Through drawing, telling, or writing, she can discuss and share cause-and-effect situations. The format is to take an effect (an event), to state it clearly in a sentence, and then to analyze the statement.

The sentence might be "I was punished for throwing milk at Bob." The teacher then asks for elaboration and receives a reply: "I was trying to talk. Bob kept interrupting me, so I lost my train of thought. I became angry. I got angrier, but I didn't say anything." The situation is then diagrammed—written or dictated—in the following way:

CAUSE: I talk. Bob interrupts. I am angry. I can't
          get words out.

EFFECT: I throw milk in Bob's face. I get punished.

The children then draw the scene: one child trying to talk and Bob interrupting; one child throwing milk at Bob.

Alternative behaviors can be acted out and then described, in speech or in writing, in terms of cause and effect:

CAUSE: I talk. Bob interrupts. I am angry. I can't get words out.

EFFECT: I am angry. I tell Bob I am angry and to stop. I walk away and discuss the problem with my teacher.

Cause-and-effect analysis can help adults become less defensive by teaching them not to personalize things. Christa felt that whenever others laughed, they had to be laughing at *her*. She took the most casual remarks personally: "You say somebody was tactless? You mean me, don't you?" By laying out these situations in the same format as the milk-throwing incident, Christa's teacher helped her to overcome a big stumbling block.

Learning to Differentiate Situations and to Set Priorities

Sometimes the social problems of the learning disabled arise from a basic inability to discriminate between different situations. The inability to see how one situation differs from another makes the person unable to set priorities. She cannot say to herself, "In this situation, action x should take priority, whereas in that situation, priority should be given to action y."

Some adults with learning disabilities do not pay attention to someone who is talking to them but just go about whatever they are doing without even looking up, and then are surprised when they are called rude.

The parents of a twelve-year-old girl could not persuade her to refrain from talking to strangers with the intimacy and affection appropriate only for close friends and family. She couldn't see the difference, because she had not learned to differentiate situations. An exasperated mother caught her teenage son heading for the basement to tinker with his greasy bike just after he had gotten cleaned up to attend his sister's graduation. When the bike seized his attention, he forgot about the graduation ceremony, not considering which was the more important, not setting priorities.

Lab School experiences demonstrate that intensive exercises on seeking similarities in different objects and differentiating one characteristic from another can help. Once students come to understand the meanings of such general concepts as *same as, equal to,* and *similar to,* based on experience with concrete things, they tend to have a little less difficulty generalizing these concepts to social situations. Phillip insisted to his teacher that $4 + 3 + 2$ could not be equal to $5 + 5 - 1$ because the numbers were not the same. He needed to hold number blocks in his hands and rearrange them before he got the point. Molly physically had to sit down on a folding canvas chair, a kitchen chair, and a beanbag chair before she could see that they were all chairs for sitting on, because to her they looked so different. Such training in seeing the similarities and differences in situations can then be followed by learning activities that apply discrimination skills to social situations.

The egocentricity that often accompanies neurological immaturity keeps a person with learning disabilities from looking closely at others, from discerning the pattern of another person's behavior, and from taking note of a person's needs. It also interferes with the give and take, the compromise, involved in most relationships. *Junior-high and high-school students with learning disabilities can become less egocentric if they learn to be of service to the hungry, the homeless, or the ill.* They have to be forced to become aware of others' needs and of society's needs. As basketball superstar Magic Johnson told the Lab School kids, "You gotta go, 'Hey, I've got a problem. I've got to take whatever means are necessary to enhance my skills.' Then, once you've conquered it, once you have met the challenge, reach back and help the next guy. Because that's what it's all about."

A democratic society needs voters. The learning disabled frequently feel their vote won't make any difference, that they don't count. Teachers and tutors of high-school students and adults must give them practice with mock voting booths, help them learn the systems just as they need to learn to fill out tax forms, open bank accounts, and take care of other adult responsibilities. The ability of the learning disabled to deal with society's issues begins with the feeling that their votes count and that they have the right and power to speak up on public issues.

APPROACHING SOCIAL SKILLS DIRECTLY

Learning Communication Skills

Relating to others depends heavily on clear communication of needs, feelings, understanding, and appreciation. For some children with learning disabilities, it takes years before they can begin to talk easily and to say exactly what they mean. Others never reach a point at which communication becomes easy, fluent, and unstrained.

Of course, language deficits contribute to problems in socialization. One adult who is learning disabled talks about his difficulty in "trapping" the words he wants. Another speaks of the trouble she has in organizing her thoughts and of the suffering that this has caused her for years. She often uses gestures instead of words or simply becomes frantic and runs out of the room. Another tells how he mispronounces words and comes up with embarrassing malapropisms. "I knew something was wrong, but I didn't know what," he says.

Before a preschooler learns to talk, she uses gestures, hitting, screaming, or other behaviors to convey her emotions. An eight-year-old with severe language problems may do the same thing because she cannot say, "I don't want to do that!" A language-impaired youngster may be unfairly punished because she could not find words to explain what caused her tantrum.

Many students with learning disabilities require intensive language therapy. Some, unfortunately, do not get it because parents and teachers do not know what language therapy can do. School systems need to provide more language therapy for the learning disabled in their individualized education programs. This does not mean merely correcting poor speech habits, such as lisping or filling one's speech with *you knows, uhs,* and other so-called paralinguistic elements. Language therapy does much more than that. It provides help in actually organizing language. A language pathologist or therapist works on syntax and language structure, on how to summarize and speak succinctly, on how to ask questions. He provides practice in daily communication skills, such as the exchange of greetings and brief chitchat, and practice in the art of conversation, which language-impaired people need. Counseling through play therapy can be helpful to language-impaired children, who cannot say what they feel. At the Lab School, a psychologist and a language therapist work with a small group of language-impaired, socially inept youngsters. If school systems don't have language therapists or if parents cannot afford to procure their services, conversation groups need to be set up with language-arts teachers and learning-disabilities specialists who can lead them.

A successful computer programmer with learning disabilities approached the speaker after a lecture on learning disabilities to discuss a point but stood too close to her and spoke *at* her rather than *to* her. The lecturer kept backing away; the computer programmer kept following, as close as ever, talking but not listening. The result was more like a dance than a conversation.

How and where to stand must be practiced. Different cultures in the world allow different amounts of personal space during conversation. Standing too close can seem threatening; standing too far away can seem cold and unfriendly. Italians usually stand closer together than English people when they talk, and Arabs and Latin Americans stand even closer. Most people pick up their cultural cues unconsciously at an early age from their families, but a person with a learning disability who doesn't process spatial relations well may miss such special cues altogether.

The fast pace of life has brought changes in family customs that almost eliminate conversation. Single-parent families and families in which both parents work are especially at risk because they often have very little time for leisurely talks. However, all families can help members with learning disabilities to develop communication skills. These are some steps that can be taken:

- Eat at least one meal together without the TV on.
- Inquire about each person's day.
- Tell what has happened. Relate news. Gossip.
- Look at family photographs together. Point out what the facial expressions and body language in these photographs convey.
- Explicitly discuss nonverbal ways of communicating. A smile, a pat on the back, or a wry laugh can be taught in the same way as communication skills.

Learning Telephone Skills

Telephone communication has become an essential part of daily life in our society. However, if a person has a language problem, the telephone is an extremely difficult instrument to master. This is because, in a telephone conversation, as in reading, there are few nonverbal clues to meaning. In the absence of facial expressions, gestures, body language, and physically present objects of discussion, the listener must rely totally on command of the language, which many people with learning disabilities do not have. The difficulty of holding a telephone conversation when language is a barrier is familiar to those who have tried making calls in countries where their native tongue is not spoken. Conversation is hard enough for a person with language problems, but using the telephone can be true punishment.

It is generally parents, not schools, who teach their children to use the telephone. However, volunteers in the school can help children with learning disabilities greatly by working intensively with them on telephone skills on a one-to-one basis. Telephone companies have equipment and materials that can be used at no cost for telephone training. In France good telephone skills are considered so important that some high schools include a course that teaches not only telephone mechanics, such as transferring calls and setting up conference calls, but also ways to handle incoming information and to deal with angry customers or unreasonable demands.

In setting up a school program, volunteers should be provided with a checklist of telephone skills appropriate to different ages so that a plan of remediation can be provided when necessary. The checklist might begin with elementary skills like these:

- dialing a number correctly
- dialing 411 to ask for information
- dialing 911 to report an emergency
- taking down a simple message
- knowing the work numbers of parents by heart

At the adult level, instruction can go as far as learning how to deal with the telephone company over an erroneous billing.

Providing Opportunities for Structured Social Interaction

People with learning disabilities often grow up without friends their own age, and they are often loners throughout life. Frequently, they avoid social situations with their peers, pretend to be people they are not, and mask their real selves as a defense against negative reactions. Thus they lose out on having comfortable peer relationships and on learning how to compromise when required, or how to put up with bumps and bruises, to shrug and then move on. The learning disabled, without social experience, tend to nurse each wound and to retreat to televisions, books, food, alcohol, drugs, or anti-social behavior. They missed the social interaction that would have taught them how to adjust their behavior to others and that of others to themselves.

To make up for lost opportunities for social interaction, many children and adults with learning disabilities need explicit social tutoring. They require friendship pairs, social trios, and/or small group experiences in social activities led by a teacher, an experienced professional, or a trained volunteer parent worker. These social-remediation groups need to offer project learning (decorating a room, cooking, running a booth at a fair, setting up a picnic or a party) with very explicit teaching goals.

High-school students need homework in the fourth R in order to learn how to infer from previous experiences what will happen in certain social situations. Literature and history assignments, as well as current events, can be looked at from the vantage point of the fourth R. Social-skills curricula are available today in many forms—computer software, film strips, television programs, and workbooks. But interactive theater techniques touch a deeper nerve. Social goals have to be included in individualized education programs at school, but it is also important to chart social goals with students and their families.

Parents can help their children better if they understand thoroughly that socialization problems may be a part of having a learning disability. Parents need to know as much as possible about learning disabilities in general and the fourth R in particular. The Lab School presents a monthly lecture/discussion series, for parents and professionals, on such topics as:

- The Fourth R—Relationships: Social Problems of the Learning Disabled
- Setbacks: Helping Children with Disappointment and Failure
- Helping Grandparents and Other Relatives Understand
- No Friends, No Fun
- Individualizing to Find Careers

Local chapters of the Learning Disabilities Association of America, as well as the Orton Dyslexia Society, continually provide similar workshops and lectures for the public in most parts of the country. See appendix 1 for a list of organizations and associations offering such services.

12

What Parents Can Do

"My parents were my saviors!"

"My parents cared almost too much. My mom used to finish my sentences and write my papers."

"Our whole family was dyslexic. None of us could write. It didn't matter. I grew up knowing from my parents that I was smart and OK."

"My folks fought everybody—doctors, teachers, principals, psychologists, college learning services. They let me know how much I counted!"

"My mom went broke paying for my tutoring, my occupational therapy, my counseling. I owe her so much."

"I hope, when I have kids, that I can give my kids the same kind of support my parents gave me, particularly if the kids have learning disabilities."

When adults with learning disabilities discuss their lives, they talk about their parents more than most adults do. That's not surprising. People with learning disabilities need more time to mature, to develop skills, and to become independent. Therefore, their parents are at the center of their lives for many more years than is usual.

All over the country, as I have talked with adults with

learning disabilities, I have heard about their parents and about the ways in which these parents did or did not advocate for their children. Although some adults are furious with their parents for not helping them enough or for helping them too much, most adults with learning disabilities are awed by the amount of time, energy, and thought their parents spent on them. They do not believe they could have made it without all this help.

Broadcast journalist Fred Friendly said, "I just think I got wired the wrong way. . . . A lot of kids did. And those kids are just as bright as anybody else. They've got all the equipment. It's just sort of in the wrong places. . . . I don't resent at all—although I think my poor mother would if she were still alive—the fact that I had such a difficult childhood, because I think I've had a very fulfilling, challenging life. But to make it, you need parents who understand that problem, understand it better than you because they're more adult, and they love you not in spite of it but because of it, and they are willing to put up with it because if they stay with it, their child will make it, just as a lot of other dyslexic people have who finally live to want to talk about it."

Actress Margaret Whitton has a similar message: "I would get terrible report cards, and it was not a lot of fun. But I had a terrific mother. She had four kids. She taught all of them how to read, and then I came along. She knew I was intelligent, and I'm amazed at what she did. At one point, she took me out of school and turned me loose in a museum. She would make flash cards and hang them all over my room. She'd read stories to me that would be like mysteries, and just at the point where we were going to find out who did it, she'd stop and leave the book. She was really supportive, wouldn't listen to all the people who said, 'She's dumb, she's lazy, she doesn't care.' She fought with them, and sometimes she fought with me. I was lucky to have her."

Scholar Roger Wilkins, head of the Pulitzer Prize Board, talked about the power of his parents in this way: "My problem was reading very slowly, and my teachers became very frustrated with me. My father was a writer, and he loved words, so I knew a lot of words, and I knew the structure of grammar better than most kids. My teachers were impressed by the fact that I talked standard English, not what they believed black people talked. My teachers would say, 'You're smart. Why do you read so slowly?' I would get very upset when they got frustrated. The thing that helped me was that my parents never gave up on me. They just said, 'Take as long as you need. As long as you're going to read, just keep at it.' We didn't know about learning disabilities then, and I think that had it not been for their faith in me, I might well have given up on myself."

Parents are often so conscious of the harm they think they may have done to their children that they rarely reflect upon all the invisible gifts they give their children. Genes do not entirely determine what sort of human being a child will turn out to be; parents of the learning disabled make a powerful difference in their children's lives. As Sheila, a Lab School graduate, said with great passion, "My mother and father not only had to reach the point where they could believe in me, but then they had to convince *me* they believed in me—no easy task!" It's not so much the words uttered by parents that adults carry with them through life as it is their parents' attitudes, values, and habits of feeling. When a person has experienced unconditional love, it goes with that person everywhere. At the Lab School galas, most of the Outstanding Learning-Disabled Achievers talked about their mothers, fathers, grandparents, aunts, and uncles who believed in them. As noted architect Hugh Newell Jacobsen said when he received his award in 1990, "At moments like this, one can only wish that one's mummy and daddy were here."

THE PARENTS' PATH

Every parenting experience is unique, just as every child with learning disabilities is. However, there are some common experiences of parents of the learning disabled that are worth examining.

I Wish My Kid Were Normal

Most parents of children with learning disabilities have to go through a process of finding out what's wrong. Sometimes it takes years because they don't want to believe that something can really be wrong with their child. It is common for people to avoid the subject altogether or to blame their children's problems on laziness, being willful, or being manipulative.

However, as a child's problems grow, so does the parents' realization that something must be done. They begin to cast around for an all-encompassing easy answer, a quick fix: if they move to another house, or even a new city, if they change schools or go to another diagnostician, perhaps the problems will go away. At another stage, parents get angry at the whole world for saddling them with these problems. Why me? Why not that person over there who's always had it easy? Some parents remain in the angry stage and fail to move on, which can have profoundly negative consequences for the child.

Sometimes parents pin the big G of guilt on themselves, castigating themselves for causing the learning disabilities. They are convinced that if they hadn't done this, that, or the other, their child would not be learning disabled. They tend to forget (or fail to absorb) that learning disabilities are intrinsic to the individual, that parents can help make them better or worse but can't cause them.

There are no parents who haven't been depressed from time to time by their own inadequacies and by the defeats suffered by their children. Parents tend to grieve for what could have been. They wish their kids did not have problems. It's a slow process to come to terms with a learning disability—for the parents, for their whole families, and for the child himself. It takes a while to be able to say, "OK, so Joey has these disabilities. But look at his strengths. Let's set up a program that works for him."

Tomorrow Has Come

Much is demanded of parents for a great many years. Eventually, the child with learning disabilities becomes the adult with learning disabilities. The longed-for tomorrow when the child will outgrow his or her problems comes and yet the child is still immature and more dependent on his or her parents than other children are. Parents cannot hurry neurological maturation. They must be patient, and they must not blame themselves for their child's immaturity. At this stage, parents often feel bad because

- their child is still not achieving in high school
- their child is still not paying attention (ADD)
- their child continues to be hyperactive and impulsive (ADHD)
- their child's learning disabilities haven't gone away

These things are not the parents' fault. They are not the child's fault, either. They are the fault of the condition, alas.

Parents who adopt youngsters who turn out to be learning disabled also tend to blame themselves for causing the disabilities. There are many adopted children with learning disabilities at the Lab School whose earliest histories are not known. Solid research needs to be done in this area. Professionals have been surprised that adoptive parents take on the guilt of causing the learning disabilities when the genetic histories of the children are very different from theirs.

THE ROLES PARENTS PLAY

Parents are the adults in charge who have to train their children to take charge of themselves. Parents are their children's advocates—lawyerlike representatives who stand up for their offspring. Parents sometimes replace the friends that the person with socialization problems wishes he could make on his own. Parents usually are the coaches who cheer their child on, stand in her corner, and tell her she can do it! Parents often are conductors who try to harmonize a whole band of uncles, aunts, cousins, and grandparents as a supporting chorus for the family member with learning disabilities. Parents are producer-directors who organize activities, expeditions, outings, and excursions to help give the one with learning disabilities a better understanding of the resources at hand.

With all these roles and responsibilities, it is not surprising that parents' self-esteem may waver. It doesn't help when an adolescent son blames most of his problems on them and on the way they brought him up. But they may feel better if they remember that all adolescents dump on their parents, whom they once thought were perfect and now find very imperfect.

Who's in Charge?

Some parents become so frail and unsure of themselves that they abdicate their essential role as the adult in charge. They accept their child's statements as gospel and suspend their own critical judgment. A child with learning disabilities is fully capable of taking advantage of a situation and of manipulating her parents. Kim came from junior high school each day for two weeks announcing that she had no homework. Her mother steamed over to the school and accused Kim's advisor of holding back her child's education. Of course, Kim had been given homework every day. The advisor showed Kim's mother the written assignments and Kim's assignment notebook. Kim's mother did not back down but said, "Kim always tells the truth. She always has!"

Adults with learning disabilities laugh at the tricks they played on their parents. Galan laughed at all the stories his mother believed: "I told her that we couldn't have gym because the gym was flooded, and she believed me. Of course, I also told my teacher I couldn't do my homework because I took my mother to the emergency room of the hospital, when I didn't. My mom paid too much attention to what I said. She kind of thought, by believing me, she was showing respect for me. Oh, well!"

Occasionally, a parent will relinquish his responsibility by becoming his child's best buddy and failing to set any limits or make any demands so that the child is forced to take over the parental role, assuming more responsibility than he can carry. My experience is that if a child is not free to be a child, he often develops into a childish, irresponsible adult who is bent on recapturing the childhood he missed.

Some children tyrannize their households and make everyone duck for cover. Their parents have not made it clear what the family will allow and what it won't allow. If a child has learning disabilities, this does not mean the child is helpless, is entitled to whatever he wants whenever he wants it, or is to be catered to, waited upon, and allowed to be rude and insatiable in his demands. This child, adolescent, or young adult can often manipulate the whole household and make everybody unhappy, including himself.

Running to Specialists

Anxiety overwhelms most parents of children who are learning disabled. Some move into a flurry of activities, running their child to every specialist, desperately seeking a panacea.

Rosemarie, aged twenty-six, said, "My parents wanted me to be *fixed*. I was dragged to eye specialists, speech specialists, reading specialists, some doctor with a long beard who tried hypnosis and gave me special pills, to faith healers, to chiropractors, to a lady who looked like a belly dancer who did transcendental meditation, a psychiatrist who gave me pills, a social worker who squeezed my hand nicely, and a holistic doctor who gave me vitamins. I was put on special diets, made to do exercises for my eyes, crawling exercises, and to sing certain sounds every evening. What I learned from all this is that my mother, and my father, too, were frantic to cure me, that they felt horrendous about my dyslexia. I tried so hard to get cured to help them, but nothing worked." The burden on Rosemarie was to try to relieve her parents' anxieties, which, unfortunately, she could not do. Then, apparently, Rosemarie decided to become a behavior problem because, she said, "it used to take their minds off my being dumb."

Instead of running so much, Rosemarie's parents might have joined the Learning Disabilities Association of America (LDA). It is basically run by parents, though professionals take an active part. It has branches in every state and most cities (see appendix 1). Parents of children with learning disabilities need to find these groups in the nearest city. They not only provide support but also are sources of valuable knowledge of the finest specialists and treatment centers in various parts of the country. National conventions of the LDA and of the Orton Dyslexia Society (see appendix 1) often have excellent workshops that can give parents specific help with their young child, adolescent, or grown child. Speakers discuss such topics as how to advocate for a child with learning disabilities in schools, how to handle social problems, how to plan estates, how to train for employment, and a host of others. The National Center for Learning Disabilities (see appendix 1) has much helpful literature.

THE PARENTS' FEARS

The parents of people with learning disabilities have a great many fears. What they fear most is that their child will not grow up and live a normal life—hold a job, find a spouse, have children, and enjoy life. It is reassuring for them to hear from adults who have succeeded despite their learning disabilities or to meet adolescents with learning disabilities who are off to the workplace or to college. Here are some of the most common fears that parents have.

Parents *fear* that their impulsive child with perseveration, attention deficit disorders (ADD), and hyperactivity (ADHD) may end up as a gambler or an alcoholic or, worse yet, in a mental institution or in jail. This is why preventive mental health is extremely important. Well-trained counselors can help parents deal with fears realistically and take steps to avoid the worst-case scenario.

Parents *fear* that their child with language problems is being treated as a retarded person when he's gifted and that he will never develop sufficient language skills to fend for himself adequately. This is why it is important to seek a language therapist who is experienced with the learning disabled.

Parents *fear* that their clumsy, awkward child, who is accident prone, will end up in an emergency room having seriously maimed himself. It is important to seek out occupational therapists and professionals in adaptive physical education to help a young person organize his body in space.

Parents *fear* that their child has no special talent and will not be able to find employment. They need to look more closely at the child to unearth his abilities and perhaps to create a special area of expertise for him.

Parents *fear* that their child will never be able to go to college. However, more and more students with learning disabilities are attending America's colleges and universities.

Parents *fear* that their friendless child will end up isolated and unhappy. It is important to search out group activities and therapies that can help him relate to others.

Parents *fear* that by setting limits they will turn off their child, that their child won't like them. It is important for parents to realize that even though their child complains, he feels safer when boundaries are clear.

Parents *fear* that if they hold their older children accountable, they will run off or rebel by getting into trouble. This might happen, but if the parents are reasonable in their requests, it usually doesn't.

Parents *fear* that their child will not be able to live independently if they should die. Parents must train their child to make his bed, shop, cook a little bit, wash up, and take out the garbage. Parents need to walk the child through these tasks at first—for example, accompanying him on the bus and subway the first few times. Knowing how to get around the city alone gives young people great confidence, just as being able to drive gives them a strong feeling of independence. Independent living is the goal.

Parents need to face their fears and take concrete action to deal with them. Parents must take a good look at their child and identify everything in his makeup that is working. Parents can tap inner resources they never knew they had. To bring up a child with learning disabilities, parents need to call upon all kinds of experiences they have lived through—experiences of battling illness, of combating prejudice, of being caught in storms and hurricanes, of surviving in jobs they hated, of standing alone and tall for something they believed in deeply. These experiences in meeting adversity helped to train them to be the parents of a child with learning disabilities.

Parents who fear they cannot give all the support, reassurance, and backup that their child needs are usually being too hard on themselves, too critical of their own performance.

Often they learn later that their children did not see them as inadequate. Actor Daniel Stern said, "I got support from my family, my parents especially, to make me feel confident and to make me feel that I was a good person."

THE STRESSES OF PARENTING

Few people realize how hard the parents of the learning disabled work. Few people know the stress of just getting a person with learning disabilities out of the house in the morning. There is much strain in being the focusing agent, the memory person, the organizer and conversation coordinator, day in and day out. Meeting with school personnel, going through deliberations regarding individualized education programs, consulting tutors and therapists—these all cause stress.

Siblings don't make it any easier to parent a child with learning disabilities. They want to have all their needs met, too. They are rivals for parental attention and have their own anxieties about brothers or sisters with learning disabilities. They need to be brought in as co-problem solvers to help the person with learning disabilities, but that has to be done with the sensitive awareness of an orchestra leader.

Husbands and wives sometimes conflict about handling the child with learning disabilities. They argue about what to do about her paying attention, her hyperactivity, her behavior, and her inability to do her homework. Traditionally, the husband feels his wife is spoiling or babying the youngster with learning disabilities. The wife feels she spends more time with the child and understands her difficulties better.

Parents feel stress from every vantage point. They feel it from their own parents and other relatives, as well as from their children, and particularly from the child who is learning disabled. They often feel stress from their mate, their boss, and their coworkers. Schools, community centers, and athletic groups can also induce stress. Deadlines of all kinds produce extreme stress. Then there are the larger issues of stress related to finances, race, religion, and politics.

The child who needs special education in after-school religious classes often does not receive it, which can sometimes undo all the good accomplished by special help in daily schooling. The child becomes victimized because he can't read his lessons, write, understand directions, speak clearly, or sing in tune. In some families it becomes a great crisis when the child refuses to go to school and one parent or grandparent insists that he must.

Athletic teams can also cause stress. Youngsters with learning disabilities tend to hate losing because they are so often made to feel like losers. Winning frightens them, too, because they are afraid of having to maintain a high level of performance. And then there's the stress of the child with poor coordination who feels that he is expected to be a good athlete or whose parents put him on teams to make sure he does become a good athlete (which doesn't happen too often). The child with learning disabilities who fails in Boy Scouts or Girl Scouts is as stressed as the parents; the same stress is felt when neighborhood groups exclude this child.

Perhaps the greatest strain of all for parents comes from having to acknowledge that their own child is learning disabled. To deal with this strain, the parents must view the learning disabilities as only part of their child's total being. *The level of comfort with which parents can accept their child's learning disabilities profoundly affects the child's perception of himself.*

How do people handle stress? There are a multitude of ways, and parents of children with learning disabilities, like everyone else, indulge in some of those listed in the following illustration.

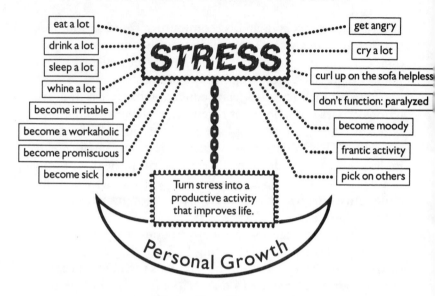

Ways of handling stress

A very normal reaction to stress is to feel angry with the burden of parenting the child, adolescent, or adult with learning disabilities. Such anger is natural; what matters is that the anger not be buried. When feelings are buried, they tend to rise up later and take over the person's life. The anger then becomes all-consuming and difficult to control. That is why we must recognize the anger when it first occurs, express it, deal with it, and then move on.

The anger and stress of parents can have affirmative effects, too. The emotion and tension can lead to change, can goad parents into making necessary decisions that, when acted upon, improve situations. Handling anger in a healthy manner can give extra energy to a parent for problem solving and trying out new ideas.

Nothing toughens a person better than the combat training of being a parent. Being a parent of a child with learning disabilities provides the parent with the training and skills to organize anything; to run an industry; to negotiate a labor contract; to become a lawyer, social worker, psychiatrist, or psychologist; to become a spiritual advisor, an advertiser, a member of a think tank, or a social leader on a cruise ship; and to do almost anything else. Never fear: few things build character better than being a parent of a child with a learning disability! As one parent said in a meeting, "Enough of this character-building stuff. I don't need any more."

WHAT PARENTS CAN DO

There is no cookbook with standard recipes for parenting kids with learning disabilities. Kids with different kinds of learning disabilities need different kinds of parenting, just as they require different kinds of educational help. However, adults with learning disabilities believe that there are some basics that apply to all:

> "My parents were there for me. They loved me with all my warts."
>
> "My mom listened endlessly."
>
> "My dad did projects with me."
>
> "They looked at the learning disability as a small part of what was *me*."
>
> "I was expected to help around the house to the best of my ability."
>
> "My folks were real clear on how I was to behave; there were clear consequences when I didn't behave that way."
>
> "I felt safe because my mom and dad were in charge."
>
> "My mother didn't say it often, but when she said no, it meant no."

"My folks were lavish with praise for all my efforts. We kind of problem-solved our way through my childhood."

The following are some other steps that parents can take.

Become a Problem Solver

Few of us receive explicit training in parenthood. Therefore, parenthood involves continual problem solving in unfamiliar territory. There are no easy answers, no solutions that fit all children. And it's ten times harder if the child is learning disabled. There's little time for parents to feel sorry for themselves because they gave birth to or adopted a child with learning disabilities. They need to pick themselves up and move on, keeping their eyes on their child.

It's not fair that certain families have to work so hard to problem-solve their way through life or that some children are born with learning disabilities. Sometimes it helps parents to help their children if they say, "We begin with the premise that the world is not fair. It is not fair that you have learning disabilities, but you have them, so let's see what you and we can do to deal with them." Not expecting the world to be fair, the child will then learn to make do with what he or she has.

Spell Each Other

One parent can be alert when the other has battle fatigue; one can assume more responsibility than the other for a while. Often there is only one parent who has to be both father and mother to the child, who has to play all roles, being the good guy and the bad guy. The single parent cannot afford to be down, because then it all falls apart. The combat training for the single parent is often too rigorous, particularly if the child is ADHD as well as learning disabled. Grandparents and relatives need to come in and rescue the single parent, not only for his or her mental health, but for the child's sake too. The mental health of both the parent and the child depends on the parent's being able to take rest and relaxation when needed.

People with learning disabilities have to learn to deal with the humiliation, ridicule, isolation, defeat, and failures that their disabilities present. Therefore, it is vital that parents begin to encourage problem solving at an early age: "Well, you can't do it this way. Let's figure out another way you might be able to do it." It's the problem-solving abilities of the learning disabled that will save them, and that is why parents should not take care of everything for them but should instead help them seek alternative strategies and solutions.

Avoid Overprotectiveness

One of the biggest difficulties of parenting in general, and of parenting the person with learning disabilities in particular, is striking a balance between overprotectiveness and underprotectiveness. College counselors tell of parents of students with learning disabilities who do all the talking for them or who actually interfere with their children's programs. Parents need to run this kind of interference in their children's early years, but they must learn to let go in the later years. On the other hand, some students with learning disabilities have been sent off to college with little guidance and backup. When Tad was floundering because he took too many courses and could not shoulder the load of reading and writing to be done, his parents said, "You're old enough to solve your own problems." He felt very unsupported. Tamara's mother, in contrast, would not have hesitated to call the dean of students, unaware that in doing so she was telling Tamara that she was incapable of taking care of herself. The most helpful route lies somewhere between these two extremes. For example, it might have worked to suggest to Tad and Tamara that they contact the head of Learning Services or to encourage them to take fewer courses.

Let Go When You Need To

Parents hurt when their children hurt. Parents tire from always having to think of the needs of others, continually anticipating problems that the person with learning disabilities might have, planning, following up, checking, taking stock, starting all over again. All this responsibility is painful.

Yet parents often find it difficult to let go. They find it painful when the caretaking has come to an end. They are used to carrying the entire load and living much of the child's life with him. They have felt the child's every bruise and ache. But as the child with learning disabilities turns into a young adult, the parent, whose life has been so intertwined with his, needs to become involved in new ventures. She needs to put a lot of energy into activities that do not have to do with her son or daughter. But she still has an eye out. She still worries.

Tad's mother, Mildred, said, "I'm not as exhausted now as I was for the first twenty years of Tad's active life. In some ways, it's as though I have been given a new lease on life. Still, I fear that Tad becomes discouraged too easily. He's been at the university for almost six years. He has three courses left. I fear he's going to quit and walk away without a diploma. It's *his* *problem.* I can't take it on. Still, it hurts!"

She is tempted to do his work for him, to speak to the authorities to garner help for him, to hire a tutor. But Tad, aged twenty-four, has to do it himself. And he needs her belief that he can do it himself; her belief is demonstrated by her doing nothing.

Sometimes parents have to let their child fall, hurt herself, and then learn to pick herself up. Adults with learning disabilities remember with pride how their parents used to say, "You can handle that. You can find a way. Try it on your own. I'll help you if you need me!"

Empower Your Children

Part of parenthood is empowering children to do well and to treat others well. It is not easy to empower a child who has many constant needs, but it can be done. Remember that helplessness and worthlessness are your child's enemies. Too often, a child comes to feel that he does not count, that he has no power. If a child can deliver a message by himself, then he feels some power. He needs to know that his voice is heard, that his opinions carry weight, and that his feelings matter. It is important for him to feel that he can change things. He has to feel that he can manage and that he can alter his own life.

Some adults at the Night School say that their parents mocked them, goaded them, punished them, or pitied them. Of course, few parents set out to hurt their child; these actions usually come from frustration, ignorance, and defeat. Happily, many adults with learning disabilities remember the moments when their fathers or mothers galvanized communities on their behalf or marched into schools to require that they be treated with respect or searched endlessly to find the proper schools, camps, and tutoring services. In some cases parents made enormous sacrifices to obtain help for their children, such as taking out a second mortgage on their home, assuming a second job, giving up money for a new car, or allotting their recreation or food money to pay for tutoring.

Fight for Your Children

If parents fight for their kids, the kids, when they grow up, will fight for themselves. They will fight to have all the opportunities they need to develop themselves as functioning and satisfied members of society.

It was militant parents who established the field of learning disabilities in the early 1960s, who fought for Public Law

94–142 and the Rehabilitation Act of 1973, and who are fighting today to prevent any weakening of these laws. They keep their eye on Congress and on the federal government to ensure that the learning disabled continue to enjoy equal opportunities and equal access to occupations that they wish to pursue.

Parents need to take good care of themselves, to keep their spirits alive. Their fire, their steadfast belief, energizes their children. It keeps them in the struggle and helps them to rise above it.

Hold On to Your Sense of Humor

Some adults with learning disabilities remember that there was a lot of fun and laughter in their homes. "School was wretched," said Dan, "but my home was a blast. We had such fun that it made me feel less bad. It wasn't so bad that I had learning disabilities!"

To make life fun for their children, parents need to carve out time to have fun themselves. The more demanding the child, the more exhausting life is for the parents, and the more the parents need to get some relief and plenty of sleep. They carry such heavy daily responsibility that they need times to be uninhibited and free from responsibilities. Parents need enjoyments to look forward to as they go through difficult periods in their lives. Children with learning disabilities can consume so much of their parents' lives that parents should make every effort to continue their own friendships. Parents also need to foster their own talents and interests.

THE PLUS SIDE OF PARENTING A CHILD WITH LEARNING DISABILITIES

Parents who have gone through the combat zone of their child's learning disabilities are usually very special people.

They have been to the depths and have risen again. They have gained a richer appreciation of life. They embrace the sun when it comes out. They don't take good times for granted but rather are grateful for them. They don't expect things to go well all the time, but they cheer when they do. For the most part, their children have been their finest teachers, teaching them to cherish divergent ways of living and learning.

I don't recommend having a child with learning disabilities in order to become an exciting, interesting, courageous personality. But when faced with the disability, many parents turn out that way. If parents can hang in there long enough, they usually will see their children grow into remarkable human beings who do them proud.

13
What Teachers Can Do

"I felt sorry for my teachers. They didn't know what to do with me!"

"If you can't learn one way, they need to try another way, and another, but most teachers won't or don't know how to."

"It's important for teachers to pull out of you what you do and don't understand."

"Classes have to be smaller. Teachers can't help you if they don't know you."

"Ask a professor for help—dog him, dog her, nag if necessary, then hope he'll take the time."

"Teachers need to learn the art of listening."

"Every teacher should be made to take a course on learning disabilities."

Many adults with learning disabilities talk of recurring nightmares about elementary school:

- being called upon and being unable to utter a word
- being asked to write something and the pencil flying out of their hands

- being asked to do a math problem, and the numbers turning into slimy creatures that squirm off the page
- sitting on a stool with a teacher pointing a stick at them

Hans Christian Andersen, author of *The Ugly Duckling*, had, in his sixties, nightmares of a schoolmaster making fun of him. Despite all their triumphs, many celebrities with learning disabilities still shudder in the presence of a teacher. Anger creeps into their words as they talk about their teachers. "He thought I was stupid and let everyone know it!" said one of them. Another got even by drawing gross cartoons of his teachers. One obliterated teachers from his mind. Still another said that his success occurred with the help of his wonderful family and friends and *despite* his teachers.

Some teachers prefer to work with the advanced, uncomplicated students who progress rapidly. They resent having to adapt their teaching methods for a student with learning disabilities. Thomas told fellow Night School students that he had experienced the impatience of these teachers, who did not want to be bothered by him or by his mother and father. One teacher calmly told Thomas that he was limited and should go to vocational school. From then on the teacher ignored him.

How could that teacher fail Thomas so totally? Perhaps the kindest answer is that many teachers, never trained to work with exceptional students, are baffled about how to help them. Many teachers are overburdened by having as many as forty-five in a class, often including at least five with special needs.

It is hard work to be a teacher, especially of students with learning disabilities, who can become all-consuming if a teacher does not have the training and support to work with them. They provoke anxiety in their teacher and make her fear that she may never reach them. Easily defeated and afraid of failure, such students resist learning and set up impenetrable roadblocks. They convince many teachers to try another career! The students' feelings of worthlessness are contagious, and teachers sometimes catch them.

Teachers are often shocked by the depths of emotion their former students express, both positive and negative. "I was going to drop out of school in eighth grade," said Felicia, "but this one teacher would not let me do it. He argued with me. He attached himself to me. He told me there was a lot that I could do to make the world a better place. He asked me to research something about the aged for him. He got me involved in a service project, where he was the advisor. He managed to have time for a Coke after the service project and to be there for me. Eventually, he and I worked with another girl who was going to quit school because her learning disabilities were dragging her down. He even managed to develop an award with a trophy—*For the Most Giving Student to Those in Need*—and made sure I won it. He gave me *so* much confidence. He was my turning point. I'd like to give him *The Extra Mile* award because he saved my life . . . at least changed it for the better. He gave so much of himself."

There are successful adults with learning disabilities who credit a few dedicated teachers who went that extra mile for them with saving them from dropping out of school. They revere these teachers. "I overcame my particular problem because of really wonderful people, most of them teachers, who care very, very much. Gradually, with a tremendous amount of hard work and patience that I still can't believe, they convinced me somehow that I could do it. They helped me to compensate for whatever my problems were. They found a way around some of my difficulties and enabled me to gain for myself some self-confidence and some belief that I could do it," said Thomas Kean, former governor of New Jersey.

WHY TEACH?

Why do people become teachers? *Certainly it is not for the money.* It is to share the world of the mind; to bring the best out in students; to help them forge ahead, acquire skills and knowledge, develop interesting lives, and excel in their chosen professions. Sometimes teachers lose sight of these goals and try to cram facts into their students' heads rather than to encourage their curiosity or to seek better ways for them to acquire learning skills.

For example, a student had handed in her best paper to date to a university teacher who glanced at the paper, threw it back to her, and said, in front of other students, "This is not college material! Why are you here?" The college student had the thinking skills of a gifted adult but, because of her learning disabilities, the writing skills of a fifth grader. She should have been given three different grades—one for content, one for effort, and one for writing skills. Her teacher was destined to become for her one of those negative memories that we saw in the preceding section.

The best teachers, the ones who become their students' treasured memories, are those with a sense of mission. They are moved by the joy of learning, and feel compelled to share that joy with others. They take pleasure in seeing a student become excited about learning and take off on her own. Such caring, conscientious, dedicated teachers give their all to their students.

All teachers who go into special education must be such people because they will be dealing with children and adults whose lives are on the line. Because the stakes are so high and the job is so difficult, such teachers need more patience than others do. They also need to be more analytical. Special-education teachers have to keep asking what works and what doesn't. They must constantly look for patterns in learning and in behavior that can be used successfully with particular students. What interests of the student can be built upon? Special education at its best is high-quality individualized education.

With a broad smile on his face, Garrett, a graduate of the Lab School who could not read until he was thirteen years old, told of "the day that everything clicked. I will never forget that feeling—like a deep rush of emotions pouring out, like fireworks exploding into magnificent color patterns in the sky. I could read a page, then another and another, and I went on and on. My teacher hugged me and turned red, and she had tears in her eyes. Even though I was thirteen years old, I hugged her. She had made it possible! And now I read at least a book a week."

The few adults at Night School who have had some *special* (that is, individualized) education seem far better disposed toward teachers than do the other students. Most of them embraced the instruction they received, and many adored their special-education teachers, even though they resented being in special classes and having to leave their friends to go to the resource room for special education. A graduate of the Lab School told students that "all teachers should be required to teach special education, particularly to teach the learning disabled, for one year, before they are allowed to teach in regular schools. Maybe then teachers would realize that there is a way everyone can learn, and they would learn to individualize and be creative."

THE SPECIAL NEEDS OF ADULT LEARNERS

The adults at the Night School have the courage to put themselves on the line. They realize that it is up to them to learn, that teachers can't open up their heads and pour in skills. They become coinvestigators into their own problems and coworkers on the solutions.

It is evening when they come in to study, most of them straight from their jobs, their families, or their universities. They are tired. Their teachers have to radiate energy and charisma. They have to arouse enthusiasm and energy in these students to ready them to start learning. And then they must deliver the very best of their knowledge and teaching. It's a tall order, night after night. Not everyone can meet the challenge.

Humor abounds at the Night School. Classes are filled with laughter and a sense of fun, which is terribly important. Students know they are with faculty who are human—who believe they can learn and will not give up on them. They rely upon being talked to very directly. They expect to be treated with respect and not talked down to. Unlike kids, who are required to go school, adults make this choice themselves. Once at school, they want the expertise of the teachers. In some ways they are more demanding than children. They wear out their teachers in a different way.

Adults with learning disabilities often have a ferocious intensity, demanding to know everything and to be able to take off in leaps and bounds. They require the most experienced, the most knowledgeable teachers, who can answer their many questions, who can explain why they are being taught in divergent ways, who can do diagnostic and prescriptive tutoring, saying, for example, "Because you tend to learn in this way, we are going to have to adapt your materials in the following way." Volunteers in literacy programs, who often know little about learning disabilities, are sometimes staggered when they encounter this intense thirst for knowledge; they don't know how to deal with it. The situation is unfair both to the volunteers and to the students unless top professionals are guiding the volunteers every step of the way.

When adults seek help at the Night School, they know that the ultimate responsibility is theirs. Faculty find it exhilarating to teach people who want to learn, who want to soak up every bit of their knowledge. They don't have to play games with their students. Everything is laid out clearly, from the plan of instruction to goals and objectives. At each session adults expect their faculty to go over with them exactly what they will do.

Teachers working with a group of five adults have to be even more organized. Each of the five, each hour, must have an organized progression of activities written down in a folder before him. The teacher switches back and forth among the five students with ease, operating from a highly organized work plan, within which she can be creative as the need arises. But the essential goal remains matching student and teacher— creating an alliance that works.

"That teacher is not my style," said one of the adult students, Julian, to the Night School director, and the director immediately went to work to find the one that would form the proper match. Julian was back a week later reporting, "She's doing everything I need to learn!" Adults give teachers the feedback they need. They can reveal what children cannot.

Although things are improving in 1991, there are few good adult materials for low-level readers. Teachers obviously don't want to give childish materials to adults, yet the materials must be simple enough that adults with reading difficulties can follow them. Children's materials will not do. Therefore, teachers of adults have to make a lot of their own teaching materials, and they have to modify materials originally intended for children. Adults want practical materials that teach them skills they can use every day. As described in detail in chapter 7, adults tend to learn best by doing, just as children do.

When working with adults, teachers need to realize that their students are often burdened with many outside problems, such as taking care of children or parents. Although they tend to do more than is required of them and often hold themselves to standards higher than their teachers expect, sometime the pressures of living, a job, a recession, or a war affect their work. The approach or the pace of a teacher's lessons may at times have to be changed.

A teacher of adults needs to keep himself from stepping over the line from being a friendly professional to becoming a dear friend. Sometimes adult students need to lean on a strong shoulder, but for the most part, teaching and tutoring sessions should be focused on work. Teachers ought not to cry on the shoulders of their adult students, though this sometimes does happen because the learning disabled are often extremely nice, sensitive, caring people.

PRINCIPLES OF TEACHING

There are a number of principles of teaching students with learning disabilities that hold for adults as well as children. These are discussed below.

Individualizing

All children and adults deserve individualized education. The individual needs and learning styles of each student must be recognized and built upon by his or her teachers. This means looking at each student and listening carefully. It also means choosing materials and methods appropriate to each student's interests, abilities, and learning style. (More about this below.)

Focusing on Strategies, Not on Problems

When a student has trouble learning, the *teacher's role* is to show her that her failure is caused by inefficient and ineffective strategies, not by lack of effort, intelligence, character, or discipline. The teacher then needs to help the student seek new strategies.

Problem Solving

A student's failure to learn means that we have not yet found the way to teach him. The teacher must keep on exploring, doing the necessary detective work, until the way is found. Older students with learning disabilities need to take an active part in this pursuit as codetectives in search of their own learning styles.

Problem solving is the essence of teaching. Teachers of the learning disabled are, by nature, problem solvers. First they must solve the puzzle of how a student learns. Then they must invent exciting ways to teach her. Teachers who are excellent problem solvers use the student's help in developing strategies that work.

Preventive questioning, a technique of problem solving, raises questions such as these:

"What part of this can you do by yourself?"

"Where will you have trouble?"

Preventive questioning alerts the student to anticipate problems that may arise.

Reframing is another technique that works. When a student says, "I'm failing everything," the teacher reframes the statement by saying, "Yes, you are failing English, but you are doing well in math and science." People with learning disabilities often have difficulties with part-whole relationships: they do not see all the parts that make up the whole, and they interpret one failure or mistake as utter confirmation of their worthlessness. If the one failure is not reframed, they tend to feel hopeless or depressed and may even back out of their academic pursuits.

Analyzing Tasks

Just as teachers need to analyze how their students learn, so they must analyze what it is they are trying to teach. A physical-education instructor hands out combination locks to his adolescent students. Does he consider what is involved in working a combination lock? José, an adult with learning disabilities, says that he failed physical education as a youth because "I wouldn't dress out [change into athletic clothes]. Why? Because I couldn't figure out the gadget, the combination lock, but, look, how did they expect me to do that when I can't tell right from left?" Part of teacher training must be in analyzing the tasks students are being asked to do. Consider the task of opening a combination lock. It can be broken down into at least seven functions demanding skills such as

- knowing left from right
- having sufficient eye-hand coordination to (1) hold the lock in one hand; (2) do the combination with the other; and (3) be able to move fingers in a direction away from the thumb
- reading symbols, recognizing numbers, seeing the spaces between each slash mark and the numbers on the lock
- remembering the combination and what to do
- understanding the sequence (left turn, right turn, left again, pull)
- having a sufficiently developed sense of timing to know when to pull the lock
- having the attention span to stick to the task

José's gym teacher expected all sixteen-year-olds to be able to do these things. He didn't notice that José had trouble with the task. If the gym teacher had taken the trouble, he could have broken down the task, found out which parts of the task José could accomplish alone, and taught José the other parts of the task. It is good practice to start teaching such a student at a little below his competence level in order to ensure success. The teacher should have asked himself questions such as

> Will José learn best by demonstration?
>
> Do I need to talk him through it?
>
> Will he learn best by hearing instructions?
>
> Would written instructions help him?
>
> Do we need to develop strategies to help him distinguish his left side from his right?

Keith told José that he put a purple sticker on the left side of his combination lock so all he had to remember was "go purple to 5, the other way to 30, purple to 7, and pull."

Varying Teaching Methods

In general, teachers need to know all the methods and approaches that have been developed to teach a particular subject so that they can pluck out the one that they need for a particular student. Individualizing means matching the methods to the student and tailoring them to fit his needs. A teacher must analyze his own patterns of learning and understand his own learning style so that he can vary it for his students. When teachers are pressured to teach too many students at once, one unfortunate consequence is that a single method is likely to be adopted and all students will be expected to conform to it. If a student has severe auditory and language problems and her school system uses a phonetic approach to reading, she is being set up for failure after failure.

In college, where classes are smaller, professors can be encouraged to help the learning disabled seek ways they can be successful. On the other hand, some college classes have more than a hundred students in them. The college's division of Academic Services or Learning Services can help students choose the classes or instructors that will best meet their needs.

Providing Structure

Regular routines, clear procedures, and customary behavior let students know what to expect in a classroom. In general, persons with learning disabilities have difficulties in establishing and maintaining inner boundaries and parameters and therefore need even more structure in their learning environment. Teachers must establish a time, a space, and a place for all things. Open shelves help students see where things belong. Younger children need to practice how to enter a room, how to leave it, how to find materials, and how to return them to their proper places.

Since people with learning disabilities can become easily overwhelmed, the teacher has to limit the amount of stimulation in the room—the amount of work, materials, procedures, choices, and talking—all without limiting the student.

Explaining and Demonstrating Tasks

With students of all ages, teaching the approach to a task, as well as the task itself, can be very helpful. This means talking through the whole procedure, giving an overview of the task, and explaining what it is and where to begin. Often it means giving the student a dry run through the task so that he can understand it based on concrete, hands-on experience.

Students with learning disabilities, who are often language impaired, need to be given clear, precise direction in a minimum of words. Teachers need to listen to the directions they give and to show students what these directions mean in terms of the actions they must take. "Half the time I mess up on the directions given to me," said Mark, a college student with learning disabilities. Yolanda said that her problems were that some professors talked too fast and were barely audible. Teachers should train themselves to use vocal inflections and pauses consistently to emphasize important points in their lectures.

Giving the Gift of Time

As discussed in chapter 6, timing and time-management difficulties must be understood by teachers who have students with learning disabilities. What is hard to realize is how slowly such students process what is heard, what is read, and what has to be written. Throughout this book, the voices of celebrities tell the reader how much longer it took them to do what everybody else could finish in minutes. Teachers need to experience what it is like to be given an assignment (written in gibberish) and to watch the people next to them (whose assignments are not written in gibberish) finish in a minute while they are still struggling. The abilities of the learning disabled often cannot be evaluated when they are held to a time limit. Such people need the gift of time.

Building on Strengths

Teachers need to pick up on anything a student enjoys, be it automobiles, football, fashion, art, TV, or cooking. All these things can provide a route to learning. Make special materials to teach what students need to know through what they like to do, want to do, and *can* do. Discover the particular talents of each student and work these talents into the life of the classroom. Make sure that the student with learning disabilities holds responsibility in the area of her strengths. Do not simply praise her talent. Depend on her.

With children, it is important to schedule any remediation classes for times when a student will not have to be pulled out of his favorite classes. Adults need to have remediation scheduled at a time that does not conflict with things they like and do well.

Making Progress Visible

Students need constant and visible proof of progress, shown, for example, on graphs or charts, in cartoons, or on checklists. Certificates of accomplishment are treasured proof of competence. Students should make comparisons with their earlier work and see with their own eyes that whereas they could read only a paragraph in September, they can read a small book in April. As discussed in chapter 7, their concreteness requires that they be able to see progress.

Parents also need to see the student's strengths in some visible form. When a teacher presents a report on the student's progress, it should be concrete. Pieces of the student's work should be picked out and patterns of errors and corrections visibly displayed to parents, who often are also concrete. Successes should be highlighted as well as mistakes.

Teaching through the Five Senses

New material needs to be linked to past knowledge and experiences. Unfamiliar material can sometimes be linked to parts of the body. For instance, the five vowels can be linked to the five fingers, each with a different function.

Simple, elementary tasks need to be presented in unique, sophisticated, and alluring ways. Students can study the early history of mathematics by pretending to be shepherds tallying their sheep with knots on a string or scratches on a rock. As the flock grows, new computing methods will have to be invented. Abstract concepts in political science, such as the global balance of power, can be demonstrated with scales.

Some students have very poor rote memories. For such students a teacher must find methods of evaluation other than examinations. Drawings, cartoons, projects, tape recordings, and papers written on computers can all be used. The learning disabled know more than they can demonstrate by traditional means. So, the teacher must find each student's proper medium and have the student use it to show what she understands. Also, memory can be strengthened if a student is given a concrete reminder, such as a tea bag to hold in an American history class to recall "No taxation without representation." A whiff of curry powder can remind students that the explorers of the fifteenth century sailed around the world looking for the spices of the Orient. Vocabulary development can be helped by studying word derivations and finding their concrete origins. For example, a picture of Nicolas Chauvin in a Napoleon hat might evoke the word *chauvinism,* meaning "a blind fanatical patriotism" such as Chauvin had for Napoleon. Reinforce what has been learned by constant repetition, in different ways, through different media, until the learning sinks into the bones and becomes automatic.

Not Catching Others' Feelings

Feelings of defeat, of fear, of anger, and of guilt are extremely contagious. Teachers need to learn not to respond in kind to their students' negative feelings but rather to use those feelings diagnostically. Edwin came into the Night School angry. He started to argue with his teacher over some insignificant point. His teacher was able to register Edwin's feelings and say, "You're angry about something. I can tell because I wasn't angry this evening, but the moment I was with you, I started feeling angry. So deal with it or talk to me about it and then get to work!" Teachers have to be enough in touch with their own feelings to be able to register the feelings of their students.

Valuing Effort

All teachers know the value of praise. *It is important to give specific, not global, praise;* to value effort and positive attitudes; to show appreciation when students are willing to be taught; to ask questions; and to be sensitive to the needs of others. For example:

"You certainly look ready to learn."

"I like the way you are looking me in the eye."

"I'm impressed that you remembered to bring everything for the project."

"You struggled. You stuck to it and came through!"

Changing Pace

Anticipation is a key to teaching people with learning disabilities. The teacher needs to anticipate when a student will start to become overwhelmed by too much material. The teacher must stay several steps ahead in order to anticipate when the student will become restless or unable to remain in a group and will therefore need to switch to another activity. Anticipation, with humor, can facilitate a transition, as when a teacher says, "Well, now, it's about time for you to throw down your pencil, grunt, and state what a dumb, boring activity this is!" If a student can laugh, his mood changes and a problem is averted.

Changes of activity and pace help hold wavering attention. Remember, the attention span of a student with learning disabilities can often be short. Teachers have to entice attention, lure it, and hang on to it in every possible way—by catching a student's eye, altering the tone and volume of voice, using dramatic gestures, touching a shoulder, and using a student's name. As one businessman with dyslexia put it, "The teacher is the seller. The student is the purchaser. He can be turned off easily unless the teacher really makes an attempt to sell especially to him!"

Always have alternative plans and backup material on hand. On some days (particularly on overcast, stormy days or right before the full moon), students become more restless, and teachers need the flexibility to drop a lesson and change plans. College professors who teach small seminars can change pace; in large lecture-hall classes, it is more difficult.

Setting Goals

With students who are learning disabled, it is important to set a few simple goals to be accomplished each year. These can be behavior goals such as not interrupting or academic goals such as mastering fractions. They can be goals of bringing homework in or remembering to bring a pencil to class. Students must take part in setting their goals. Teachers and students need to check in periodically through the year to see how these goals are being met. Students do best having some goals but not too many.

Adults with learning disabilities need to set different goals, such as improvement on the job or movement to another job in a few years. Such goals help them to reach higher and not be complacent. Successful adults with learning disabilities tend to have had very specific goals that they strived to achieve. Success didn't just happen to them. They aimed for it.

Innovating

When teachers use unusual, innovative teaching methods, students tend to be more interested and to learn more. The American Constitution can be taught as if to a Russian student just learning about democracy. Tyranny can be studied in the persons of Adolf Hitler, Idi Amin, and Saddam Hussein: if they were in charge, how would they change the United States? If poetry is being studied, an Indian drum can be used to convey rhythm in the works of such poets as Vachel Lindsay and Gerard Manley Hopkins. Originality on the part of the teacher encourages individuality on the part of the student.

A sense of adventure should pervade what happens in school. Trips of the mind and the soul should take place. Surprises, from time to time, should provide delight (even though the learning disabled have trouble dealing with changes in routine). Education must be a journey into ideas, not just an acquisition of facts. All the senses need to be engaged.

The intellect needs to be challenged through using the senses. Imagination needs to be tapped to gain the total involvement of a student. The use of the absurd to get across a point works with the learning disabled. Laughter is an important teaching tool. It commands attention. It motivates. It tells the student that his troubles with studies are not catastrophic.

Teachers need to emphasize the importance of diversity and divergent thinking, not only by having students study the different backgrounds and customs of various countries but also, for instance, by encouraging them to come up with as many ways as possible

- to describe a storm
- to protect America's water supply
- to draw a map
- to protect an animal threatened with extinction
- to celebrate birthdays

Obviously, people who do not learn in orthodox ways profit from unorthodox teaching methods. A lot of the talents developed by the celebrities who appear in this book were overlooked in school. These talents could have been detected and developed sooner if their teachers had taught in more innovative ways.

It is time to bring art forms back into the classroom so that crafts, drama, puppetry, music, dance, filmmaking, and ceramics can join the computer as learning tools. The hidden talents of students are waiting to be explored. Teachers can explore and nurture these talents, but they need supervisors who will encourage and help them. They need principals who will lead the way, encouraging their staffs to discover and use new tools. They also need school boards that will rely less on quantitative measures such as test scores, since nontraditional learning often cannot be measured annually but tends to show results only over longer periods of time.

The following charts can help teachers look for their students' strengths and weaknesses.

If a person has a preponderance of checks in the last two columns, he or she may be demonstrating a number of attentional, organizational, and social immaturity problems similar to learning-disabled students, and needs to be referred for testing.

CLASSROOM BEHAVIOR	USUALLY	SOMETIMES	SELDOM	NEVER
Extraordinarily observant				
Listens well to instruction				
Follows oral directions well				
Speaks to the point				
Well focused on tasks				
Completes tasks within time frame				
Is on time to classes				
Homework handed in on time				
Follows written directions well				
Tests well, particularly multiple choice				

CLASSROOM BEHAVIOR (cont.)	USUALLY	SOMETIMES	SELDOM	NEVER
Good use of space on a page				
Moves well (not clumsy)				
Knows left from right side				
Good handwriting				
Takes good notes				
Neat desk				
Brings necessary materials to class				
Follows procedures carefully				
Good follow-through on projects				
Consistent in responses to questions				
Remembers information well				
Good with symbols and codes				
Good with foreign language				
Good with algebra and chemistry				
Good at organizing work				
Alphabetizes well, uses library well				
Self-starter				
Adjusts well to changes in routine				
Moves easily from one activity to another				
Can do several things at once				
Welcomes new approaches				
Eager for new information				
Sensitive and considerate of others				
Takes turns easily				

Copyright © 1986 Sally L. Smith

THE CHANNELS OF LEARNING

What channels does each student use? Look for patterns of strengths and deficits, know the deficit areas, and build on the strengths.

ACTIVITY	VISUAL/ SPATIAL CHANNEL		VISUAL/ MOTOR CHANNEL		AUDITORY/ LANGUAGE CHANNEL	
	Strong	Weak	Strong	Weak	Strong	Weak
LISTENING SKILLS Listens attentively						
Trouble following directions						
Asks for repeats of information						
Learns best from lectures						
Difficulty rhyming						
Memorizes by repeating out loud						
Doesn't like to be read to						
Prefers to see pictures than listen						
Does not like to deal with telephone calls						
Quickly hears difference between "b" and "v"						

ACTIVITY	VISUAL/ SPATIAL CHANNEL		VISUAL/ MOTOR CHANNEL		AUDITORY/ LANGUAGE CHANNEL	
ORAL EXPRESSION Excellent vocabulary						
Difficulty asking questions						
Good storyteller						
Cannot remember the correct word						
Problems organizing thoughts, speaking clearly						
Uses grammar and syntax well						

ACTIVITY	VISUAL/ SPATIAL CHANNEL		VISUAL/ MOTOR CHANNEL		AUDITORY/ LANGUAGE CHANNEL	
	Strong	Weak	Strong	Weak	Strong	Weak
ORAL EXPRESSION (cont'd)						
Has good social language (pragmatics)						
Creates pictures with words using descriptive vocabulary						
Prefers to draw than talk						

ACTIVITY	VISUAL/ SPATIAL CHANNEL		VISUAL/ MOTOR CHANNEL		AUDITORY/ LANGUAGE CHANNEL	
READING SKILLS						
Excellent retention of words seen (sight vocabulary)						
Mixes up b, d, p, and g						
Sees patterns in words (e.g., pat, cat, rat)						
Good sounding out of words						
Blends sounds well						
Doesn't learn from phonics						
Poor memory for consonant and vowel sounds						
Skips, omits, and adds words						
Poor comprehension of reading material						
Cannot keep place in the book						
Applies rules of syllabication						
Does not see details in words (e.g., vowel sounds)						

ACTIVITY	VISUAL/ SPATIAL CHANNEL		VISUAL/ MOTOR CHANNEL		AUDITORY/ LANGUAGE CHANNEL	
WRITING SKILLS (written expression and handwriting)						
Spells phonetically						

ACTIVITY	VISUAL/ SPATIAL CHANNEL		VISUAL/ MOTOR CHANNEL		AUDITORY/ LANGUAGE CHANNEL	
	Strong	Weak	Strong	Weak	Strong	Weak
WRITING SKILLS (cont'd)						
Accurately forms and spaces letters						
Good at art, poor at writing letters						
Writes 41 for 14, "saw" for "was"						
Difficulty copying from blackboard or book						
Poor note taking						
Traces letters well						
Poor spelling						
Poor coloring, pasting, cutting						
Doesn't like to do puzzles, mazes, word searches, follow-the-dot exercises						
Mixes up sequences within a word (e.g., *gril* for *girl*)						
Good handwriting						
Likes to write messages to everybody						

ARITHMETIC SKILLS						
Remembers multiplication tables easily						
Accurately forms and spaces numerals						
Mixes up signs of + × ÷ −						
Can't align numbers properly in columns						

ACTIVITY	VISUAL/ SPATIAL CHANNEL		VISUAL/ MOTOR CHANNEL		AUDITORY/ LANGUAGE CHANNEL	
	Strong	Weak	Strong	Weak	Strong	Weak
ARITHMETIC SKILLS (cont'd) Difficulty with word problems						
Misplaces decimal points in math problems						
Trouble identifying and producing geometric shapes						
Difficulty seeing angles						
Understands *components* of algebraic statements, but gets lost when completing full problems of several lines						

ACTIVITY	VISUAL/ SPATIAL CHANNEL		VISUAL/ MOTOR CHANNEL		AUDITORY/ LANGUAGE CHANNEL	
LEARNING CONTENT (e.g. geography, history, chemistry, biology) Mixes up South America and Africa on map						
Poor recall of geographical terms						
Able to take good notes						
Does well following picture sequences of experiments						
Trouble following oral directions for procedures						
Difficulty reading charts						
Good recall of historical dates						
Poor recall of chemistry symbols						
Good fund of general information						

14
What the Learning Disabled Can Do for Themselves

"I'm good at listening. I can't write without a computer, but I've trained my mind to take notes."

"My SAT score went up 300 points when I could take the test by listening to the questions on tape, and take as much time as I needed."

"Other people come to me with their problems. Imagine! I'm known as a good problem solver. Well, I guess I've had enough practice at it!"

"I know how to help myself. Now I have to learn how to make use of all the resources that are there for me."

"My goals are pretty clear. I'm on track! Someday I want to help others who have troubles like mine."

At first, adults with learning disabilities usually try to hide their problems. Only gradually do they learn to seek help. Often the initial impetus to do so comes from an advocate or ombudsman in the person's life—usually a parent, teacher, mentor, spouse, partner, or friend. From that point on, it's a long, winding trek for that person to become an advocate for himself or herself. A lot of exploring and growing has to take place between first recognizing that one has learning disabilities and then learning to live a full, independent life.

ACCEPTING LEARNING DISABILITIES

Because he was quick-witted, clever, and outstandingly successful on the football field, Dexter Manley was able to hide from everyone, even his wife, the fact that he could not read. But when Washington Redskin quarterback Joe Theismann broke his leg, Dexter wondered what he would do if he were in the same spot and could no longer play football. So, Dexter admitted to his wife and to a few others that he needed to learn to read. His wife's mother had read in a Chicago newspaper about The Lab School of Washington's Night School, where Manley appeared one day, asking if he could be helped. His enrollment was kept confidential for three years, until Dexter, pleased that he could read the newspaper at last, let the public know. His openness helped many people find the courage to seek similar help.

Talcott, who worked on a trade magazine, felt better having a name to put to all his eccentricities. Joan, a lab technician, gave a sigh of relief when told that her cluster of difficulties constituted learning disabilities. In contrast, Claude was appalled to discover at his university that he had a learning disability. He had done decent work in high school, which was a less demanding environment, but at the more complex university, his unexpected failures led him to the university's Learning Services Department. He couldn't bring himself to believe that a part of him was defective, and it took a few years before he could wrestle it all out.

Mario, on the other hand, had become the manager in a printer's shop by age forty. His gregarious personality, generosity, and industriousness endeared him to all his workers. He covered his slow reading and his inability to write by wearing a number of masks (see chapter 3). When he heard me answering telephone call-ins on the Larry King radio show, he called my office and said, "How did you know me? You just described me and my worst fears. You know the masks I wear. Is it too late for me to learn?" First we got Mario to a psychologist who understood learning disabilities. Mario was indeed diagnosed as learning disabled, which relieved him greatly because he had secretly worried that he was brain damaged or retarded. He felt he had passed as normal at work. When last heard from, Mario had hired a tutor and was reading more proficiently; the writing was slower in coming.

With the acceptance of their learning disabilities, people frequently become less hard on themselves emotionally and tougher on themselves with respect to accomplishing their goals.

Henry had not been able to keep a steady job. He worked in construction, in gardening, as a guard, and in a factory. He was strong as an ox and very good looking. He had traveled all over America. Even though Henry could not read or write and could do only basic math, he had a huge storehouse of information. However, he kept this information to himself, appearing truculent and slow-witted instead. When Henry was given the Woodcock-Johnson Psychoeducational Battery (a test of intellectual potential and academic achievement for all age groups), he scored at the highest level (above twelfth grade) on general knowledge; he clearly had a keen intelligence. Yet his achievement scores were on a preschool level. Henry, who had always been written off as dumb, was learning disabled.

He was also the father of a four-year-old boy who was learning letters. Henry wanted to learn to read to his boy. Determined to gain the requisite skills, Henry attended a municipal literacy course, gave up when it didn't help him, and then tried a church-sponsored course but failed that, too. He ended up at the Night School, which the D.C. Vocational Rehabilitation Department paid for him to attend.

By this time Henry had a big chip on his shoulder. Each teacher he met was greeted with "I'm sure you can't teach me, but I'll give you a try." Within two and a half years, Henry was reading at an eighth-grade level, well enough to read to his boy. Still gruff and defensive, still the clown and the cynic, he was proud enough of his accomplishments to talk about the process of learning with fellow adults with learning disabilities. Then he was invited to speak on a panel to a large group of professionals and parents of children with learning disabilities. He became afraid that he was doing too well and that the D.C. Vocational Rehabilitation people would not fund him anymore. They joined the Night School staff in encouraging Henry to go to college and agreed to pay for him to take the "Guided College Study" course at the Night School for the first year while he attended college. By acquiring the skills he so desperately wanted to learn, Henry began to like himself more and became more relaxed with the people around him. He is in college today, preparing for a business career.

Eric, aged twenty-eight, moved from Connecticut specifically to attend the Night School and to prepare for college. He knew he was learning disabled because he had severe language disabilities, lacked fluency in speaking, and could not "trap" words he knew. He was always tense and could not speak at all in public. His writing was poor. His reading was barely literate. A year at the Night School helped Eric come to terms with his learning disabilities and ferret out what he did well. He was an excellent problem solver. People turned to him for advice. He was more organized than most of the students, even overorganized, and had a talent for dealing with numbers. His math skills were at close to college level. He wanted to run his own construction business. He hired a spokesman who negotiated for him and an executive secretary who wrote for him. When he was last heard from, Eric's business was solid, and he felt good about what he had chosen to do.

LEARNING TO LIKE ONESELF

Learning to like oneself brings a fundamental change in the way one views the world. When people like themselves, everything seems possible. A person who feels good about himself dares to step out on a limb at times and risk failure. A fall won't alter his basic view of himself. He will acknowledge his clumsiness and move on.

How does a person with learning disabilities come to like himself? The most important step is to drop that model of perfection that so many of us grow up with. None of us is as attractive, intelligent, charming, funny, or compassionate as we would like to be. There are bulges and lines, quirks and foibles, that we have to learn to accept about ourselves. People with learning disabilities have to come to terms with who they are. Artist Robert Rauschenberg has said, "You know, you have to be aggressive in your own self-esteem. I don't mean arrogant or anything, but you have to get that idea out of your system that you're less! You have to go about feeling your own excellence."

Until he can accept his learning problem, a person is likely to believe that events just happen to him, that he is jinxed, or, if he has good luck, that he'll make his way willy-nilly. As author Elizabeth D. Squire says, "It certainly is more inspiring to think of yourself as a person with a problem you can get around by working a little harder, trying alternatives, and not giving up, than to think of yourself as an awkward klutz who is jinxed and has bad luck. After all, it was the tortoise and not the hare who won the fabled race. We tortoises love that story."

A tortoise must stick its neck out from under its shell and make itself vulnerable to injury if it is to see where it's going and so get on in the world. Likewise, a person with learning disabilities needs to stick her neck out, to stretch herself, to take risks. However, doing so requires first coming to love oneself, in the words of Oliver Cromwell, "warts and all."

BECOMING AN AGENT OF CHANGE

A person with learning disabilities cannot remain passive but needs to take control actively. Only then will he no longer view himself as a victim of fate, battered by bad luck or miraculously saved by good luck. He can make things happen! He can change situations and affect the course of events. *He has to see himself as an agent of change.* Then he will be able to view problems as opportunities. He will be able to say, for example, "This is what I'm good at; this is what I experience difficulty with. So maybe we could try it another way."

When Matthew was getting his scuba-diving training, he had to pass a test to show that he understood the workings of a pressure gauge. The students were handed a diagram showing all its parts, but Matthew, who has a moderate learning disability, could not decipher diagrams. So he asked the instructor to open a pressure gauge and let him look inside it. He easily understood how it worked, and thus was able to pass the test orally.

Taking the initiative in one's own life can have dramatic effects. Curt, for example, was determined to find a job in advertising because he was a fine artist and was clever at creating slogans. However, he had a tendency to slouch and walked in a halting way that did not inspire confidence. Curt's résumé got him eleven interviews, but he was turned down each time. Curt decided to ask his roommate to coach him. He practiced talking in a voice that sounded firm and confident, and he strode around the apartment with his shoulders back and his head held high. He remembered exercises he had practiced with an occupational therapist fifteen years before and what his sports teachers had said about his posture. He soon appeared more in command of himself. On his thirteenth try, Curt landed a job in an advertising agency, where he is working today and moving up the ladder.

Hannah and Philip, two adults with learning disabilities,

felt powerless to change their lives. They felt that everything just happened to them, and that it wasn't fair. They comforted each other by finding daily proof that the world was picking on them. The two of them would gripe for hours. Naturally, they infected each other with their negativism, and sometimes they took out their antagonism spitefully on others. Hannah went to a tutor to help improve her writing skills. As she became more competent, she began to feel more confident. She changed jobs and felt more capable at work. She met with a social worker for an hour a week to talk about her unhappiness, what her previous boss had called her *attitude*. As Hannah grew more in charge of herself, she realized she could change what was happening to her. She and Philip grew apart because he continued to layer himself with powerlessness and negativism, refusing to reach out to improve his situation in any way.

High-school students with learning disabilities who feel that they are victims of chance sometimes need to be allowed to work, closely supervised by a master teacher, with younger children who are severely learning disabled. By studying child development and observing how the little ones learn, the older ones tend to tune in to their own learning styles. They need to be guided to look for what a child does well so that they can appreciate how deftly Michelle puts together puzzles, how well Andrew verbalizes, and how much skill Rae demonstrates in her dancing.

High-school students placed in such situations often make such comments as, "I avoided work more cleverly than he does" and "You know that kid feels stupid, just the way I did, and he's not stupid!" Encouraged to tell the child that he's smart, the older youth reinforces that knowledge in himself.

Planning is a large part of teaching, and planning for children helps older students plan better for themselves. It helps them to advocate intelligently for themselves, to make a realistic assessment of their own strengths and weaknesses, and to plan for their own success in life. The experience teaches them, as Gil said, that "there's a lot you can do with your own life. I gotta take charge of where I'm going and what I'm doing. I'm sure I can handle it."

One freshman in college wrote about his drive and willpower, which saw him through all kinds of difficulties. After mentioning his dreadful time with spelling, writing, math, catching balls, and paddling canoes, he explained that he had found ways to handle his problems: he typed his papers, thus eliminating the need for legible handwriting; he used a calculator, thus eliminating any careless arithmetic errors; and he got assignments done early, thus reducing the pressure on himself.

Artist Chuck Close said, "I think accomplishment is figuring out your own truth, your own idiosyncratic solutions . . . knowing yourself. Accomplishment is being able to do what you want to do, even if you don't do it the way everybody else does it."

SECURING ACCOMMODATIONS

A person who cannot walk requires a wheelchair, ramps, and other special facilities to function in daily life. A deaf person needs an interpreter, often a telephone system called TDD, and sometimes a dog specially trained to react to sounds. A blind person cannot function properly without recorded books, books in Braille, a cane, and a guide dog. These are called *accommodations*.

Section 504 of the Rehabilitation Act of 1973 protects the rights of people with disabilities, and gives them access to educational facilities that had not been open to them before. Any college or university that uses federal funds is required to follow this law and to offer special accommodations for the learning disabled. The Americans for Disabilities Act, passed in July 1990, provides for access to employment. It requires employers to provide accommodations to ensure that they are not discriminating against persons with disabilities. People with learning disabilities have benefited greatly from these laws and will continue to do so. These laws say that people who are qualified to study in universities or to work in an occupation may not be held back by disabling conditions that can be corrected by equipment, building modifications, and human services.

Typical accommodations needed by college students with learning disabilities include

- access to computers inside as well as outside the classroom and occasionally to take tests
- access to tape recorders for taking notes
- access to calculators to speed up calculations
- access to talking books and recordings for the blind to help them with reading material
- extra time on tests and lab assignments
- oral rather than written tests
- tutoring in areas of need
- waiving of the foreign-language requirement
- a reduced course load
- permission to take exams in a separate room, with fewer distractions
- access to a single dormitory room to limit distractions

Information about such accommodations and permissions to use them can usually be obtained at a college or university's Student Services Department, Learning Center, or Learning Services Department.

Typical accommodations needed on the job by adults with learning disabilities include

- access to computers with spell checkers
- access to tape recorders to take notes and to record instructions from supervisors
- access to calculators to speed up calculations
- written directions for work to be performed
- models of performance or samples of work
- permission to take more time to accomplish tasks (which often means working overtime just to get the work done)
- access to a quiet office with a minimum of distractions

Of course, many adults with learning disabilities select occupations that build on their strengths and avoid their areas of weakness:

- Mel, a computer programmer, never has to write reports by hand.
- Lucian, an assistant to a dentist, does not have to write at all.
- Roy makes silver jewelry and rarely has to read anything.
- Arthur, who teaches art at a community college, does not have to deal with math, except for that involving his banking.
- Tia said, "I needed accommodations in college, but I accommodated myself by choosing a job that hit all the things I do well. I'm a landscape architect. I love going to work!"

USING MENTORS

One Night School adult related that she had had a mentor in junior high school who changed the course of her life. This teacher convinced her that she could do almost anything she set out to do, and she found that to be true. Other Night School students told about their role models, heroes, or mentors. Katie described how she followed a girl in college named Lois wherever she went. Katie tried to imitate how Lois walked, chose the same kind of clothes she wore, and attempted to copy the warm, casual way Lois greeted everybody. "I'm so intense. I have one thing on my mind, and I dash to get it done," she said. "So I screen out everything else, and I miss a lot of the life going on around me. Lois was so smart, and she seemed to have such a good time, and everybody loved her, so I decided to emulate her. It took a year before people could see the difference in me! But in the end they did!"

Others talked admiringly about their bosses. Marcia told how she practiced speaking like her boss, to the point where clients often said that they did not know which of them was speaking on the phone. A group of men shared how they tried to take on the mannerisms of their bosses because they wanted to project more forceful personalities.

A youngster with learning disabilities sometimes finds a mentor in a camp counselor, a scout troop leader, a teacher, or an athletic coach. A mentor is someone who sees the potential in a youngster and encourages her to reach further and aim higher. When the mentor's encouragement, help, and confidence are translated into self-confidence, the life of a young person with learning disabilities can be aimed toward success.

USING SUPPORT NETWORKS

It takes a good deal of maturity to know when and how to ask for help. Arthur, aged twenty-five, says, "I find asking for help real hard. It kind of makes me feel stupider."

The learning disabled need a lot of support from

parents   mates
grandparents   friends
relatives   roommates
                         tutors and teachers
                 counselors and psychiatrists
                             social groups
                            interest groups

Maggie, in her first year of college, felt intimidated by her Ivy League institution, particularly by her professors. She could not find the courage to approach them and explain her dyslexia, even though she needed arrangements to survive in their courses. The head tutor of Learning Services came to her rescue. He served as her advocate by talking to the professors. Maggie found she had support in the Learning Services Department, that she could turn in times of distress or simply for advice.

Specialists in learning disabilities continue to hear from former students, even some from decades before. These students seem to need to keep in touch with those who knew them when. In addition, many people with learning disabilities need access to periodic counseling. Continuing support networks for them should be built into community colleges and mental-health systems whenever possible. As they become their own advocates, they seem quicker to recognize when they need help in the form of job counseling, tutoring, or assistance with study skills, but often they don't know where to turn.

In an ideal world, each person with learning disabilities would be able to turn at any time to a case manager in the local clinic or to a university counselor who would point him toward the appropriate service. People with learning disabilities need continually available resources throughout their lives. But in the real world, this doesn't happen. When an adult with learning disabilities can afford and does use special services, such as tutoring or psychotherapy, on a regular and continuing basis, this augurs well for him in the long run. Turning to the tutor or the therapist only during crises does not produce the same results. For example, Amanda saw her tutors only when she was preparing a paper or studying for a test, and not regularly to improve her skills. She often dropped out of classes and finally quit her college studies.

Some adults thrive in peer groups and group therapy. Many feel comfortable in the format of Alcoholics Anonymous, though some find this a punishment. Interest groups such as photography clubs, singing groups, and amateur sports teams help some adults and provide support as well as excitement.

- Patrick goes to a bowling group once a week.
- Fred has a racquetball evening.
- Florence goes birding every Saturday morning and has met fascinating people through this social group.
- David has found an acceptance, unequaled by anything else in his life, among the strategists in his chess club, who share his passion for the game.
- Gabriella joined the local theater group for fun, because she had always loved dramatics. She not only made friends there but also found that she had so much talent that she left her job and became a paid member of the staff. Aimee made props there, while Ted became the assistant to the lighting specialist in the same group.

Some people with learning disabilities find support in volunteering to help those in dire need.

- Peter works at a food station for the homeless. On Saturdays, he makes sandwiches all evening. On Wednesdays, he hands out food. He is beginning to care for others and is receiving a lot of recognition and support for his volunteer work.

- Bud works with senior citizens, maneuvering their wheelchairs, helping them eat, and talking with them for hours. They love him, and he feels needed.
- Miriam works in a hospital play room with young children recuperating from serious illnesses. She, who used to talk nonstop, has become a caring listener. The nurses at the hospital have congratulated her on her talent at listening to and helping the children.

DEALING WITH MATES, LIVE-INS, ROOMMATES, AND FRIENDS

The best support for many people with learning disabilities comes from those already involved in their lives.

People who live together have to adjust to one another's needs, likes, and dislikes. The inflexibility of some people with learning disabilities makes them poor candidates for group living and rather risky as a partner in a couple. Still, deep friendship and love often overcome many barriers.

The disorganization that plagues people with learning disabilities causes friction in living situations. Their extreme messiness and lack of organization, which affects everything from cereal boxes to clothes to litter, can drive a mate crazy. The putting off of repairs, not noticing the loose doorknob or missing buttons, can exasperate a close companion. If the companion understands that such behavior is part of the learning disabilities and not a form of aggression, it helps. The person who has compensated for disorganization by compulsively keeping everything in its place at all times can also cause friction with roommates. In all cases, the problems need to be talked out to see how they can be resolved.

- Christa's live-in boyfriend does all the bookkeeping and cleaning up. He asks Christa to cook and to decorate the house, which she does very well. He is happy to help her by taking on the chores that she can't take on.
- Oliver so completely takes over the house that Anna feels as though he's her father and she is a little girl. Anna doesn't like it, but she sighs helplessly and says, "That's just the way it is, I guess!"
- Courtland's wife provides all the structure in his life; he says meekly, "I do whatever my wife says."
- Barbara, on the other hand, is very conscious of her foibles—"my LD-isms," she calls them—and tries to accommodate them where she can. She doesn't watch where she's going, bumps into things, drops plates, and spills coffee. She loses her belongings. Her husband, Bob, can tolerate most of it. They have worked out signals to let Barbara know when her behavior starts to exasperate him. They have a good relationship, with much laughter over their trials and tribulations.

Roommates can often say things to people with learning disabilities that parents have been unable to get across. Peers usually become more important to adults with learning disabilities than the old folks are. Roommates who are nonjudgmental and generally kind can help a person with learning disabilities to grow up. Friends can tell him that they won't put up with his lateness. They can, without screaming, tell her that she must do her own shopping each week and that there's no excuse for not doing it.

Friends can give each other deep acceptance. "No matter what I look like or how stupid I act," said Alice, "Elaine is there for me. She makes me feel good about myself, and together, we'll take on the world." Damian said the same thing about his girlfriend, Mary Catherine.

After a certain age, mates, live-ins, roommates, and friends usually can do much more than parents to foster the personal growth of an adult with learning disabilities. That adult must become boss of himself. Until he can do that, he cannot be a boss of others.

BECOMING BOSS

Many adults with learning disabilities fail at menial jobs because they cannot cope with the strict demands placed on them. They have trouble sticking to a company line. They are better at making it up, deviating from it, or creating a spinoff. Many people with learning disabilities make first-rate entrepreneurs.

Entrepreneurs with learning disabilities are more likely to set up work environments where they receive all the support they need.

- Judd, as head of a record company, hired an accountant because he is very poor at math and an assistant to manage the multiple details of public relations. His executive secretary spells and writes for him. Judd reads well, negotiates magnificently, and outthinks all his employees.
- Hassan is excellent at math, overorganized, and very neat. He is a chief bookkeeper, with six employees to help him.
- Nancy runs a boutique. She has a flair for fashion and the charm and salesmanship she needs. She has taken on employees to do all the things she cannot do.
- Sven has his own building company. He could have been an architect, had he been able to read, write, and do math. Instead, he puts his sense of design and love

of houses to use by building them. His wife does all the bookkeeping, including drawing up contracts. His chief employee does all the reading and writing to keep up-to-date on new materials. Sven supervises his other employees extremely well and is a true artist when it comes to the creative part of building.

An entrepreneur with learning disabilities who hires good accountants and writers is using the same talent for problem solving that propels people to the top in the business world. She is shrewd in accommodating her needs. She knows how to apply her own talents to the fullest possible extent, and she is buoyed up by the talents of the people she has so carefully hired. Perhaps she is more effective than people without learning disabilities who do not have equally impressive support systems.

Many adults with learning disabilities, once they have risen above their painful childhoods, find that they are experts at grappling with problems. They have lived daily with adversity and have triumphed. People who have experienced normal childhoods but meet hardships later often turn to the learning disabled for help and succor. "I never thought that my grueling childhood would give me better preparation for adulthood than my peers, but you know, it seems to be true," said Dennis, a Night School student. He then described how many people had asked him to listen to their plights and to give assistance. He laughed as he told the Night School group that he pulled out of his unconscious all the techniques his parents and mentors used to employ:

"Let's look at three ways to handle that situation!"

"Have you looked at it from the other person's point of view?"

"Perhaps there are several different approaches that could work here."

"Let's take one approach, step by step, and see where we land!"

Problem solving is key. A person must keep asking himself what he can do to make himself better. How can he keep on growing and feeling successful? Much of the joy in life is in solving its problems.

BEING SELF-DIRECTED

Adults who set up reasonable goals for themselves achieve more than those who just let themselves be swept up in the routine of daily demands. The process of establishing a few goals requires thinking. It involves analyzing yourself, tapping your resources and passions, and deciding where you want to be in one or five years. The adults interviewed in this book emphasize repeatedly that sitting back and letting life happen doesn't work. Their lives demonstrate that they have had to become pro-active. They have had to force themselves to become agents of change. They had to risk failure.

Many adults with learning disabilities have become successful because they took charge of their lives and did not succumb to rules or follow procedures that played on their deficits. When a person accepts responsibility for his life, there is no place for blaming, accusing, or pointing the finger. Bearing responsibility means being accountable, asking questions, looking, listening keenly, trusting feelings, relying on inner resources and ingenuity, and doing the very best possible.

The search for miracle cures is over. The quick methods, the unique gimmicks, the special treatments, the medications, and so on are no longer counted on to fix reading, writing, or math problems. They can't be counted on to bring a beautiful, productive life into being. The instant fix turns out to be a life-long effort.

Being learning disabled doesn't have to keep a person from chasing his dreams. It just means that he chases them differently, often along unorthodox valleys and streams. Sometimes he meets obstacles and has to find ways around them. He has a passion, or at least an interest, and involves himself in it. As actress Margaret Whitton said, in talking to Lab School children, "I don't want you to think that our sense of success is kissing Michael J. Fox or getting a column in the newspaper. You really have to find something in this life that you want to do and that you enjoy and are good at. That's what I would call a great accomplishment and a great way to spend your life."

Learning disabilities should be a cause neither for shame nor for pride. They are simply one of the facts of life—part of the way in which some people operate. The disabilities are like architectural modifications on the basic plan of being. No matter what we do, we are in charge of ourselves as we chase our dreams. The responsibility for learning and growing rests with us. That's what adulthood is all about!

To learn about and secure the accommodations they need, people with learning disabilities must formulate and ask a lot of questions. The next few pages suggest some questions that they can ask professionals whom they consult about their learning disabilities or whom they see when applying to college or for a job.

QUESTIONS AN ADULT WITH LEARNING DISABILITIES CAN ASK A DIAGNOSTICIAN

When an adult thinks that she has a learning disability, the first step to take is to have an educational evaluation. A supervisor at work or a close friend or relative may suggest a testing center or a particular specialist. It is essential that the diagnostician be skilled in testing and knowledgeable in the field of learning disabilities. *Before* testing is scheduled, ask the following questions:

1. Have you tested other clients for a learning disability?
2. How much does it cost?
3. Will you give me a written report? Will you write specific recommendations?
4. Will I be able to use your report to receive special accommodations at work or in college?

After diagnostic testing, ask the following questions:

1. What are my strengths?
2. What are my weaknesses?
3. Is any type of medical testing recommended as a result of the testing that was done?
4. What kind of help do I need?
5. Do I need classes or one-to-one tutoring? Where can I get this help?
6. What approach to teaching do you think will work best for me?

QUESTIONS TO ASK A TUTOR

A tutor *must* have a strong background in learning disabilities. Diagnostic-prescriptive tutoring works best with the learning disabled. The following questions should be posed to a prospective tutor:

1. Have you tutored clients who were learning disabled?

2. Can you tell from my testing what my strengths and weaknesses are?

3. What methods will you use?

4. How often should I be tutored each week?

5. What can I do to help the tutoring be successful?

6. What goals are reasonable for the first two months of tutoring?

7. What kind of progress can I expect after six months or a year of tutoring?

8. How often do you write a report on my tutoring?

9. How much do you charge?

10. If I can't afford one-to-one tutoring, are there any alternatives?

QUESTIONS TO ASK ONESELF IF CONSIDERING COLLEGE PROGRAMS

1. Why do I want to go to college?

2. Am I ready for a four-year college or university, or should I start by going to a community college or technical school?

3. How far away from home should I consider going?

4. Are there special admissions requirements for students with learning disabilities? If so, what are they?

5. Are standardized tests like the SAT or ACT required? If so, what scores will I need for admission?

6. How might I describe my learning disability to an admissions counselor?

7. What size college will I do best in?

8. Do I want a coed or single-sex college?

9. Do I want to be in or near a big city, or would I prefer a small college town?

10. Is there a college that offers a major in my special interest (for example, photography or drama)?

The list of colleges available to students with learning disabilities ranges from Ivy League schools to small community or technical colleges. Just as mainstream students do, a student with learning disabilities must take into account the college's admissions criteria and then decide if, in fact, these criteria can be met or almost met. A student with a low grade point average, low SAT or ACT scores, and average recommendations cannot expect to get into a top school, whether or not it has excellent services for the learning disabled. Sometimes colleges are willing to waive or to put little emphasis on standardized test scores or basic subject requirements if a student with a learning disability is especially gifted. If the applicant comes with a strong grade point average, excellent recommendations, and some exceptional talent that the school is interested in, her opportunities are good.

QUESTIONS TO ASK OF THE COLLEGE ADMISSIONS OFFICER

1. What are the admissions requirements?

2. How are advisors assigned to students with learning disabilities?

3. Are there classes expressly for students with learning disabilities?

4. Are there special courses that students with learning disabilities are required to take? Do these courses count for college credit?

5. What is the average class size? for freshman classes? Are the introductory freshman lecture classes very large?

6. How do I go about discussing my learning problems with my professors?

7. What kinds of tutorial or counseling programs are available on campus? Do they involve one-to-one help or group work?

8. Are there any other services for students with learning disabilities?

9. Is there an additional fee for services for the learning disabled?

10. How many credits per semester are required in order to be considered a full-time student? Is it possible for me to take just three courses a semester?

11. How many students with learning disabilities are now being served?

12. May I speak to a student with learning disabilities who is enrolled here?

QUESTIONS TO ASK ONESELF WHEN APPLYING FOR A JOB

1. Should I tell the person who's interviewing me that I have a learning disability?

2. How should I describe my learning disability?

3. What kind of work do I enjoy doing? Do I like working with my hands? with computers? with numbers? with people? outdoors?

4. What kind of work can I do best?

5. What kind of workplace do I need? Do I need quiet? Do I need structure?

6. Do I work best independently?

7. What salary do I need to pay my expenses?

QUESTIONS TO EXPECT AT A JOB INTERVIEW

During an interview, a person can expect to be asked some of these questions. Go over the list with a teacher or a friend and come up with answers with which you are comfortable. Then, when you go in for a job interview, you won't be caught off guard.

1. What kind of a person are you? Tell me about yourself.

2. Describe your learning disability.

3. Will you need special accommodations because of your learning disability? If so, what are they?

4. What do you think you might like about this job?

5. What are your main strengths (skills, abilities, personal characteristics)?

6. What do you consider to be your main weakness?

7. Tell me about your past work experience.

8. Tell me about your last job and what you liked or didn't like about it.

9. Why should I hire you?

10. Tell me what you know about the job you're applying for.

11. Why would you like to work for this company?

12. How well do you work under pressure?

13. Tell me about the times in your work history when you were unemployed. What did you do during those times?

14. Have you ever been fired from a job? Why?

15. You don't seem to have stayed at any job for very long. Can you tell me why? How long do you plan to stay on this job?

16. What are your salary expectations?

17. When would you be available to start working?

18. Would you be willing to work overtime and on weekends?

19. Do you have any questions about this job?

QUESTIONS TO ASK A THERAPIST

Often as the result of years of being told that he is inadequate and inept, an adult with learning disabilities will feel the need to get professional help. It is important that the psychiatrist (MD), psychologist (Ph.D), or social worker (MSW) have had experience with clients with learning disabilities. Asking specific questions will be helpful in making the right choice of counselor.

1. Have you worked with the learning disabled in the past?

2. What do you see as the primary purpose of this therapy?

3. I have difficulties expressing myself in words; will that be a problem in my treatment?

4. How do I know that therapy will be useful to me in my work situation? in my social relationships?

5. Under what circumstances do you recommend medication? Do you decide whether I need medication? What if I don't want any?

6. I've tried therapy in the past, and it hasn't worked. Do you think it might work now?

7. Will my medical insurance cover the cost of my therapy?

8. One of my greatest problems is getting along with people and being comfortable in social situations. Are there groups specifically for the learning disabled?

9. Can I trust you to keep our sessions confidential?

10. How do we decide when I'm ready to end my therapy?

15
Strategies for Success

"My mind is like a sieve. Things go through it, and I don't remember anything. I have tricks to remember everything."

"I use certain tunes to remember number combinations."

"I use the shapes of words to remember them."

"The day of the week and the time are on my watch."

"I listen best when I'm drawing."

"I dictate my reports on a dictaphone, and someone types them for me."

"I've tried five strategies to keep my bankbook straight, and I finally found one that works!"

*A*ccommodations are what people with learning disabilities need from the *outside* world in order to be successful. *Strategies* are what people have to develop from the *inside* in order to compensate for whatever is not working properly. I hope you know by now that the learning disabled can achieve almost anything they want, as long as they work harder than other people and use strategies appropriate to their own needs and abilities.

STRATEGIES FOR COLLEGE

The following are some strategies developed by college students with learning disabilities. Each student, of course, has to design his own, and nobody needs them all.

Choosing Courses at College

- Know your abilities and your learning disabilities.
- Know what accommodations you require.
- Be sure the classes you choose have professors who are willing to make those accommodations.
- Choose courses that you really will attend. You cannot afford to miss classes.
- During the first year, limit the number of courses you take, preferably to three each semester.
- Combine your knowledge of how you learn best with the style of the professor.
- If you have a good auditory memory, find lecture courses.
- If you learn best from textbooks, find a professor who teaches from books.
- If you learn best by doing, seek out classes that are project oriented.
- Do a lot of research by talking to people in Special Services or Handicapped Services; interview professors when possible; go to department offices and ask questions.
- Do not take *all* the difficult, required courses at the same time. Spread them out with classes that you know you can handle easily.
- Seek out other students with learning disabilities and ask their opinions.
- Be prepared to take more than the usual amount of time to complete your degree requirements. Many stu-

dents with learning disabilities need six years to complete their bachelor's-degree programs.

Knowing When to Ask for Help

- Ask for help with studies from the moment you arrive at college. This should be a basic rule for students with learning disabilities. It is a kind of preventive medicine.
- Find out what special services and resources you can call on. If you don't know where to ask, start at the dean's office.
- Asking for help shows that you are a mature person who recognizes that learning disabilities require different methods of teaching, learning, and studying.
- Remember: you are number one! Whatever age you are, you made the decision to study for an advanced degree because you want to achieve specific goals. Get the help set up from the start, use it, and grow.

Organizing Materials

- Use a three-ring binder notebook with a section for each class; this way you have to remember only one notebook. As another option, use a separate notebook for each class, with covers of different colors for each subject.
- A pencil case keeps pencils, pens, and highlighters in one place, easy to find if you remember to put them back.
- Keep a small assignment book in your pocket and cross off assignments when completed.
- When you finish a course, put your lecture notes and papers in a file for future reference.

Establishing a Work Space

- Find a quiet corner, perhaps a carrel in the library.
- Put your desk facing a wall to minimize distractions.
- Keep your workplace clear of junk. Have a large, well-lighted surface, and use it *only* for study and writing.
- Try to have a clear space right in front of you, and sit in a comfortable chair.

Keeping Track of Time

- Mark in red the due date for an assignment on a monthly calendar, and mark each day between the assignment date and the due date in green so that you will remember to work on the assignment continually instead of just on the night before it's due.
- Keep the monthly calendar in a place where you can't avoid looking at it, even if it must go in the bathroom.
- Make a daily list called "To Do."
- Have an alarm clock that will buzz when an hour is up.

Demonstrating Interest to Lecturers and Professors

- Get to class early and sit up front. Try to maintain eye contact with the professor.
- Listen actively. Nod from time to time. Sit forward in your chair. Respond. Smile.
- Give the message through your behavior that you are interested.

Paying Attention

- Hold something in your hand, like a soft ball, that you can squeeze whenever you notice your attention wandering.

- Develop a little voice in your head that keeps reminding you to pay attention.
- Sit up front so you can watch the speaker's face as he talks. Keep your eyes on him.

Keeping Eyes Focused on a Task

- Put the point of your pencil where you want your eyes to focus on the page.
- Cut a window in an index card and put it over the diagram or chart you are studying, like a frame.
- Change your way of seating to encourage a fresh focus.
- Highlight what you are looking at by putting large dots next to it.
- For contrast, put a big piece of bright red construction paper underneath an ordinary sized piece of white paper.
- Try placing a piece of blue- or gray-tinted plastic over the page you are reading and see if this helps you focus.
- Underline or highlight the main points you have to study. Frame the most important material.

Following Oral Instructions

- Listen carefully and repeat them to yourself.
- Write down the numbers 1, 2, and 3 if there are three parts to the instructions, to focus your mind on the first, second, and third parts.
- Ask the person to repeat the instructions to you, and visualize yourself doing them.
- Say, "Let me see if I understand you correctly," and repeat the instructions back to the speaker for verification.
- Try to anticipate what the next instruction will be.

- Listen for signal words: *next* and *furthermore* refer to the future; *however* and *since* refer to the past.

Following Written Instructions

- Read the entire set of directions twice before beginning to work. This gives you an overview of what is expected of you. It is like previewing a chapter in a textbook.
- Read the instructions to find out what action you are supposed to take.
- Circle or underline words such as *explain, list,* and *compare,* and put a 1, 2, 3, or 4 beside them. Getting the assignment right helps you succeed in the course.

Taking Notes

- Jot down the key words that will help you remember the lecture. If you have read all the material and have underlined key words and important facts, you will be familiar with the subject and will need only a few notes.
- Create a series of pictures that represent words so that these pictures remind you of what the professor said.
- Get permission to use a tape recorder with a counter on it; tape the whole lecture, but take the best notes that you can. When you can't keep up, put the number from the tape counter in your notes and leave a space. Later you will need to replay only the parts of the lecture you had trouble with, not the whole hour or two.
- Check with your counselor or teacher to see if your learning disabilities entitle you to have a notetaker.
- Get a friend to take notes for you in exchange for your typing them.
- Take a laptop computer into a business lecture or class.

- Work on expanding your memory. There are many excellent books on memory training techniques currently available.
- Have special pockets built into your clothing for a small tape recorder or dictating machine.

Reading College Books

- Break down reading assignments into small chunks. Set aside on your calendar an hour or two for reading each day. Check off assignments as you complete them.
- Skim through a chapter to preview it before reading it carefully.
- If skimming is too difficult, read the first sentence in each paragraph to get an idea of the material.
- After skimming a chapter, talk it over with somebody. You have probably learned more than you thought.
- Recite the material you have read out loud; this helps to fix it in your mind.
- Try to get the syllabus several weeks before classes begin so that you can start reading and studying early.
- If you read slowly, you can get recordings for the blind or Library of Congress talking books.

Using Textbooks

- Read the summary of the chapter before anything else.
- Study the questions at the end to see what the author expects you to know.
- Study the table of contents to determine the overall organization of the book.
- Read the glossary.
- Read the introduction.
- Then read the chapter.

- Pay close attention to the headings and subheadings. They may provide a skeleton outline for your notes.
- Study any charts, graphs, or pictures.
- Organize historical facts into time clusters. If you have to remember all the American presidents, cluster them into five groups: from the American Revolution to the War of 1812, then to the Civil War, then to the First World War, then to the Second World War, and then to the present. Thus you need to remember only a few at a time.
- Try tricks (called *mnemonics*) to jog your memory. HOMES recalls the Great Lakes (Huron, Ontario, Michigan, Erie, Superior). To recall the nine planets in their correct order, memorize (and visualize!) this sentence: My Very Educated Mother Just Served Us Nine Pickles (Mercury, Venus, Earth, Mars, Jupiter, Saturn, Uranus, Neptune, Pluto). You can make up your own mnemonics.

Taking Exams

- Find a tutor to teach you how to take tests, and practice taking tests on your own.
- If possible, obtain copies of previous tests. Take the test. Then check your answers with an answer sheet. If you don't learn the correct answers, you probably will continue to make the same mistakes.
- Ask for as much time as possible when taking a test.
- Study for forty minutes a day during the two weeks before the test. This is usually enough preparation.
- Study efficiently. Ask yourself whether the material you are studying is pertinent to the class and to the style of the professor. Do not try to remember everything ever mentioned in class. This will overload your memory.

- Make a checklist with your tutor or classmates. List everything you need to study.
- Group facts into categories to keep yourself from being overwhelmed by too much material.
- Go over the material aloud with a fellow student.
- Practice following written directions.
- Multiple-choice questions and filling in blanks are difficult for people with learning disabilities. If you face this kind of test, study regularly from the beginning; do not try to cram at the end.
- Mark up test questions. Put boxes around directional words (explain, compare, choose); put boxes around question words (what?, when?). Underline key nouns. Circle qualifiers (3 out of 4, most important). Use the wording of essay questions to begin the answers.

STRATEGIES FOR EVERYDAY LIFE

Adults at the Night School often share strategies with one another during my Tuesday-night seminars with them. There are so many areas to cover that I have touched on only a few here. Chapter 11 covers some of the strategies necessary for social life. Chapter 14 probes some of the strategies needed for independent living.

Keeping Track of Money

- Carry a tiny notebook and jot down every expense. At the end of the week, add up what you spent on transportation, food, movies, supplies, and so forth, and set up a budget for the next week.
- Ask the bank for the type of checkbook that has a carbon copy for each check.

- On payday, divide up your money and put it into envelopes, marking what each one is for (for example, rent, car payment, personal expenses).
- Have a friend check your bankbook weekly; in return, you can do favors for your friend. Or forget the bankbook and use a money machine, which always tells how much money you have in the bank.
- Carry a calculator with you.
- See if your employers can issue paychecks as direct deposits, transferring your salary directly into your bank account.

Sustaining Energy

- Get enough sleep to compensate for your hard work. You have to put in ten times as much work as other people to achieve what you do. Eight hours will probably be sufficient, though some people actually need more.
- Get enough exercise. Walking and exercising help battle fatigue.
- Eat sensibly, because good nutrition also helps ward off fatigue. Avoid a diet of fast food and junk food.
- A part of each day needs to be set aside for something that you like to do and that you feel competent doing.

Self-monitoring

Ask yourself . . .

- What is the one goal I want to achieve this week? What am I doing to make it happen?
- Did I understand what my friend (doctor/professor/boss) said to me? Let me paraphrase it.
- Did I say what I meant to say?

- Stop. Think. What am I supposed to do now?
- Did I follow the instructions I was given? Let me repeat them. Let me look at them again.
- Did I bring all the materials I need for work? Let's see what I need. Let me plan for tomorrow.
- Did I finish the whole task? Let me go back and look.
- I won't panic. I can break these instructions down into small steps. What am I going to do first? Which step comes second? What is the last step?
- Did I say anything to irritate that person? Let me repeat what I said and listen to myself.

Remembering Left and Right

- Remember which hand you use to pick up a pencil, and visualize that action when you must identify left or right.
- Look at the ring on your right hand before following the direction to make a right turn.
- Check the watch on your left hand before turning left.
- Put a mark on your left thumb. (You don't have to go as far as Ken, who put a tatoo on his left hand.)
- Check for an unusual feature on your left hand, like a knuckle that sticks out, and look for it.

Remembering Telephone Numbers

- Tap out a rhythm.
- Use *chunking* (divide the number into groups of two or three).
- Visualize the pattern of numbers on the block of touch-tone buttons.
- Use an electronic device that fits in your wallet to record telephone numbers, including your own.

Shopping

- Do your household shopping in the same store or supermarket so that you know the layout well.
- Don't be too embarrassed to ask store employees where to find what you need. They are used to answering such questions.
- Make a list before you go and check off each item as you purchase it.
- Remember the colors and designs on cans and packages so that if you can't read the fine print, you'll still recognize the product.

Doing Household Chores

- Mark garbage day on your monthly calendar and hang the calendar prominently in the kitchen.
- Make a monthly schedule of things to be done in the house, such as mopping the kitchen floor, vacuuming, and making small repairs.

Keeping from Knocking Things Over

- Get up and look before you move. Shift the chair that might get in your way. Move the water glass that might spill. Move the butter before your sleeve gets into it.
- Imagine a red ALERT button that lights up when you enter a room, one that reminds you to stop and look for obstacles before proceeding.
- Remind yourself to look down at your feet from time to time to see if there's an obstacle in your way.

Writing Thank-You Letters

- Telephone your thank-you.
- Send a picture, flowers, a computer graphic, or a homemade construction.

- First write your thank-you note on a computer. Use a spell checker. Mail the printout, or if you have good handwriting, copy it out by hand on personal stationery and send it.

Keeping Track of Time

- Remember to set the alarm clock.
- Have signs by your bed reminding you to set the alarm.
- Set the buzzer on your watch to go off at specific intervals.
- Keep a big calendar by your bed or desk and mark significant events in red.
- Have a friend phone you, if necessary, to get you up at the correct time. (Of course, this works only if you answer the phone!)

Finding the Way

- Know where you are going the first day of work. It helps to rehearse. Do a dry run and time it. You need to know how long it takes to get there.
- When asking directions, ask for landmarks ("Turn left at the third traffic light"; "Go past the tennis courts and take a right at the gas station").
- Notice the names of shops near where you need to turn.
- Ask questions if you're not sure.
- Call the transit information service to find out how to get from one place to another on public transportation.
- Get a schedule of subway and bus routes. Have your tutor go over such schedules with you.

Not Forgetting or Losing Items

- Always put keys in the same spot in the house or in the same pocket.

- Put a heavy ball or chain on the keys so that their weight tells you where they are.
- Put your briefcase next to the front door or at the bottom of the stairs where you will trip on it if you don't pick it up.
- Leave a "Things to Remember" note on the bathroom mirror.
- Tape reminders such as "Buy gas" and "Buy stamps" to the steering wheel of your car or the handlebars of your bike.

Projecting an Image

- Look neat.
- Look alert and energetic.
- Look employers in the eye.
- Stand or sit straight.
- Speak clearly.
- Look cheerful and, when you can, enthusiastic.

Remembering Information

- Fix a piece of information in your mind by visualizing pictures.
- Say it out loud. If that doesn't work, try walking as you say it out loud. If that doesn't work, type it or tell somebody else in conversation what you have been studying and what you want to remember.
- Put rhythm or music to facts that you want to remember.
- Organize facts into categories. Then you have to store away only a few categories, and you can remember the facts in each category by association.

STRATEGIES FOR DESCRIBING LEARNING DISABILITIES

The biggest strategy that a person with learning disabilities has to pull out of his inner being is how he will describe his problems to others. Will he simply say, "I'm learning disabled?" Many people will not understand that.

Billy doesn't tell people on the job that he's learning disabled. He simply describes what he can and cannot do. Like Billy, Betsy explains, "I'm very good at selling things to people, and I'm good with money. However, I hope I do not have to write on the job because I spell poorly and my handwriting is hard to read."

Pat explains to her boss that she has trouble following oral directions and that if he can write things down for her, she will be more efficient. Mike tells everybody to "please let me know precisely what you want done on the job. If you are vague, I become confused."

Karen did explain during her job interview that she had learning disabilities. "What that means," she said, "is that I have some specific difficulties which I will explain to you, but they will not prevent me from being a first-class art director for you. I'll work like a dog. I'm very experienced and an innovative artist, as my references show. I have a lot of good contacts with clients. I get along well with people. I'm highly organized in every area but one: I'm terrible at math. I'll need substantial help making budgets and doing any financial management." Karen was hired!

A person with learning disabilities should describe her strengths, always projecting a competent image. The decision whether or not to use the words *learning disabled* depends on the person and the situation. Some of our Night School adults find that they get a better reception using the word *dyslexic*. Jeannie says that *dyslexic* sounds more intellectual and that people are less likely to question how smart she is when she uses this word instead of *learning disabled.*

The more descriptive you can be, the less you will need to use labels. The more positive you can be, the more the other person will be positive. Adults with learning disabilities need to advocate for themselves and explain their strategies when necessary. It can be done, lightly. Humor helps!

- Ronnie used to say, "It's too bad I can't tie my mother to my head, listing all the things that I have to do today and what I must not forget to do!"
- Everett made up an "I'm Not Stupid—I'm LD" rap.
- Joanne used to make people laugh by saying, "I have always reversed things so badly that I would read the word *small* as *llamas.* No wonder I work in the zoo!"

TURNING NEGATIVE INTO POSITIVE

Positive thinking builds on strengths. It makes us concentrate on the best in ourselves and opens us up to infinite possibilities. The founder and president of Kinko's copy shops, Paul Orfalea, said, "Everybody has a bit of the Rainman in them. I consider my disability an opportunity."

Actress Margaret Whitton put it this way: "When I think of it as a learning *ability,* it makes me look at things differently and maybe solve problems differently. When I was in school, it was really frustrating and embarrassing, but I don't think that way anymore. I don't really think of it as a *disability.* It's just a different way of thinking, another way of getting information."

When talking to Lab School children in 1988, Cher said, "You have to learn how to turn a negative thing into a positive thing. You guys know you have the ability to be supercreative. And that's kind of what you have to do. You have to turn, like make a left turn into a straight road."

THE ULTIMATE MATURITY

The ultimate maturity is knowing when you need help and daring to ask for it. Often pride prevents us from asking for what we need. We frequently choose to suffer for hours by ourselves rather than turn to the person who can answer our questions and point us in the direction we need to go. *College students with learning disabilities who ask a lot of questions and seek support are more likely to graduate than those who don't.*

An adult with learning disabilities often fears that his questions sound dumb and decides he must struggle on his own. Some adults with learning disabilities have difficulty in phrasing questions. Others, like entrepreneur Paul J. Orfalea, claim that they made their way in the world by asking a lot of questions. Many learn by being briefed and then asking difficult questions that demand in-depth answers.

The Lab School of Washington's Outstanding Learning-Disabled Achievers have tended to come up with a continual stream of cogent questions that get right to the point. They have trained themselves to listen well and to remember. Memory is a muscle, and they have worked seriously on strengthening it. They knew when they needed help in certain areas and quickly went about seeking it. Adults in the Night School are learning to do the same thing. They join me in giving the following advice:

You are the person who can make things happen.

You need to recognize your strengths and weaknesses.

You need to know what accommodations you need.

You need to invent your own strategies.
You need to know what you know.
You need to know what you don't know.
You need to be able to ask for help when you need it.
You are the person who can make things happen!

APPENDIX I

Resources for the Learning Disabled

BIBLIOGRAPHY

Learning Disabilities in General

Bos, C., and S. Vaughn. *Strategies for Teaching Students with Learning and Behavior Problems.* Boston: Allyn and Bacon, 1988.

Brutten, Milton, Sylvia Richardson, and Charles Mangel. *Something's Wrong with My Child.* New York: Harcourt Brace Jovanovich, 1973.

Bryan, Tanis H. *Understanding Learning Disabilities.* Palo Alto, CA: Mayfield Publishing, 1986.

Critchley, Macdonald. *The Dyslexic Child.* London: Heinemann Medical Books, 1969.

Featherstone, Helen. *A Difference in the Family: Living with a Disabled Child.* New York: Penguin Books, 1981.

Hammill, D., and N. Bartel. *Teaching Children with Learning and Behavior Problems.* Boston: Allyn and Bacon, 1990.

Ingersoll, Barbara. *Your Hyperactive Child: A Parent's Guide to Coping with Attention Deficit Disorder.* New York: Doubleday, 1988.

Johnson, Doris, and Helmer Myklebust. *Learning Disabilities: Educational Principles and Practices.* New York: Academy Press, 1967.

Kronick, Doreen. *New Approaches to Learning Disabilities.* Philadelphia: Grune and Stratton, 1988.

Lerner, Janet W. *Learning Disabilities: Theories, Diagnosis and Teaching Strategies.* Boston: Houghton Mifflin, 1989.

Levine, Melvin D. *Developmental Variation and Learning Disorders.* Cambridge, MA: Educators Publishing Service, 1987.

Levy, Harold. *Square Pegs Round Holes: The Learning Disabled Child in the Classroom and at Home.* Boston: Little, Brown, 1973.

Lewis, Richard S., A. Strauss, and L. Lehtinen. *The Other Child: The Brain Injured Child, a Book for Parents and Laymen.* New York: Grune and Stratton, 1960.

Lynn, R., N. Glukin, and B. Kripke. *Learning Disabilities: An Overview of Theories, Approaches, and Politics.* New York: Macmillan–Free Press, 1979.

Mercer, Cecil D. *Children and Adolescents with Learning Disabilities.* Columbus, OH: Charles E. Merrill, 1979.

Moss, Robert A. *Why Johnny Can't Concentrate.* New York: Bantam Books, 1990.

Osman, Betty. *Learning Disabilities: A Family Affair.* New York: Random House, 1979.

———. *No One to Play With: The Social Side of Learning Disabilities.* Boston: Houghton Mifflin, 1979.

Rawson, Margaret. *The Many Faces of Dyslexia.* Baltimore: Orton Dyslexia Society, 1988.

Siegel, Ernest. *Educating the Learning Disabled.* New York: Macmillan, 1982.

Silver, Larry. *The Misunderstood Child: A Guide for Parents of Learning Disabled Children.* New York: McGraw Hill, 1984.

Smith, Sally L. *No Easy Answers: The Learning Disabled Child at Home and at School.* New York: Bantam Books, 1981.

Stevens, Susan H. *Classroom Success for the Learning Disabled.* Winston-Salem, NC: Blair Publishing, 1988.

———. *The Learning Disabled Child: Ways Parents Can Help.* Winston-Salem, NC: Blair Publishing, 1980.

Ungerleider, Dorothy Fink. *Reading, Writing and Rage*. Rolling Hills Estates, CA: Jalmar Press, 1985.

Vail, Priscilla L. *About Dyslexia: Unraveling the Myth*. Rosemont, NJ: Modern Learning Press, Programs for Education, 1990.

Wender, Paul H., and Ester H. Wender. *The Hyperactive Child and the Learning Disabled Child: A Handbook for Parents*. New York: Crown Publishers, 1978.

Westman, Jack C. *Handbook of Learning Disabilities*. Boston: Allyn and Bacon, 1990.

Woodward, Delores, and Delores Peters. *The Learning Disabled Adolescent*. Rockville, MD: Aspen Systems, 1983.

Learning Disabilities—Adults

Alley, G., and D. Deshler. *Teaching the Learning Disabled Adolescent: Strategies and Methods*. Denver: Love Publishing, 1979.

Cordoni, Barbara. *Living with a Learning Disability*. Carbondale, IL: Southern Illinois University Press, 1987.

Cruickshank, William, William Morse, and Jeannie Johns. *Learning Disabilities: The Struggle from Adolescence toward Adulthood*. Syracuse, NY: Syracuse University Press, 1980.

Johnson, Doris J., and Jane W. Blalock. *Adults with Learning Disabilities: Clinical Studies*. Orlando, FL: Grune and Stratton, 1987.

Lewis, Richard S. *The Other Child Grows Up*. New York: Times Books, 1977.

Siegel, Ernest. *The Exceptional Child Grows Up*. New York: E. P. Dutton, 1975.

Spreen, Otfried. *Learning Disabled Children Growing Up: Coping with Attention Deficit Problems*. New York: Oxford University Press, 1988.

Zwerlein, Rayna, M. Smith, and J. Diffley. *Vocational Rehabilitation for Learning Disabled Adults*. Albertson, NY: Human Resources Center, 1984.

Personal Stories—Learning Disabilities

Hampshire, Susan. *Susan's Story*. New York: St. Martin's Press, 1982.

Hart, Jane, and Beverly Jones. *Where's Hannah?* New York: Hart Publishing, 1968.

Keller, Helen. *The Story of My Life*. New York: Doubleday, 1902.

MacCracken, Mary. *Turnabout Children*. Boston: Little, Brown, 1986.

Simpson, Eileen. *Reversals: A Personal Account of Victory over Dyslexia*. New York: Washington Square Press, 1981.

Educational Theories

Boyer, E. L. *High School: A Report on Secondary Education in America*. New York: Harper and Row, 1983.

Bruner, Jerome. *Actual Minds, Possible Worlds*. Cambridge: Harvard University Press, 1986.

———. *The Process of Education*. New York: Random House, 1960.

Dewey, John. *Experience and Education*. New York: Collier Books, 1963.

Gardner, Howard. *Frames of Mind*. New York: Basic Books, 1983.

Glasser, William. *Schools without Failure*. New York: Harper and Row, 1969.

———. *The Quality School: Managing Students without Coercion*. New York: Perennial Library, 1990.

Montessori, Maria. *The Secret of Childhood*. New York: Ballantine Books, 1981.

Pulaski, Mary Ann. *Understanding Piaget: An Introduction to Children's Cognitive Development*. New York: Harper and Row, 1967.

Sizer, Theodore R. *Horace's Compromise*. Boston: Houghton Mifflin, 1983.

Sternberg, Robert J. *Learning and Individual Differences: Advances in Theory and Research.* New York: W. H. Freeman, 1989.

Arts

Allen, Anne, and George Allen. *Everyone Can Win.* McLean, VA: EPM Publications, 1988.

Dewey, John. *Art and Education: A Collection of Essays.* 3rd ed. Merion, PA: Barns Foundation Press, 1954.

Edwards, Betty. *Drawing on the Right Side of the Brain.* Los Angeles: Jeremy P. Tarcher, 1989.

Gardner, Howard. *Art, Mind and Brain: A Cognitive Approach to Creativity.* New York: Basic Books, 1982.

College Searches

College and the Learning Disabled Student: A Guide to Program Selection, Development and Implementation. Charles T. Mangrum and Stephen Strichart. Orlando: Grune and Stratton, 1984.

Colleges with Programs for Learning Disabled Students. Charles T. Mangrum and Stephen Strichart. Princeton, NJ: Peterson, 1988.

Community Colleges and Students with Disabilities: A Directory of Services and Programs.
American Association of Community and Junior Colleges
80 South Early Street
Alexandria, VA 22304

From High School to College: Keys to Success for Students with Learning Disabilities. 1988.
The National Center on Employment and Disability
Human Resources Center
Albertson, NY 11507

Lovejoy's College Guide for the Learning Disabled. Charles T. Straughn II. New York: Monarch Press, 1988.

National Directory of Four Year Colleges, Two Year Colleges and Post High School Training Programs for Young People with Learning Disabilities.
Partners in Publishing
Box 50347
Tulsa, OK 74150
(918) 584-5906
These directories of schools and programs for the learning disabled are updated every two years.

Unlocking Potential: College and Other Choices for Learning Disabled People: A Step by Step Guide. Barbara Schieber and Jeanne Talpers. Bethesda, MD: Adler and Adler, 1987.

What Do You Do After High School?
Skyer Consultation Center
Box 121
Rockaway Park, NY 11694
A nationwide guide to residential, vocational, social, and college programs serving the adolescent, young adult, and adult with learning problems.

General

Ayers, Jean. *Sensory Integration and the Child.* Los Angeles: Western Psychological Services, 1979.

Bower, Eli M. *The Handicapped in Literature: A Psychosocial Perspective.* Denver: Love Publishing, 1980.

Elklind, D. *The Hurried Child: Growing Up Too Fast Too Soon.* Reading, MA: Addison Wesley, 1988.

Gordon, Sol. *Living Fully: A Guide for Young People with a Handicap, Their Parents, Their Teachers, and Professionals.* New York: John Day, 1975.

Lyman, Donald E. *Making The World Stand Still.* Boston: Houghton Mifflin, 1986.

Vail, Priscilla. *Smart Kids with School Problems.* New York: E. P. Dutton, 1987.

INFORMATION CENTERS AND ORGANIZATIONS

American Speech-Language-Hearing Association
9030 Old Georgetown Road
Bethesda, MD 20014
(301) 897-5700
(800) 638-8255 (action line)
This organization provides technical assistance to professionals needing resources for diagnostic services. The Consumer Action Line is available to the public and attempts to answer speech-, language-, and hearing-related questions.

Association on Handicapped Student Service Programs in Postsecondary Education (AHSSPPE)
Box 21192
Columbus, OH 43221
(614) 488-4972
AHSSPPE is a professional organization for educators committed to promoting full college participation for individuals with disabilities. AHSSPPE has material for teachers and counselors who work with the learning disabled.

Center on Postsecondary Education for Students with Learning Disabilities
University of Connecticut
249 Glenbrook Road
Storrs, CN 06269-2064
(203) 486-4036
The center offers technical assistance on developing support services for students with learning disabilities in colleges and post-secondary programs throughout the country.

Children with Attention Deficit Disorder (CHADD)
1859 North Pine Island Road
Suite 195
Plantation, FL 33322
(305) 587-3700
CHADD offers a support group for parents who have children with attention deficit disorder (ADD) through its 215 chapters across the

country. There is a monthly newsletter, *The Chadderbox,* and a biannual magazine, *The Chadder.*

Higher Education and Adult Training for People with Handicaps (HEATH)
HEATH Resource Center
1 Dupont Circle, Suite 800
Washington, DC 20036
(800) 544-3284
(202) 939-9320
This national clearinghouse on postsecondary education for individuals with handicaps develops publications and responds to inquiries. Free publications include information on colleges and universities with support services for students with learning disabilities.

International Reading Association
Dept. TE, Box 8139
Newark, DE 19714
(302) 731-1600
This association holds international reading conferences and works with issues of the learning disabled.

Learning Disabilities Association of America (LDA)
4156 Library Road
Pittsburgh, PA 15234
(412) 341-1515
A national membership organization of professionals and parents focused on advancing the education and well-being of children and adults with learning disabilities. Free information is available, which includes a listing of state learning-disability associations and a bibliography of resources.

National Center for Learning Disabilities (NCLD)
99 Park Avenue
New York, NY 10016
(212) 687-7211
NCLD publishes *Their World* and *NCLD Guide* to increase awareness about learning disabilities. There are divisions for grant mak-

ing, legislative advocacy, and publications. Training seminars assist employers, parents, educators, physicians, nurses, and mental-health workers in this country and abroad.

National Council of Independent Living Programs (NCILP)
Access Living
815 Van Buren, Suite 525
Chicago, IL 60607
(312) 226-5900
A professional association for member centers, which disseminates information about independent living and relevant legislation through its network.

National Information Clearinghouse for Handicapped Children and Youths (NICHCY)
Box 1492
Washington, DC 20013
(703) 528-8480
A free information service to help parents, educators, care givers, advocates, and others improve the lives of children and youths with handicaps. NICHCY develops and distributes information through fact sheets and newsletters.

National Network of Learning Disabled Adults (NNLDA)
808 North 82nd Street, Suite F2
Scottsdale, AZ 85257
(602) 941-5112
NNLDA provides information and referrals for adults with learning disabilities who are involved with or in search of support groups and networking opportunities.

Orton Dyslexia Society (ODS)
8600 La Salle Road
Chester Building, Suite 382
Towson, MD 21204
(800) 222-3123
(301) 296-0232
A professional and parent membership organization offering leadership in dyslexia-related language programs, research, and publications.

Project Literacy U.S. (PLUS)
4802 Fifth Avenue
Pittsburgh, PA 15213
(412) 622-1491
This organization focuses on adult literacy problems in the United States. PLUS works with the National Center for Learning Disabilities on cooperating with learning-disability specialists.

Specialized Training of Military Parents (STOMP)
12208 Pacific Highway SW
Tacoma, WA 98499
(206) 588-1741
This is a training and information center providing workshops on the special needs of children of military parents. Questions are answered about local, state, and federal regulations in the United States and abroad. An excellent referral system for military families is provided.

U.S. Department of Education Office of Vocational and Adult Education: Division of Clearinghouse on Adult Education
MES Building, Room 4416
400 Maryland Avenue SW
Washington, DC 20202-5515
(202) 732-2410
Several publications are available for adult learners with special needs: a fact sheet on adult learners with disabilities, a listing of federally funded projects for adult learners with disabilities, *Directory of Resources for Adults with Disabilities,* and *Bibliography on Adult Education Resource Materials.*

PERIODICALS, PAMPHLETS, AND NEWSLETTERS

Career Development for Exceptional Individuals
1920 Association Drive
Reston, VA 22091
A scientific and archival journal devoted to original contributions on career development for individuals with exceptional characteristics and needs, including research and systematic reviews of research literature.

College HELPS Newsletter
Partners in Publishing
Box 50347
Tulsa, OK 74150
(918) 584-5906
This newsletter has articles of interest to parents of students with learning disabilities and also lists colleges and other programs for students who are learning disabled.

The Exceptional Child
1920 Association Drive
Reston, VA 22091-1589
(703) 620-3660
The Exceptional Child publishes articles on development of infants, toddlers, children, and youths as well as articles on professional issues of concern to special educators.

The Exceptional Parent
Psy-Ed Corporation
1170 Commonwealth Avenue, 3rd floor
Boston, MA 02134
(617) 730-5800
A journal for parents of and professionals who care for children with a disability.

Intervention in School and Clinic (formerly Academic Therapy)
PRO-ED
8700 Shoal Creek Road
Austin, TX 78758-6897
(512) 451-3246
An interdisciplinary journal directed to an international audience of teachers, parents, educational therapists, and specialists in all fields who deal with day-to-day aspects of special and remedial education.

Journal of Learning Disabilities (JLD)
PRO-ED
8700 Shoal Creek Road
Austin, TX 78758-6897
(512) 451-3246

A multidisciplinary publication containing articles on practice, research, and theory related to learning disciplines.

LDA Newsbriefs
4156 Library Road
Pittsburgh, PA 15234
(412) 341-1515
A bimonthly newsletter for parents, professionals, and adults that includes up-to-date research findings, information on current publications, and a list of scheduled conferences.

Learning Disabilities: A Multidisciplinary Journal
4156 Library Road
Pittsburgh, PA 15234
(412) 341-1515
This biannual publication put out by LDA and directed to parents and professionals is a scholarly journal representing the major disciplines concerned with learning disabilities.

Learning Disabilities Research and Practice
1920 Reston Drive
Reston, VA 22091
(703) 620-3660
This journal provides a forum for the presentation of current research in the field of learning disabilities and a vehicle for the dissemination of information important to practitioners in the field.

Learning Disability Quarterly
Council for Learning Disabilities
Box 40303
Overland Park, KS 66204
(913) 492-8755
The *Quarterly* publishes educational articles with an applied focus on learning disabilities, such as reviews of professional and teacher-training materials, practical needs of the learning-disability practitioner, and information on state and federal legislation.

National Network of LD Adults Newsletter (NNLDA)
808 North 82nd Street, Suite F2
Scottsdale, AZ 85257
(602) 941-5112
A quarterly publication focused on adults who are learning disabled, incorporating news, views, and information resources.

Perspectives on Dyslexia
8600 La Salle Road
Chester Building, Suite 382
Towson, MD 21204
(301) 296-0232
This quarterly newsletter developed by the Orton Dyslexia Society has articles on people, education, and medical research. It also gives information about meetings, seminars, workshops, and conferences on the subject of dyslexia.

Steps to Independence for People with Learning Disabilities
by Dale S. Brown
Instructional Support System of Pennsylvania
150 South Progress Avenue
Harrisburg, PA 17109
(717) 657-5840
A free pamphlet that contains practical information for the learning disabled on getting along at home, with friends, and at work.

EDUCATIONAL TESTING SERVICES

It is now possible for the learning disabled to have special arrangements made when taking standardized tests for admission to institutions of higher education. To take advantage of the accommodations that are offered, call or write to the services listed below.

American College Test (ACT) Administration
Box 168
Iowa City, IA 52243
(319) 337-1332

Students with a documented learning disability are permitted to make special arrangements to take this test. Untimed tests, tests on cassettes, and reader services are available.

Educational Testing Service (ETS)
Princeton University
Princeton, NJ 08541
(609) 734-5068
Through ETS, special administrations of the Scholastic Aptitude Test (SAT), Graduate Records Exam (GRE), and Graduate Management Admissions Test (GMAT) are offered.

GED Testing Service
American Council on Education
1 Dupont Circle
Washington, DC 20036
(202) 939-9490
The GED (General Educational Development) Test is administered by this service. Adaptations and accommodations can be made for students with learning disabilities.

CAREER-RELATED RESOURCES

Center on Education Training for Employment
Education Resources Information Center (ERIC)
1900 Kenny Road
Columbus, OH 43210
(800) 848-4815
(614) 292-4353
The center provides a wide range of materials for *professionals* about curriculum development, technical education, career planning, and preparation for employment.

Job Accommodation Network
809 Allen Hall
Box 6123
West Virginia University
Morgantown, WV 26506-6123
(800) 526-7234

This is an information and consulting network that serves people with disabilities and their employers in the United States and Canada by assisting with job accommodation recommendations.

Lovejoy's Career and Vocational Schools. Clarence E. Lovejoy. New York: Simon and Schuster, 1982.

Materials Development Center
Stout Vocational Rehabilitation Institute
University of Wisconsin–Stout
Menomonie, WI 54751
(715) 232-1342
The center disseminates information to *professionals* about vocational rehabilitation and training of disabled students. Materials include information on vocational evaluation, work adjustment, job placement, and independent living.

National Association of Trade and Technical Schools (NATTS)
2215 Wisconsin Avenue NW
Washington, DC 20007
(202) 333-1021
Free material includes a pamphlet with information on choosing a career school for the student with a disability and *Trade and Technical Careers and Training: A Handbook of Accredited Private Trade and Technical Schools.*

National Center on Employment of the Handicapped
Human Resources and Abilities Center
201 I.U. Willits Road
Albertson, NY 11507
(516) 747-5400
The center puts out a handbook, *Vocational Rehabilitation for Learning Disabled Adults,* which is for rehabilitation professionals.

The President's Committee on Employment of People with Disabilities
1331 F Street NW, 3rd Flr.
Washington, DC 20004

The President's Committee works on public issues but does not provide direct services to adults with learning disabilities. The organization has many publications that address aspects of employment for adults who are learning disabled. Most publications and information are free.

An example of publications is Dale S. Brown's *Pathways to Employment for People with Learning Disabilities,* a report of a national consensus-building conference held in May 1990.

Vancouver Association for Children and Adults with Learning Disabilities
2590 Granville Street, Suite 105
Vancouver, BC V6H 3H1
Canada
(604) 732-8006
This organization provides *Employment of the Learning Disabled: An Annotated Bibliography of Resource Materials for Education and Training,* an index of employment and related services available in Canada and the United States.

Woodrow Wilson Rehabilitation Center
Box 125
Fisherville, VA 22939
(703) 332-7000
The center provides excellent programs in social skills and job training for handicapped individuals including those with learning disabilities.

ADVOCACY

Council for Exceptional Children
1920 Association Drive
Reston, VA 22091-1589
(703) 620-3660
The advocacy focus for young adults is on the educational rights and appropriate vocation and transition opportunities for students coming out of secondary institutions.

**Disabilities Rights, Education and
Defense Fund**
2212 6th Street
Berkeley, CA 94710
(415) 644-2555
This nonprofit organization primarily provides advocacy services for learning-disabled adults in California. Technical assistance can be given to those who live outside the California area.

**Learning Disabilities Association of
America (LDA)**
4156 Library Road
Pittsburgh, PA 15234
(412) 341-1515
LDA serves as an advocacy organization focusing on adults in the workplace and in higher-education settings. A brochure for employers of individuals with learning disabilities is available.

**National Association of Protection and
Advocacy Systems**
900 Second Street NE, Suite 211
Washington, DC 20002
(202) 408-9514
Clients can receive information for contacting a state office and/or a referral for assistance from other agencies or individuals. Eligibility criteria must be met to receive services.

BOOKS ON TAPE

Recording for the Blind (RFB)
20 Roszel Road
Princeton, NJ 08540
(609) 452-0606
RFB records eduational textbooks for those individuals with learning disabilities who meet eligibility requirements. Contact RFB for application materials.

Services for the Blind and Physically Handicapped
Library of Congress
1291 Taylor Street NW
Washington, DC 20542
(800) 424-8567
(202) 707-5100
Current books and magazines are on tapes and records for individuals whose disability prevents the use of printed material. Applicants must have a documented disability to receive this service. Call or write this agency to determine eligibility requirements.

APPENDIX 2

The Lab School of Washington

THE DAY SCHOOL

Since its founding in 1967, The Lab School of Washington has provided a unique educational opportunity for many of the Washington, D.C., area's intelligent school-age children with learning disabilities. The tuitions of this nonprofit school are paid either by the parents or, in the case of 76 percent of the students, by the school systems of the District of Columbia, Virginia, and Maryland under Public Law 94–142. The Day School has 250 students. The average student-teacher ratio in the classroom is five to one.

Each child's problems are different, so The Lab School of Washington carefully tailors its activities and programs to meet individual needs. The school's success can be clearly measured in results. Of its former students, all but one went on to complete high school, most go on to college, and some are now in graduate school and law school. Over the years former Lab School students have graduated from Brown, Bard, Guilford, Oberlin, Syracuse, the University of Maryland, the University of Vermont, Emory, Colorado, Spellman, the Maryland School of Art, Ithaca, the University of the District of Columbia, Howard, Washington University, and other fine colleges and universities. Lab School graduates are now artists, engineers, businesspeople, electricians, tradespeople, lawyers, computer programmers, and educators.

Within the Day School there are four divisions:

The Primary Program. For students five to six years old who are at high risk for learning disabilities and who need two years of intensive remediation before returning to regular school.

The Elementary School. Ungraded groups I through IV, Early Elementary; Ungraded groups V through IX, Intermediate Division.

The Junior High School. Seventh and eighth grade.

The High School. Grades nine through twelve.

The Day School prides itself on having an outstanding staff, highly trained and experienced in diagnostic-prescriptive teaching and in intensive academic remediation. The Lab School is the only primary and elementary school in the country for students with learning disabilities that employs all the art forms to teach basic academic skills. Half the day takes place in highly individualized classrooms focusing on reading, math, spelling, and oral and written language, while the other half is in the arts. The foundations of reading, oral and written language, math, and eye-hand coordination are further developed through the graphic arts, woodwork, filmmaking, music, dance, drama, jewelry making, and puppetry. Youngsters with learning disabilities lack the neurological maturation required for academic success. The arts are employed at the Lab School to build organizational skills and to enhance the process of neural maturation. The arts help build important competencies and a sense of worth. Experiential education is also considered vital. As part of the innovative Academic Club curriculum, members of the Caveman Club learn history, geography, science, archaeology, literature, all the arts, and the social organization of prehistoric man by pretending to be cave dwellers. Each year students move up to another club to take on the next period of history.

Junior high school and high school students follow a more traditional academic curriculum emphasizing study skills, supplemented by classes in the arts and experiential learning opportunities. In their humanities class, junior high students study three countries and their continents, always ending with the setting up of a restaurant where they cook the food from the country and serve and sell it. High school students run the school store, have a student council, and publish their own literary journal, arts brochures, and yearbook. Eleventh graders work as apprentices two hours a day in jobs related to their interests. Twelfth graders study human development and can tutor elementary-school students or work with senior citizens. There are intramural sports: competitive soccer, basketball, and softball. There is an after-school program of sports and art for all age groups (K–12).

At the same time as intensive remediation takes place, Lab School students are given a quality education—a full academic curriculum taught through projects, activity learning, and experiential education. Talking books for the blind and homemade tapes introduce good literature to nonreaders and poor readers. Lab School students usually return to the mainstream well ahead of their peers in general knowledge. Lab School students are educated, not just remediated.

OTHER SERVICES

There is an annual six-week Summer School attended by students from all over the country. There is a Tutoring Service for all age groups, employing Lab School–trained tutors. There is a Career and College Counseling Service specifically for the learning disabled. Clinical Services, including psychological and diagnostic services, occupational therapy, and speech and language therapy, are taken care of by a large staff of highly trained specialists.

THE NIGHT SCHOOL

Since January 1984, this pioneering postsecondary program, now serving close to ninety students a semester, aged eighteen and up, has helped adults to enter or reenter college, to pass the GED test, or to upgrade their employment skills. Taught two nights a week by an outstanding group of master teachers, Night School adults rapidly increase their academic skills and computer proficiency. Incredible results take place. With a student-teacher ratio of five to one, courses are highly individualized. The adult students act as coinvestigators and planners in their own programs. Courses offered include Reading, Math, Phonics/Spelling, English and Composition, Literature, Study Skills, Life Skills, and Job-Seeking Skills, as well as a Guided Study course supporting students currently enrolled in college classes. Students meet other adults with learning disabilities, share experiences, problem-solve together, and help dispel feelings of isolation while creating motivation for achievement and success.

A NATIONAL RESOURCE

In addition to serving the local community, The Lab School of Washington is a national resource for students, educators, and lawmakers concerned with the needs of the nation's 10 million or more learning-disabled children and untold number of adults. The Lab School director is the professor in charge of The American University's Graduate Program in Learning Disabilities. Each year approximately twelve to fifteen graduate students from The American University serve their practicums under master teachers at the Lab School. Howard University, George Washington University, and Mt. Vernon College also use the Lab School as a training site. The Lab School was featured on the CBS Magazine Show *West 57th* in mid-April 1988, and Lab School administrators often appear on radio and television. Consulting services and workshops on learning disabilities can be contracted from the Day School, the After-School Program, the Night School, Career and College Counseling, Tutoring Services, and Clinical Services.

The Lab School has set up a Conference and Materials Department due to the number of requests we have received from around the country and abroad for our audiotapes, videotapes, articles, and books.

Index

Abstract thinking
   demonstrating, 215
   difficulty with, 90
   Piaget on development of, 109
Absurd, sense of, 219
Academic Club Method, of Lab
      School, 114
Acceptance of learning disabilities,
      227–229. *See also*
      Acknowledgement of learning
      disabilities
Accommodations for learning
      disabled
   defined, 233, 252
   securing, 233–235
Accountability, 191, 243. *See also*
      Responsibility for oneself
Achievers, 84–85. *See also*
      Celebrities with learning
      disabilities; Success; *and names*
      of individuals
Acknowledgement of learning
      disabilities, 20, 22–24, 25,
      31–33, 53–54
   success and, 147
Acting out, 48–49
Activity, mask of, 50
Adaptive physical education, 190
ADD. *See* Attention Deficit Disorder
ADHD. *See* Attention Deficit
      Hyperactivity Disorder
Adulthood, preparing for, through
      learning to accept responsibility
      for oneself, 132–144
Adults with learning disabilities,
      20–34
   acceptance of their learning
      disabilities, 227–229
   appropriate teaching materials
      for, 208

   as coinvestigators and
      coworkers, 206
   experiential teaching methods for,
      129–131
   extra efforts needed for everyday
      coping by, 64–65, 79–80,
      81–82
   goal setting by, 218
   help-seeking by, 226
   individualized teaching
      prescriptions for, 129
   questions to ask diagnosticians,
      244–245
   special needs of, 206–209
   support networks for, 236–242
   teachers of, 207–208
   versus learning-disabled adults, 35
Adventure, sense of, in learning, 219
Advocacy
   resources for, 285–286
   self-, 267
Agent of change, becoming, 231–233
Alcohol abuse, 152–154
American University, The, 126–127
Andersen, G. Chris , 27, 48, 57
Anderson, Hans Christian, 68, 203
Anderson, Harry, 28, 48, 146
Anger, 83, 148, 152
   of parents, 194
Anxiety, 148
   chronic, 151
Appearance, 231, 265. *See also* Image
   unkempt, 87–88, 164, 239
Apprenticeships, student, 136
Architects, 60–61
Art activities, organization and
      planning of, 138
Artistic talent, 59, 60–61
   signs of, 63–64
Artists, 60–61

Athletic talent, 57–62. *See also* Sports
  neglect of academic skills and, 58–59
Attention problems, 217
  strategy for dealing with, in college, 255–256
  types of difficulties, 6
Attention Deficit Disorder (ADD), 186, 190
  in relation to learning disabilities, 12
  terminology, 12
Attention Deficit Hyperactivity Disorder (ADHD), 74, 186, 190, 196
  effect of, on family, 162
  in relation to learning disabilities, 12
  terminology, 12
Attitude, importance of, 232
Automobile driving, 93, 139–140
  alternative to, 103
  possible difficulties in, 93, 140

Badness, mask of, 48–49
Bancroft, Ann (explorer), 28, 31, 57
Bartlett, F. C., 123
Belafonte, Harry, 29, 40–41
Berryman, John, 150
Birth
  problems after, 14
  problems before, 13
  problems during, 14
Blacks with learning disabilities, 42
Bodily-kinesthetic intelligence, 36
Body language, problems in understanding, 168
Body movement, in learning, 115–117
Bono, Chastity, 29
Books, on learning disabilities, 270–275
Books-on-tape, 286–287
Boredom, mask of, 51
Boundaries, imposing. *See* Limits, setting

Brothers and sisters. *See* Siblings
Bruner, Jerome, 110–111

Calendars, marking and color coding, 92
Caperton, Gaston, 29, 57, 76–77, 84
Careers. *See also* Jobs; Workplace
  choice of, 141, 235
  resources pertaining to, 283–285
Caring, lack of, as mask, 49
Categorization, consequences of, 38–42
Cause and effect, learning to relate to, 172–174
Celebrities with learning disabilities, 24–33
Central-nervous-system dysfunction, 3, 4
  inexact correlation with learning disabilities, 14
  perseveration and, 74–75
  single-mindedness and, 79
  trouble with coping with abstract concepts and, 90
Change(s)
  of activity and pace, 217–218
  adaptation to, 171–172
  becoming agent of, 231–233
Channels of learning, identifying, 222–225
Character traits, 38
Cher, 25, 27, 29, 40, 45, 95, 130, 267–268
Choices. *See* Decision-making
Classification of learning disabilities, 6–10
Cleanliness, 164
Close, Chuck, 28, 30, 39, 103
Clown, mask of, 45
Clubs, 128, 238
  academic, 114
Coffey, Donald S., 29, 57, 59–60, 65–66, 74, 146
Cognition problems
  social development and, 169, 170–172
  types of 8–9

Cognitive development
  Piaget's stages of, 108–110
  stage of, and teaching mode,
    110–117
Cohen, Richard, 28, 30, 97
College(s), 190
  accommodations for learning
    disabled, 233–234
  admissions requirements, 247
  choice of, 141, 247
  choice of classes at, 212–213,
    253–254
  considerations, 246–248
  help-seeking at, 254
  notetaking in, 97
  over- versus underprotectiveness
    and, 197
  questions to ask admissions
    officers at, 247–248
  studying at, 254–260
  success at, 101–102, 137, 268
Combat readiness, 143–144
Comedy. See Humor
Communication skills
  learning, 177–178
  socialization problems and, 168
  teaching, in family, 178
Competence, super-, mask of, 46
Compromises, difficulties with,
  171–172
Computers, 124–126
  as organizational aids, 102, 104
  outlining programs, 125
  teaching use of, 126
  word processing programs, 124
Concept formation, 110. See also
  Abstract thinking
Concrete experiences, 213. See also
  Experiential teaching methods
  as key to early learning, 107
  learning through, 106–131
  visible proof of progress, 215
Concrete operational stage, 109–110
Concrete thinking, 66, 90,
  170–172, 231
  in childhood development,
    109–110

memory and, 216
  visible proof of progress and, 215
Conning
  intelligence shown by, 67
  mask of, 47–48, 67–68
Contempt, mask of, 50–51
Control over others, masks and,
  43–44
Control over self. See Self-control
  skills
Coping strategies. See also Strategies
  development of talents as, 64–68
  need for, 88
Counselors, choosing, 250–251
Creativity, of people with learning
  disabilities, 62, 63
Critical thinking, training in,
  141–142
Cruise, Tom, 27, 57, 130, 84

Decision-making, 140–142
  about careers, 141
  about college, 141
Defense mechanisms, 44, 148
Depression, emotional, 151–152
  sleep and, 133, 134
  therapeutic treatment for,
    151–152
Desktop-publishing programs, 124
Determination to succeed, 72–74
Developmental learning, 108–113
  cognitive development and,
    108–113
Developmental learning
  disabilities, 13
  in DSM III, 12
Dewey, John, 111
Diagnosis of learning disabilities,
  244–245
Diagnostic and Statistical Manual of
  Mental Disorders, III-R, 11–12
Diagnosticians, questions to ask,
  244–245
Directions, how to ask for, 264
Directness, 66
Discrimination, in social situations,
  174–176

Disorganization. *See also*
    Organizational difficulties
    fear of, 98–99
    friction in living situations caused
        by, 239
    socialization problems and,
        168, 239
Distancing
    mask of activity and, 50
    mask of not caring and, 49
Diversity, importance of, 219
Divorce, 162
Doyle, William, 29, 130–131
Drill-and-practice programs, 125
Drive, 71–85
    toward success, 79–84
Drug abuse, 152–154
*DSM III. See Diagnostic and
    Statistical Manual of Mental
    Disorders, III-R*
Dunkle, Frank, 28, 54–55, 80, 81,
    104, 157
Dyslexia, 150
    versus learning disabilities, 12, 13
    social acceptability of term, 12–13
    use of term, 12–13, 266–267
    verbal retention and, 95

Edison, Thomas A., 2, 51, 68, 117
Educational testing centers, 282–283
Effort, valuing, 217
Egocentricity, 168, 173, 175
Emotional effects of learning
        disabilities, 145–155. *See also*
        Anger; Anxiety; Depression,
        emotional; Frustration
    combat readiness, 143–144
    diagnostic use of, 216
Empathy, 36, 66, 154–155
    positive and negative uses of,
        154–155
Energy. *See also* Fatigue
    productivity and, 74–76
    strategies for sustaining, 261
Entrepreneurs with learning
        disabilities, 59, 241–243

problem-solving experiences of, 242
Evaluation, educational, 244–245.
    See also Tests/testing
Everyday life, strategies for, 260–265
Examinations, taking, at college,
    259–260
Experiential teaching methods,
    113–131
    for adults with learning
        disabilities, 129–131

Failure(s)
    fear of, 149–150
    learning from, 127–128
Families
    conversation in, 178
    high-achieving, learning
        disabilities in, 19–20
Family relationships, 156–165
    effect of child with learning
        disabilities on, 161–163
Fatigue
    as mask, 52
    organizational problems and,
        99–100
    strategies for combating, 261
Fears of parents, 190–192
Feelings. *See* Emotional effects of
        learning disabilities
Filing system, mental, and preschool
        learning, 107–108
Fitzgerald, F. Scott, 2
Flanagan, Marc, 29, 45, 67
Flaubert, Gustave, 1–2
Focusing on task, 256
Forgetting, strategies for avoiding,
    264–265
Frames of Mind (Gardner), 36–37
Friendly, Fred, 29, 33, 75, 183
Friends, support from, 240–241
Frustration, 83

Games
    diagnostic-prescriptive, 114
    playing, 142
Gardner, Howard, 36–38

Geography, experiential teaching of, 119–121
Goal setting, 136–137
  by students and teachers, 218
Gold, Tracey, 28, 81–82
Good Samaritan, mask of, 47
Goodridge, Malcolm, III, 28, 57, 73, 80, 81
Grandparents, 159, 196
Grief, of parents, 186
Group therapy, 238
Guilt feelings, of parents, 185

Hampshire, Susan, 149
Haseltine, Florence P., 90, 92–93, 102, 105
Helpfulness, mask of, 47
Helplessness, mask of, 52
Help-seeking, 226, 268
  at college, 254
Hereditary factors, 13
Heroes, 236
Hidden handicap, learning disabilities as, 2–3, 19
High-achieving families, learning disabilities in, 19–20
History, learning through re-creating, 114, 118–119
Horner, John R., 29, 60, 75–76
Household chores, strategies for doing, 263
Humor, 66–67, 200, 219, 267
Hypertext, 125

Identification of learning disabilities, and dropping masks, 53–54
Illness, as mask, 52
Image, projecting, 265, 266
Imagination, 219
Impulsivity, 63, 66, 173
Individualized education, 206, 209, 212–213
Inflexibility, 71, 72–74, 78, 98–99, 170
Information
  difficulties in expressing, 96
  organizing into categories, 265
  remembering, 265
Information centers, 276–279
Initiative, importance of, 231–233
Innovation, in teaching, 218–220
Insight, 36, 66
Instructions
  oral, following, 256–257
  written, following, 257
Intelligence
  Gardner's theory of types of, 36–38
  in relation to learning disabilities, 37–39, 54
  tests of (IQ tests), 37
Interactive theater techniques, 180–181
Interest, demonstrating, to college instructors, 255
Interest groups, 238
Interests. See also Talents and abilities
  building on, 214–215
  following, 244
  supporting, 69–70, 83–84
Interpersonal intelligence, 36, 66
Intimacy, fear of, 164–165
Intrapersonal intelligence, 36–37
Intuition, 154
Invisibility, mask of, 53
Involvement, as key to learning, 114
IQ tests, 37

Jacobsen, Hugh Newell, 29, 60, 66, 184
Jenner, Bruce, 28, 49, 57–58, 64
Jobs, applying for, 248–250, 266–267
  questions to ask, 248–249
  questions to expect, 249–250
Johnson, Magic, 28, 41, 57, 175–176

Kean, Thomas H., 28, 43, 204
Keller, Helen, 121

Lab School of Washington, The (Washington, D.C.)
  about, 288–292

Lab School of Washington, The
    (Washington, D.C.) *cont.*
  apprenticeship program, 136
  approach to learning of, 113–115
  celebrities with learning
    disabilities and, 24–33
  Day School, 288–290
  discrimination skill learning
    activities, 175
  experiential teaching methods of,
    120–122, 124
  Night School, 20–25, 206–208,
    228–229, 260, 291
  Outstanding Learning-Disabled
    Achiever Award recipients,
    24, 25–26, 27–31, 40, 184,
    268–269
  school store experiences, 139
  teaching of goal-oriented behavior
    by, 136
  various services of, 290–291, 292
Labeling, 2, 35–36, 38, 41
  consequences of, 38–42
Landau, Emily Fisher, 28
Language development, in
    children, 109
Language problems, 96–98, 190, 213
  communication and, 97
  and other types of
    disorganization, 98
  socialization problems and, 168,
    176–177
  subtle, 98
  telephone skills and, 179
  types of, 8, 96–97
Language therapy, 177, 190
Learning. *See also* Developmental
    learning
  active, 113–115
  by doing, 106–131
  modes of, and modes of
    thought, 108
Learning channels, identifying,
    222–225
Learning disabilities. *See also* Adults
    with learning disabilities
  in relation to ADD and ADHD, 12

areas of, 5
causes of, 13–14
defining, 3–4
as group of conditions, 5
as invisible handicap, 1, 2–3,
    19, 150
new view of, 33–34
not in *DSM III*, 11–12
perceiving as an advantage, 33, 34
strategies for describing, 266–267
taxonomy of, 6–10
Learning Disabilities Association of
    America (LDA), 189
Learning materials, age-
    appropriate, 108
Learning style
  preferences in, 69–70, 78–79
  of teachers, 212
Left-right confusion, 6
  strategies for dealing with, 262
Legislation, 199–200
Letting go, 198
Life experiences, as teaching tool,
    129–131
Limits, setting, 100, 188, 191
Linguistic intelligence, 37
Listening skills, 95
Literal-mindedness, 66, 171–172.
    See also Concrete thinking
Living situations, friction in, 239. *see
    also* Families
Logical operations, development
    of, 109
Logical-mathematical
    intelligence, 37
Loneliness, 19, 22, 191
Losing things, strategies for avoiding,
    264–265
Louganis, Greg, 25, 28, 147
Love, of self, 230

Macho men, 47
Manipulation, 43–44, 67, 188
Manley, Dexter, 29, 57, 58–59, 227
Marina B., 28, 30–31
Marriage, 163–165

Mask(s)
  of activity, 50
  of being bad, 48–49
  of boredom, 51
  of clown, 45
  of conning, 47–48, 67–68
  of contempt, 50–51
  defined, 43
  destructiveness of, 43–44
  of Good Samaritan, 47
  of helplessness, 52
  of ill health/vulnerability, 52
  of invisibility, 53
  need for, 43–44
  of not caring, 49
  of outrageousness, 45–46
  passive, 43–44
  of seduction, 46–47
  of super-competence, 46
  taking off, 53–54
  of the victim, 51–52
Mates
  dealing with, 239
  support from, 240–241
Maturity, ultimate, 268–269
Memory, 94–95, 264–265
  aging and, 95
  anchoring of, through sensory
    learning, 119–123
  computer as aid to, 102
  schemata and, 123
  strategies to aid, 262–265
  strengthening with concrete
    reminders, 216
  tricks to aid, 95, 259
  types of difficulties, 7
  understanding approaches to, 111
Mentors
  defined, 236
  using, 235–236
Messiness, 87–88, 164, 239
Metaphors, extended, 129
Mnemonics, 259
Model building, 121
Money, strategies for keeping track
  of, 260–261
Motivation. See Drive

Motor problems, types of, 7
Movement activities, learning to
  organize, 93–94
Musical talent, 36, 61

National Center for Learning
  Disabilities, 189
National Joint Committee on
  Learning Disabilities, definition
  of learning disabilities, 4
Negativity
  channeling of, into positive
    actions, 69
  mask of, 50–51
Negotiation skills, 171
Neurological dysfunctions. See
  Central-nervous-system
  dysfunction
Nightmares, recurring, 44, 202–203
Note-taking, 257

Obstacles, strategies for
  avoiding, 263
Occupational therapy, 93, 190
Olav, king of Norway, 27
Opportunities, viewing problems
  as, 231
Optimism, 267–268
Order. See also Organization
  extreme, 98–99
  need for, 86–105
Orfalea, Paul J., 29, 267
Organization. See also
    Disorganization;
    Organizational difficulties;
    Order; Planning; Structure
  of materials, at college, 254
  of movement activities, 93–94
  need for, 86–105
  of time, 88–92
Organizational aids, 102, 103–104
Organizational difficulties. See also
    Disorganization;
    Overorganizing
  bypassing, through alternative
    solutions, 102–105

developing own solutions to,
102–105, 149
fatigue caused by, 98–99
types of, 9
as cause of failure, 86
getting rid of, 87–88
language problems and, 98
Organizations and associations,
189, 276–279
Orton Dyslexia Society, 189
Outlining programs, for
computer, 125
Outrageousness, mask of, 45–46
Overorganizing, 98–99, 239
Overprotectiveness, avoiding, 197

Pace, changes of, 217–218
PageMaker, 124
Parents of children with learning
disabilities, 182–201
anger of, 194
appreciation of life gained by,
200–201
basic parenting skills for,
195–200
dependence of children upon, 159
divorce of, 162
fears of, 190–192
grief of, 186
guilt feelings of, 185
and learning-disabled children,
19–20
letting go by, 198
level of comfort of, 193
militant, 199–200
need for relaxation, 200
need for separating from child,
159–160
as problem solvers, 196
roles and responsibilities of,
187–189
sense of humor, 200
sharing responsibilities, 196–197
single parents, 196–197
skills developed by, 194–196
stresses of, 192–195

Patton, George S., 2, 46,
117–119
daughter of, 68, 118–119
Peer groups, 238
Perceptions, of people with learning
disabilities
freshness of, 63
unique, 62
Perceptiveness, in interpersonal
relationships, 66
Periodicals, 279–282
Perseveration, 74–75
Piaget, Jean, on cognitive
development, 108–110
Planning, 137–139. See also
Organization
as key to success, 137
learning, 232–233
Play, use of, as teaching
method, 115
Play therapy, 177
Positive thinking, 267–268
Power, masks and, 43–44
Praise, specific, 217
Prenatal factors, 13
Preschool learning, 107
Preventive questioning, 210
Priority-setting, learning,
174–176
Problem solving
as background experience for
entrepreneurship, 242–243
teaching techniques of, 210
training in, 141–142
Procrastination, 89–90
strategy for coping with, 90
Progress, providing visible proof
of, 215
Psychiatric Handbook. See
Diagnostic and Statistical
Manual of Mental Disorders,
III-R
Psychiatrists, 250
Psychologists, 250
Psychotherapy for people with
learning disabilities, 151–152
for depression, 151–152

Public Law 94–142 (The Education for All Handicapped Children Act), 199, 288
learning disability as defined by, 3–4

Quark Xpress, 124
Questionnaire, 15–18
Questions, phrasing, 268
Quietness, as mask, 55

Rauschenberg, Robert, 28, 38–39, 45–46, 61, 95, 112, 230
Reading college books, how to, 258
Reading comprehension, and schema theory, 123
Reframing, 210
Regulation, self-. See Self-regulation
Rehabilitation Act, 199
Section 504, 233–234
Reinforcement of learning, 216
Relationships, personal, 155. See also Family relationships; Social development; Support networks
most important skills for, 166–167
Remediation classes, scheduling, 215
Remembering. See Memory
Repetition, reinforcing through, 216
Resourcefulness, 73–74
Resources for learning disabled
advocacy resources, 285
books, 270–275
books-on-tape, 286–287
career-related resources, 283–285
educational testing centers, 282–283
information centers and organizations, 276–279
periodicals, pamphlets, and newsletters, 279–282
Responsibility for oneself, 132–144, 191, 243
adults with learning disabilities and, 207

self-monitoring as prerequisite for, 135–136
teaching, 134–144
Reversals (Simpson), 150
Right-left confusion. See Left-right confusion
Rigidity. See Inflexibility
Risk-taking, 65–66, 230
Rockefeller, Nelson, 2
Rodin, Auguste, 2, 68
Role models for learning disabled, 27, 236

SAT tests, 27
Schema theory, using, in teaching, 122–124
Schemata, 123
Schooling, 202–225. See also Teachers
traditional, problems caused by, 38–42, 64, 202–203
Scientific interests, 59–60
Seduction, mask of, 46–47
Self-acceptance, 230
Self-control skills, 135–137
Self-direction, 243–244
Self-esteem, 55
untapped, 54–55, 145–149, 230
fear of intimacy and, 164–165
improvement of, 147
masks and, 43
sports and, 49, 57–58
success and, 145–146
Self-image, and IQ and SAT test scores, 37
Self-monitoring, 135–136
strategies for, 261–262
Self-regulation
learning, 133–135
overregulation and, 143–144
Senses
schema development and, 122–123
teaching through, 215–216
using to anchor memory, 119–122
Sensory defensiveness, 163

Sensory-integration therapy. *See* Occupational therapy
Sensory-motor development, 109
Sexist stereotypes, use of, 47
Sexual relationships, 163–165
Shame, feelings of, 19–20, 22, 25, 26–27
    masking, 35–55 [*see also* Mask(s)]
Shopping, strategies for, 263
Siblings, 156–159
    informing, about sibling with learning disabilities, 158–159
    and parents, 157
Silence, 101
Simpson, Eileen, 150
Single-mindedness, 76–79, 81, 170–172
    disadvantages of, 78
    losing track of time and, 88–89
Sisters and brothers. *See* Siblings
Sizer, Theodore, 111–112
Sleep
    and depression, 133, 134
    recurring nightmares, 44, 202–203
Social behavior problems
    causes of, 167–170
    language problems and, 176–178
    neurological dysfunction and, 169–170
    types of, 9–10
Social development, 166–181. *See also* Relationships, personal; Social skills
Social skills, 167
    learning, 176–180
    needed by persons with learning disabilities, 166
    teaching, 180–181
Social workers, 250
Socialization, 166–180
Socializing, planning, 138
Space, structuring use of, 138–139
Spatial intelligence, 36
Spatial organization, difficulties with, 92–94

Spatial perception. *See* Visual-spatial perception
Specialists in learning disabilities, 237
    diagnostic testing by, 244–245
    disagreements of, 4–5, 11–12
    running to, 188–189
Spell-checking programs, for computer, 124
Sports, 77–78. *See also* Athletic talent
    and self-esteem, 49
    and stress, 193
Squire, Elizabeth Daniels, 70, 123–124, 171, 230
Star, Nonnie, 78–79, 163
Stereotypes, sexist, use of, 47
Stern, Daniel, 28, 57, 59, 192
Sternberg, Robert, 37, 38
Stimulation, limiting, in classroom, 213
Strategies
    for college, 253–260
    defined, 252
    for describing learning disabilities, 266–267
    for everyday life, 260–265
    focusing on, 209
Strauss, Richard C., 28, 43, 48–49, 59, 95, 104, 130, 147
Street smarts, 37, 66
Strengths and weaknesses, identifying, 220–221. *See also* Talents and abilities
Stress, emotional, 148–149
    anticipation of situations causing, 148–149
    of parenting, 192–195
    ways of handling, 193–194
Strong, silent type, mask of, 49–50
Structure
    through alternative action, 102–105
    imposed from without, 100–102
    through organizational aids, 102
    providing, in classroom, 213

Stubbornness, 72–74, 78–79, 81–83
single-mindedness and, 77
Studying suggestions, for college, 254–260
Substance abuse, 152–154
effects of, and symptoms of learning disabilities, 153–154
Success
accepting responsibility for self and, 243
alternate methods of learning and, 232–233
asking questions and, 268
at college, 268
dedicated teachers and, 204
drive for, 71–72, 79–85
fear of, 149–150
goal setting and, 218
learning disabilities as cause of, 34
obsession with, 76
risks necessary for, 65–66, 230
self-direction and, 243–244
self-esteem and, 145–146
strategies for, 252–269
structuring for, 100–105
unorthodox roads to, 244
views of, 32
Suggestibility, 152
Sullivan, Annie, 121
Support networks, 236–241
employees as, 241–242
family and friends as, 239–241
using, 236–239
Symbol-learning problems, types of, 8

Tactile defensiveness, 162–163
Talents and abiliites, 56–70
importance of recognition of, 59, 61, 64
building on, 214–215
criticism of, 62–63
identifying, 220–221
innovative teaching methods and, 219–220
nurturing of, 57
obvious, 57–62
potential, overlooking, 54–55, 57, 59, 62, 64
supporting, 68–70
unique ways of perceiving world and, 61–62
Tasks
analyzing, 127, 211–212
focusing on, 256
organizing, 91–92
teaching approach to, 213–214
Taxonomy of learning disabilities, 6–10
Teachers. See also Teaching
of adults with learning disabilities, 207–208
baffled or overburdened, 203–204
dedicated, 204
experience of learning-disabled world by, 126–127
learning style of, 212
need for anticipation by, 217–218
organizational abilities of, 100–101
professional attitude of, 209
role of, 209
training of, 126–127, 211–212
what can be done by, 202–225
Teaching. See also Teachers; Teaching methods
at Lab School Night School, 206–208
motivation for, 205–206
principles and techniques of, 209–220
Teaching materials
for adults, 208
backup, 218
Teaching methods
best, learning, 54
experiential, 113–131
innovative, 218–220
varying, 212–213
Teaching modes, in relation to stage of cognitive development, 110–117

Teasing, effects of, 41
Telephone skills
  learning, 178–180
  strategies for remembering phone
    numbers, 262–263
  teaching, 179–180
Telephone system for deaf
  (TDD), 233
Tenacity. *See* Stubbornness
Testing centers, 282–283
Tests/testing
  for diagnosing learning
    disabilities, 15–18
  IQ, 37
  of street smarts, 37–38
Textbooks, reading, 258–259
Thank-you letters, 263–264
Therapists, questions to ask,
  250–251
Thomas, Lewis, 11
Time
  as abstract concept, 90
  losing track of, 88–89, 153–154
  organizing, 88–92, 138–139
  strategies for keeping track of, 264
Time-management difficulties,
  88–92, 153–154
  need for teachers to
    understand, 214
Torrence, Mark, 28, 31, 104–105
Totten, Mrs. James, 68, 118
Transportation, public, 264
Trial and error approach to learning,
  111–112

Tutoring, diagnostic-prescriptive,
  245–246
Tutors, questions to ask, 245–246

Ventura Publisher, 124
Victim, mask of, 51–52
Visual thinking, and artistic
  talent, 61
Visual-spatial perception
  difficulties with, 6–7, 92–94
  unkempt appearance and, 87–88
Vocabulary development, 216
Volunteering, 238–239
Voting, practicing, 176
Vowels, teaching, 215
Vulnerability, mask of, 52–53

Whitton, Margaret, 28, 57, 130, 154,
  183, 244, 267–268
Whole person, looking at, 68
Wilkins, Roger W., 28, 42, 84, 184
Wilson, Woodrow, 2
Winkler, Henry, 28, 41, 45, 147
Word-processing programs, for
  computer, 124, 125
Work experience
  benefits of, 130
  on-the-job training, 130
Work space, for studying, 255
Workplace, accommodations for
  learning disabled in, 234–235

Yeats, William Butler, 2
Youngest Science, The (Lewis), 11